COMMITTED TO MEMORY

1/98

COMMITTED TO MEMORY

How We Remember and Why We Forget

REBECCA RUPP

Crown Publishers, Inc.

NEW YORK

Published by Crown Publishers, Inc., 201 East 50th Street, New York, New York 10022. Member of the Crown Publishing Group.

Random House, Inc. New York, Toronto, London, Sydney, Auckland
www.randomhouse.com/

CROWN and colophon are trademarks of Crown Publishers, Inc.

Printed in the United States of America

Design by Cathryn S. Aison

Library of Congress Cataloging-in-Publication Data
Rupp, Rebecca.
Committed to memory : how we remember and why we forget / Rebecca Rupp. — 1st ed.
Includes bibliographical references and index.
1. Memory. 2. Recollection (Psychology). 3. Mnemonics.
I. Title.
BF371.R84 1997
153.1'2—dc21   97-28722
CIP
ISBN 0-517-70321-1

10 9 8 7 6 5 4 3 2 1

FIRST EDITION

For Randy

CONTENTS

ACKNOWLEDGMENTS

I AM INDEBTED TO all the many persons who provided help and support in the writing of this book, especially Joe Spieler and John Thornton of the Spieler Agency; my editors, Peter Ginna and Ayesha Pande; and the innumerable talented scientists whose research is described in these pages.

INTRODUCTION

MEMORY, IN GREEK MYTHOLOGY, was the province of the goddess Mnemosyne, the deity who—after an adulterous interlude with Zeus—gave birth to the nine Muses: Clio, the Muse of history; Urania, the Muse of astronomy; Melpomene, tragedy; Thalia, comedy; Terpsichore, dance; Calliope, epic poetry; Erato, love poetry; Euterpe, lyric poetry; and Polyhymnia, songs to the gods. (In an earlier and less prolific incarnation, Mnemosyne produced only three daughters, among them Polymatheia, the Muse of what today would be called general education.) The Muses were believed to be the moving forces behind ancient Greek creativity, inspiring artistic compositions and performances that depended heavily on the prodigious exercise of memory. From Mother Mnemosyne comes our word *mnemonics*—the collective term for methods and devices used to improve memory—and surely among the earliest of these were the rhythmic cadences of poetry, each rolling line laden with cues that cemented themselves firmly in the minds of the reciting bards. Homer's blindness was not a professional handicap: the Greek poets spoke from memory.

The value of memory in the ancient world is exemplified by the awful tale of the unwise bard who challenged the Muses to a singing contest. He should have known better: Greek mythology is peppered with accounts of human braggarts brought low by Olympian competition. The overconfident Arachne, for boasting that her weaving was more skillful than the goddess Athena's, spent the rest of her days as a spider; the luckless Marsyas, insisting that his flute-playing surpassed that of Apollo, ended up tied to a plane tree and skinned alive. Despite such obviously foreboding precedents, the bard persisted—and the Muses, in revenge for his presumption, destroyed his memory. It was, for a bard, a fate worse than death.

Almost all of us complain about our memories. My own is quirky and unpredictable, with an annoying fondness for the superfluous, the trivial, and the uselessly absurd. It allows me to remember effortlessly the date of the Spanish Armada, the Japanese word for persimmon, and the Henderson-Hasselbalch equation—informational pearls that, sadly, are seldom called forth in casual conversation—but strands me at the supermarket with no recollection of what I intended to buy there, abandons me in the airport parking lot with no hints as to where I left the car, and once, in the course of a stunningly dreadful telephone interview, evaporated entirely for several hideous instants, taking with it my self-esteem, my social equilibrium, and all my children's names.

For all its infelicitous failures, however, most of us remain stubbornly fond of our memories. Memory, built up over years and decades, is one of the few human creations that is entirely and inimitably one's own. Like fingerprints, of which all five and a half billion sets on the planet are unique, no two human memories are the same. Each is a wholly individual construct, a personal museum of once and present fascinations, as crammed with treasured odds and ends as the sixteenth- and seventeenth-century *Wunderkammer*. These "cabinets of wonder" were the forerunners of modern museums: eccentric collections amassed by the rich and curious, populated with elephants' tusks, Chinese slippers, stuffed penguins, madonnas made of feathers, Turkish toothbrushes, mummified bats, and silk-knit gloves said to have belonged to Anne Boleyn. Just so, each human brain holds an idiosyncratic assemblage of rarities. All of us are avid collectors of memories.

Unlike the artifacts in the conventional wonder cabinet, however, our mental collectibles are relatively protected from loss. If this house burned down tomorrow, taking with it diaries, photograph albums, scrapbooks, souvenirs of summer vacations, my great-grandfather's rocking chair, and the yellow bunting that all our children in turn wore home from the hospital, still—through memory—we could rebuild our pasts from the ashes. What can be remembered never entirely disappears.

We see this time and again, on small to grand scale. Families pass down stories of their pasts, handing memories on full-blown from generation to generation. Immigrants cherish memories of their homelands, teaching remembered traditions to their children. At the root of San Francisco's gaudy Chinese New Year, Boston's Saint Patrick's Day Parade, San Antonio's Cinco de Mayo celebrations, and New Orleans's Mardi Gras is a vast web of shared memories.

Memory, individual or collective, not only makes us what we are, but in a sense gives us the power to travel through time, projecting ourselves into the future. Our stories—at least some of them—will outlive us. And it's not hard to imagine a scenario in which our stories—our memories—become overwhelmingly important. This is a favorite theme of apocalyptic science fiction. In this destructive genre, the world, beset by malevolent alien invaders, irresponsibly ignited missiles, or hellish and highly contagious plagues, comes to an end. Humankind, in Stephen King's *The Stand,* is polished off by a brutal brand of flu; in John Wyndham's *The Day of the Triffids,* we fall to a combination of blinding green comets and lethal walking plants. In the works of John Christopher, a master of obliteration, we are variously eradicated by famine, ice, or sinister cone-shaped extraterrestrials. Traditionally in such literature a handful of hardy survivors is spared, to be collectively confronted with the overwhelming task of repopulating the planet, building the future, and rebuilding the past.

Put yourself in their precariously placed shoes: there you would find yourself to be, like the Homeric bards, the repository of an entire culture. From your rich accumulation of memories, you would shape the future, passing on a lifetime's supply of internalized input to your children and grandchildren, and all the other struggling members of your post-technological tribe. From memory you would resurrect, like so many mental phoenixes, nursery rhymes and folk songs, proverbs and parables, Greek myths, Bible stories, and the long-loved legends of Robin Hood, Cinderella, and Huckleberry Finn. You would transmit riddles, jokes, and recipes; home remedies; holiday traditions; weather lore; the rules of checkers, chess, hopscotch, and baseball; the names of trees and stars; the alphabet; Arabic numerals. The story of the first Thanksgiving. The know-how for planting a garden. And even, perhaps, if you've had a thorough grounding in literature, the soul-satisfying words of William Shakespeare, John Donne, Emily Dickinson, Robert Frost.

While clearly capable of monumental feats of reconstruction, human memory, in the overwhelmingly electronic Information Age, has come to be an undervalued commodity. Its tasks are seemingly done for us by more precise and efficient outside agents; information these days is indelibly engraved on the printed page or the floppy disk. The relegation of memory to last place in the pecking order of intellectual activities may result from its association with rote learning, represented by the relentless repetitious drone with which students of the last century absorbed their lessons.

"We ask ourselves, and our children, to remember nothing these days," writes Clara Claiborne Park ruefully in her essay "The Mother of the Muses: In Praise of Memory," which appeared in 1980 in *The American Scholar.* "Not the multiplication table, for we have calculators; not the presidents or the periodic table or the great dates of history; not 1066, not 1453, not 1517, not 1789, not even, perhaps, 1914 and 1917 and 1939. We may make an exception for things we really care about— baseball statistics, for instance. The educated man, however, need not burden his memory. He has learned how to look things up." Still, looking up—though an undeniably useful skill—lacks the mental resonance of memory. No quick flip through the encyclopedia stirs up the warm glow of familiarity that once led a poet to write: "My mind to me a kingdom is." As we fill our minds with poetry, prose, and verbatim quotations, we gain a familiarity with the beauty of language and an expansion of perception that comes in no other way. Paraphrase, says Park, is cold and ungainly stuff, a faint and feeble echo of the true memorable phrase.

In the bookless society of the future portrayed in Ray Bradbury's novel *Fahrenheit 451*, an elderly woman is caught concealing a cache of forbidden books. Rather than surrender herself to the book-burning Firemen, Bradbury's indomitable book-lover chooses to incinerate herself along with her confiscated library. As she strikes the fatal match, she delivers a defiant quotation: *"Play the man, Master Ridley; we shall this day light such a candle, by God's grace, in England, as I trust shall never be put out."* The words were first spoken in the early days of the Protestant Reformation by Hugh Latimer, onetime Bishop of Ely, as he and Nicholas Ridley went to be burned at the stake for heresy. The power of great language, thundering from martyr to martyr down the centuries, clutches the heart and mind as no paraphrase can ever do. Verbatim memory is our link to historical greatness, the means by which we share the triumphs, torments, and inspirations of other minds and make them our own. Great words move us like bars of music.

Chief Joseph, stone-faced in surrender, in the mountains of Montana: *"Hear me, my chiefs. I am tired; my heart is sick and sad. From where the sun now stands, I will fight no more forever."*

Winston Churchill, rallying Britain to battle: *"Let us therefore brace ourselves to our duties and so bear ourselves that if the British Empire and its Commonwealth last for a thousand years, men will still say, 'This was their finest hour.'"*

John Donne: *"No man is an Island, entire of itself; every man is a piece of the Continent, a part of the main; if a clod be washed away by the sea, Europe is the less, as well as if a promontory were, as well as if a manor of thy friends or of thine own were; any man's death diminishes me, because I am involved in Mankind; and therefore never send to know for whom the bell tolls; it tolls for thee."*

The Book of Ecclesiastes: *"To every thing there is a season, and a time to every purpose under heaven."*

And William Shakespeare:

> *This story shall the good man teach his son;*
> *And Crispin Crispian shall ne'er go by,*
> *From this day to the ending of the world,*
> *But we in it shall be remembered;*
> *We few, we happy few, we band of brothers.*

Through such words in memory, we stand, like Newton, on the shoulders of giants.

Memory has many faces, and not all have the poetic power to tug at our souls. Some functions of memory are purely prosaic, comfortable carpet-slipper-like activities that we casually take for granted as we go about the business of our daily lives. Memory allows us to recognize friends, neighbors, and acquaintances and call them by their names; to knit, type, drive, and play the piano; to speak English, Spanish, or Mandarin Chinese. It allows us to identify the tune of "The Star-Spangled Banner" and respond to it by leaping patriotically to our feet, to find our way home from office, school, or grocery store, and to show up on time for our dentist's appointment next Thursday afternoon.

In the following pages, I will describe the many facets of memory, discuss the ways in which we learn, recall, and remember, and offer some suggestions for those interested in what the ancients called the "art of memory": techniques for locking information firmly and unforgettably in the mind. Along the way, I hope to convince you that the art of memory is a far from arid art. Much of what we remember—or must remember—is trivial, the small change of every day, but memory can provide us with far richer rewards.

If thou of fortune be bereft
And in thy store there be but left
Two loaves—sell one, and with the dole
Buy hyacinths to feed the soul.

So wrote James Terry White in 1907 in "Not By Bread Alone," a poem so unmarked that it only merits a footnote in small print in Bartlett's *Familiar Quotations*. White wasn't thinking about memory, but its essence nonetheless is there. Memory provides us with our mental daily bread. But cultivated, it can give us hyacinths to feed the soul.

Remembering

"The horror of that moment," the King went on, "I shall never, never forget."
"You will, though," the Queen said, "if you don't make a memorandum of it."

Lewis Carroll,
Through the Looking-Glass

Isaac Newton's Dinner and
15,000 Chinese Telephone Numbers

Memory, for most of us, is a maddeningly squeaky—if not downright immovable—wheel. We forget, with blithe egalitarianism, names, dates, and telephone numbers, birthdays, wedding anniversaries, the definition of *solipsism*, the significance of the Missouri Compromise, and wherever it was that we last dropped the car keys. These dismaying evaporations of information lie behind such memory-prodding inventions as the appointment book, the crib sheet, and the electronic key-tracking beeper, and such face-saving social practices as the prominent wearing of name tags at class reunions. This last, researchers find, is a necessary precaution: by three months after graduation, we'll have forgotten 85 percent of our erstwhile classmates' names.

Memory lapses, depending on when and where one has them, range from the privately insignificant to the publicly spectacular. Actors, stricken on stage, forget their lines; musicians, victimized in mid-measure, forget their melodies; professors, a legendarily absentminded company, forget socks, lecture notes, social engagements, and umbrellas. Sir Isaac Newton routinely became so absorbed in his work that he forgot dinner; Adam Smith, author of the economic classic *Inquiry into the Nature and Causes of the Wealth of Nations*, periodically forgot to get dressed, once abstractedly arriving at church clad only in his nightgown. A classic tale of memory lapse is told of Sir Thomas Beecham, the flamboyant British conductor and founder of the London Philharmonic Orchestra. Beecham, the story goes, happened upon an acquaintance in the lobby of a Manchester hotel, an elegant woman whose face he recognized but whose name annoyingly escaped him. In the course of conversation, he remembered vaguely that she had a brother. Hoping to jog his recalcitrant memory, he asked how the brother was and if he was pursuing the same line of work.

"Oh, he's very well," the woman replied, "and still king."

> British author G. K. Chesterton was renowned for his absentmindedness. Once, while on a lecture tour, he sent his wife an urgent telegram: "Am in Birmingham. Where ought I to be?"
> His wife wired back: "Home."

At the opposite end of the scale are those who, elephantlike, never seem to forget. Themistocles, the Athenian leader who trounced the Persians at the Battle of Salamis, is said to have known the names of all 20,000 citizens of Athens; Xerxes, king of the vanquished, could name each one of his 100,000 soldiers. Homer and his poetic heirs could recite all 27,000 lines of *The Iliad* and *The Odyssey*, a performance that, if delivered nonstop, would have taken close to two solid days. The African *griots*—tribal historians—memorize family genealogies extending back centuries, a catalog of begats that may include thousands of names. The Maori talking chiefs of New Zealand, half a world away, memorize royal ancestries going back two thousand years. One Gou Yan-ling of Harbin, China, whose memory feats are listed in *The Guinness Book of World Records* (sandwiched between the world's "Largest Brain" and "Most Expensive Skull"), managed to memorize 15,000 seven-digit telephone numbers; Hideaki Tomoyori of Japan can reel off the value of pi to 40,000 places, a dull but impressive numerical performance that takes over seventeen hours. John Dean, star of the 1973 Watergate hearings, recalled in his near-endless testimony the details of several years' worth of shady governmental meetings, eventually summed up in a 245-page document, a memory display so spectacular that awed members of the press promptly dubbed him "the human tape recorder."

Conductor Arturo Toscanini, who had a phenomenal musical memory, is said to have known—by heart—every note of every instrument for 250 symphonic works, plus the words and music to one hundred different operas. At a concert in St. Louis, just as the orchestra was preparing to go on stage, the second bassoonist discovered that a key on his instrument was broken: he was unable to play his lowest note. Frantic, he presented his dilemma to Toscanini, who frowned a moment in thought, then said, "It is all right—that note does not occur in tonight's concert."

Theodore Roosevelt could read two books a night—and quote passages from them, verbatim, five years later. He could also recite the entire *Song of Roland* in the archaic French.

Perhaps the most famous of memory Olympians, however, by far outshining all of the above, was a Russian journalist known to the psychiatric literature simply as S. His real name was Solomon-Veniaminovich Shereshevskii. S was the second of the many children of a Jewish bookstore owner from a small town near Moscow. As a young man, he had hoped to become a professional violinist, but his ambitions were squelched by an ear infection that left his hearing permanently impaired.

Instead, he became a newspaper reporter, and it was his editor at the newspaper office who, in the early 1920s, set him on his road to psychological stardom. The editor's custom was to meet each morning with the members of his staff to dispense the day's assignments, which included long and detailed lists of instructions, directions, names, addresses, and telephone numbers. The other reporters, cowed by this inundation of information, promptly wrote everything down; S conspicuously never took notes. When taken to task for this—the editor was getting nervous—S defended himself by reeling off the entire morning's list, number by number, word for word. He could also, it turned out, reproduce the previous day's list and the list for the day before that—or, for that matter, all the lists he had ever heard, including the list from ten months ago, Tuesday. "Does not everybody remember everything?" he is said to have asked.

Everybody, of course, doesn't, and the impressed newspaper editor, who knew a mental find when he came across one, sent S to have his memory analyzed at the laboratory of the famous clinical psychologist Aleksandr Luria. Thus began a fruitful twenty-year association, eventually culminating in a book devoted to S: *The Mind of a Mnemonist: A Little Book About a Vast Memory*. Just how vast left Luria, a man who had seen a great deal of the outer limits of human behavior, in awe. S, without batting an eye, was able to memorize a list of several hundred random nonsense syllables—an interminable string of "ma na va sa na sa ma va"—and to recall them perfectly, not only immediately after learning, but fifteen years later. After only a few minutes of study, he could recite lengthy tables of scrambled letters and numbers, or reproduce immense and totally meaningless mathematical formulae; and he was able to repeat, after a single reading, stanza after stanza of *The Divine Comedy* in Italian, a language he did not understand. "When I began my study of S," wrote Luria, "it was with much the same degree of curiosity psychologists generally have at the outset of research, hardly with the hope that the experiments would offer anything of particular note. However, the results of the first tests were enough to change my mind and leave me, the experimenter, rather than my subject, both embarrassed and perplexed. . . . I simply had to admit that the capacity of his memory *had no distinct limits;* that I had been unable to perform what one would think was the simplest task a psychologist can do: measure the capacity of an individual's memory." S's monumental memory ability is a condition generally known as hypermnesia—super-memory—and one can't help but be secretly pleased that his possession of it saved him from all the embarrassments and perplexities suffered by run-of-the-mill psychological subjects.

Memory Is a Many-Splendored Thing

EVEN ORDINARY HUMAN MEMORY, however, is a many-splendored—and multifaceted—thing. Its capacity is immense and its powers legion: we can, in the blink of an eye, conjure up visual images of the Eiffel Tower, Mount Fujiyama, and the Emerald City of Oz; recall the numbers of the exits on the Washington Beltway; recognize—in fractions of seconds—thousands of individual faces. We can remember impressions and sensations as disparate as the pattern of the wallpaper in our grandmother's kitchen, the smell of the ocean, and the sound of a sousaphone. We can pack away the know-how for riding a bicycle, juggling, and playing the harmonica; and amass vocabularies of up to 100,000 words, often in more than one language. We can identify Vincent van Gogh's *Starry Night*, recognize the tune to "I've Been Working on the Railroad," and recall the plot of *The Scarlet Pimpernel*.

Memory is a versatile all-purpose tool, a mental Swiss Army knife, with which we conduct and create our daily lives. Even as routine an operation as stumbling off to work in the morning is an impressive feat of memory, no matter how blearily we may rise to greet the day. We use the information in our memory banks to read the time threateningly advancing on the face of the bedside alarm clock, to operate showers, zippers, shoe buckles, and electric coffee machines, to navigate our way around the house, to recognize the members of our families, to read the thermometer on the porch and predict the need for an extra sweater, to unlatch the sticky and uncooperative deadbolt on the back door, and to drive the car. Some of us may require an occasional memory-prodding nudge to get us going—a Gary Larson *Far Side* cartoon, for example, shows a just-awakened person sitting helplessly on the edge of his bed facing an enormous sign that reads FIRST PANTS, THEN SHOES—but for most, memory for the many processes of daily living is there on demand.

Memory not only rolls us through our daily grooves; it also performs a deeper and more pervasive function. We lay it down in sediments over the years of our lives; it solidifies to form the bedrock of our being. Through memory, we shape our characters, build our careers, forge our relationships, and write our mental autobiographies, the unique and irreplaceable histories of ourselves. Without it, we are hollow persons, not only empty of a past, but lacking a foundation upon which to build the future. Our memory is so much a part of our being, said author Vladimir Nabokov, that an afterlife without it would be unthinkable; it would be as though only one's left foot could be admitted into heaven.

Our accumulated memories—our personal reservoirs of triumphs and tribulations, joys and sorrows, loves and hatreds, and experiences, real and imagined—coalesce to form our personhoods and stretch across the years to give us what Nobel laureate John Eccles called "continuity of self." There, packaged between our ears, is the time we stood up to the second-grade playground bully, the year we spent in a potato commune in Arizona, the semester we flunked calculus, our awful first love affairs, our job promotions, the births of our children, our scratchy relationships with our mothers, the motorcycle trip we once took through Idaho. Integrated over time, our memories supply evidence for what we believe ourselves to be: winners, losers, successes, failures, brave, adventurous, caring, conscientious, clumsy, crochety, kindhearted, or cocksure. We make and remake ourselves through memory; we move through time like whales, filtering experience from our surroundings, digesting, repackaging, deciding what to keep and what to throw away. We assemble ourselves, piece by piece, from recollections. We are what we remember.

> In many ways, the past is a writer's capital. Your first glimpse of the sea, the first crack in your heart, the flower that bloomed on a favorite aunt's windowsill—these are uniquely yours.
> Susan Shaughnessy,
> *Walking on Alligators*

> When I was eight or nine, I first heard the phrase "Stop the World, I Want to Get Off." I remember perfectly the moment when I read the words for the first time, in an advertisement, and stopped dead in my skimming of the Sunday Times. It was, I think, one of my first real encounters with what I called then "deep thinking" (the other times came when I first considered Death—my own, negative numbers, and "What came first, the chicken or the egg?").
> Joyce Maynard,
> *Looking Backward*

While, like fingerprints, no two persons' memories are alike, aspects of each may be shared. From culture to culture and country to country, individual memories overlap like Venn diagrams. These overlaps are collective or communal memories, joint remembrances of historical experiences that reinforce group memberships and bind us together as tribes. Such shared memories are the roots of religious rituals, the sources of patriotism, familial loyalty, and ethnic pride. In memory of a common past, Jews celebrate Passover and Yom Kippur, Christians reenact the Last Supper; and Muslims turn daily toward Mecca and fast in the month of Ramadan. The Irish, remembering the Emerald Isle, march through the streets of Boston on Saint Patrick's Day; the British, remembering the Gunpowder Plot, burn effigies of Guy Fawkes on the fifth of November; and the French, remembering the Revolution, shoot off fireworks on Bastille Day. Americans variously remember the *Maine*, the Alamo, Pearl Harbor, Bunker Hill, and the Red River Valley; we are linked by communal national recollections of Benjamin Franklin ("We must all hang together or assuredly we shall all hang separately"), Abraham Lincoln ("A house divided against itself cannot stand"), Franklin Delano Roosevelt ("The only thing we have to fear is fear itself"), and Will Rogers ("All politics is applesauce"). Jointly, we consume turkey and pumpkin pie on Thanksgiving Day; hang out the flag on the glorious Fourth of July; and burn an eternal memorial torch on the Tomb of the Unknown Soldier. Every small-town museum and historical society, with its jumble of quilts and candleholders, undersized military uniforms, rusted kettles, flintlocks, forks, and china-headed dolls, is a tribute to the power of group memory. Our personal memories distinguish us from one another; our communal memories bind us together.

> *The adoration of the moosehide britches of our ancestors is a defining characteristic of New England.*
> Howard Mansfield,
> *In the Memory House*

Squirrels, Eels, and Elephants Never Forget

H UMAN MEMORY MAY BE the richest and most prodigious on the planet, but it's not the only one. All creatures great and small, from the lowly worm to the legendarily retentive elephant, possess some form of memory. Birds, at least in part, remember their migratory paths: young geese and whooping cranes must follow some knowledgeable elder until they learn the north-south route for themselves; and homing pigeons have been shown to use remembered visual cues to find their way back to the home loft. Salmon remember their spawning grounds; eels, who return annually to breed there, recall the taste of the water in the Sargasso Sea.

Squirrels, whose deceptively scatty behavior can trick one into believing that they have no brains at all, have superb memories for the burial sites of their nuts. The average gray squirrel, *Sciurus carolinensis,* a thrifty and farsighted creature except for its habit of gnawing suicidally on electrical wires, buries between one thousand and ten thousand nuts each autumn, one at a time, in little cup-shaped holes about three inches deep. Past dogma has held that squirrels only manage to retrieve their hidden loot through the winter months by serendipity, helped along by a discriminating sense of smell. Recent research by biologists Lucia Jacobs and Emily Liman at the Institute for Advanced Study in Princeton, New Jersey, however, indicates that there's more to the seemingly scatterbrained squirrel than meets the eye. Nut disinterment, in practice, involves a phenomenal exercise of memory. To demonstrate this, Jacobs and Liman allowed assorted gray squirrels to do what comes naturally: bury hazelnuts. The burial site, however, was a restricted outdoor enclosure, and the obliviously busy squirrels were closely monitored by the investigators, who carefully recorded which squirrel buried which nut where. Once their hoards were safely stashed away, the squirrels were removed from the site of action and caged for periods of up to twelve days, before being returned to the enclosure—hungry—to forage. If the squirrels zeroed in on the buried goods by smell alone, the researchers theorized, retrieval would be a matter of snatch-and-grab with no respect for personal property rights; if memory played a decisive role, however, the squirrels should prefer their own caches to those of others. The latter proved to be the case, and Jacobs and Liman took the squirrels' behavior—somebody else's nut hidden practically at one's feet was ignored in favor of a far-distant nut of one's own—to indicate that the squirrels, from memory, constructed complex mental maps of their burial sites. It's a humbling lesson for those of us who, year after year, lose the family snow shovel somewhere beneath the winter's first snowfall and are unable to find it again until the following spring.

The elephant, whose ponderous species shares (with women) a stellar reputation for memory, likewise has a substantial mental armamentarium. The popular view of the perspicacious elephant appears in a Rea Irvin *New Yorker* cartoon of 1926 titled "An Elephant Never Forgets." The first frames picture a beastly small boy in a Sunday suit feeding a cake of soap to a trusting elephant. Decades later the deceived elephant has its revenge: identifying the boy, now an elderly man with spectacles, a frock coat, and a long gray beard, on a sidewalk during a parade, the elephant breaks ranks, pursues the ex-tormentor home, chases him into the bathroom, and gleefully feeds him a retributional cake of soap. Wildlife biologists, observing independent elephants, on the loose in the wild, have found them to possess notable spatial memories, which allow them to recall the locations of widely distant desert watering holes, even if they haven't been anywhere near the place in months. This same mental skill, in people, allows us to learn routes from road maps, commute long distances to work, and find our way home from Colorado to Connecticut in time for Thanksgiving dinner. Men and women, incidentally, despite politically correct pressure to the contrary, display marked differences in spatial memory abilities. Men tend to learn long-distance routes more readily than women—a trait that persists, some psychologists hypothesize, from the days when males ranged far and wide in search of game—while women, though generally less ept with the atlas, have better memories for landmarks encountered along the way. Elephants, observers suspect, navigate female-style, maintaining within their memories landmark-studded mental maps of the local terrain. Researchers at the Indianapolis Zoo, where elephants have shown themselves to be cunningly clever at recalling the locations of apples concealed in covered buckets, are attempting to study this phenomenon in small scale.

> *"Are you lost, Daddy?" I asked tenderly.*
> *"Shut up," he explained.*
> Ring Lardner

> *Map me no maps, sire; my head is a map, a map of the whole world.*
> Henry Fielding

> *I hate women because they always know where things are.*
> James Thurber

Folk artist Alice Freeman of Newfane, Vermont, is a custom cartographer, a creator of memory maps. These colorful paint-and-papier-mâché constructions (see examples on pages 16–17) trace the landscapes of lifetimes: contour maps of remembered places are sprinkled with personal landmarks, mementos, photographs, notes, and quotations. Ms. Freeman's own memory map, a two-foot-square reproduction of the country around her hometown of Newfane, includes—along with the mountains, roads, and rivers—the site of a lost tooth, an encounter with a snake, a favorite diner and ice cream stand, and a button with the message "We Don't Care How They Do It in New York."

Among the earliest formal assessments of elephant memory were those conducted in the 1950s by German researcher Bernhard Rensch, whose interest was initially inspired by the elephant's sheer size. Rensch's original investigations in the memory field centered on the crass advantages of bulk. Larger animals, early studies had indicated, have better learning abilities than small ones. Giant Indian squirrels are better learners than dwarf Indian squirrels; large-sized breeds of chickens are smarter than small-sized breeds; rats have quicker wits than mice. The elephant, Rensch enthusiastically predicted, should by extrapolation be a memory prodigy: size-wise right at the top of the terrestrial scale, the adult elephant can reach a weight of six and a half tons, and possesses the largest brain of any land animal, weighing in at thirteen pounds plus. Tales of elephantine intelligence, inventiveness, and, occasionally, fiendish cleverness abound. Rensch repeats—but personally doubted—a story that domesticated elephants have been known to silence the bells around their necks by stuffing them with mud before slinking out at night to snitch bananas.

Results, which sadly neglected to deal with the bell-and-

Why I'm Here (1989)

Sixties Pre-Beatles Youth Subculture at Play (1989)

New Hampshire Got All the Lakes (1989)

Geier Map (1990)

bananas story, did show that elephants indeed very seldom forget. The ordinary blue-collar elephant, at work in the forests and on the roads of India, reliably remembers up to twenty-four different spoken commands, among them "Go forward," "Stop," "Squirt water under your belly," and "Break the obstacle," while the trained circus elephant retains up to a hundred. Controlled experiments with elephants are difficult—even Rensch himself pointed out, in a *Scientific American* article of 1957, that the elephant "is not particularly convenient as a laboratory animal," but he eventually managed to obtain a cooperative subject, a five-year-old female, resident at the Münster Zoo. Rensch and colleagues taught their elephant to discriminate among twenty different pairs of cards, variously patterned with dots, circles, stripes, crosshatched lines, letters of the alphabet, and, in one case, drawings of a bird and a bee. One card of each pair, the "correct" card, was matched during the training period with a food reward, a slice of bread. The investigators also gave hints at first, yelling *"Nein!"* when the elephant moved toward the wrong card. The elephant, so encouraged, quickly acquired the forty-card "vocabulary" necessary for discrimination tasks. Furthermore, she remembered her lessons. When the tests were repeated a full year later, she still performed almost perfectly. American zoo elephants, similarly trained, still remembered their cards after an eight-year hiatus. It's not yet proof that elephants *never* forget, but the evidence is on their side.

> *Prince, a precept I'd leave for you,*
> *Coined in Eden, existing yet:*
> *Skirt the parlor, and shun the zoo—*
> *Women and elephants never forget.*
> Dorothy Parker,
> *"Ballade of Unfortunate Mammals"*

Big Brains, Small Brains

THOUGH BRAIN ANATOMY inevitably plays a crucial role in the ability to remember, among individual humans size is not the defining feature of memory. (Football players remember no better than ballerinas.) During the late nineteenth century, a flare of interest in craniometry—the measurement of heads and brains—led scientists worldwide into a frenzy of brain-weighing in hopes of demonstrating that the best and the brightest were also the biggest. Most prominent among craniometers was French surgeon Paul Broca who, with scales, calipers, and creative statistics, managed to prove that the average French brain was larger than the average German brain. This was attributed in part to the German consumption of beer, which made Germans "much more fleshy" than the svelte wine-sipping French, and thus saddled them with a smaller brain size relative to total body mass. Other researchers, depending on prevailing local bias, demonstrated that white brains were larger than black brains, male brains larger than female, and rich larger than poor. One-on-one measurements of the brains of the successful and famous, however, put a spoke in this metrological wheel: against an average European brain size of 1,300–1,400 grams (about twice the weight of a basketball), the brain of poet Walt Whitman was found to weigh a measly 1,282 grams, that of author Anatole France, 1,017 grams, and that of Albert Einstein—arguably the best and brightest brain of the twentieth century—a definitely unremarkable 1,230 grams. Size differences within the human species clearly don't mean much. Among species, on the other hand, size seems to have some significance. *Homo sapiens*, the smartest, though not necessarily the most sensible, animal on earth, has the largest brain mass–body mass ratio in all the animal kingdom. The brain-to-body mass ratio generally follows a reproducible formula, allowing scientists to predict with reasonable accuracy brain sizes of anything from the pygmy shrew and the field mouse to the buffalo and the blue whale. Human beings, however, are way off the formulaic scale, boasting brains four times bigger than, mathematically speaking, they ought to be. Similarly off-scale is our nearest runner-up, the dolphin.

While people and dolphins may share the most intelligence and richest memories on the planet, even creatures with heads the size of the proverbial pin demonstrably possess some form of memory. Consider the ant, a minuscule being whose total body weight, on average, hovers around .04 gram. (Translate this into nonmetric, and you get 10,000 ants to the pound.) Ants, despite the handicap of a brain smaller than a grain of salt, have excellent memories for their nestmates' smells. Ants recognize each other by body odor. Each species has its own unique scent, generated by a combination of hydrocarbons on the surface of the skin. This scent, a chemical recognition signal, is the difference between acceptance and attack: a visiting ant redolent of the wrong hydrocarbon recipe is a goner. The young, however—as is so often the case—are more tolerant of odoriferous differences than are the old. If young ants of two different species are raised together, they socialize happily, in the course of which their scents meld, as chemicals are transferred back and forth among insects by proximity and inter-ant grooming. Separate the species, however, and the original homegrown odors gradually reassert themselves.

French biologist Christine Errard and colleagues at the University of Paris recently exploited this homogenization and subsequent reestablishment of skin smells to study ant memory.

Adolescent ants of two different species—*Formica selysi* and *Manica rubida*—were raised together for three months, then separated. At intervals, ants of the once-mixed group were then either rejoined with their old nestmates—a sort of ant college reunion—or combined with strange ants who had been raised in strictly conventional single-species groups. In the latter case, all went well until the mixed smell wore off: then mixed-group-raised *F. selysi*, now giving off an unmistakably alien whiff, were attacked by single-species-raised *M. rubida,* and vice versa. Old mixed-group members, however, never attacked one another, even after eighteen months of separation, by which time all mixed-smell cues were long gone. The conclusion reached by the French researchers was that during those three formative months, the mixed-group ants had learned one another's individual chemical signatures and had retained this information in long-term memory.

While this is all fine and good, most animals—from the selfishly human point of view—don't have all that much to remember. We humans live in a much more taxing world, a society not only based on but positively inundated by information. E. D. Hirsch, Jr., in the formidable Appendix to his best-selling *Cultural Literacy,* lists 4,545 bits of rock-bottom information that every American needs to know just in order to communicate effectively with everybody else. James Trefil lists *1,001 Things Everyone Should Know About Science,* spread over the fields of classical biology, evolution, molecular biology, physical science (classical and modern), earth science, and astronomy, with an occasional pop quiz thrown in just to make sure you're paying attention. James Garraty comes up with *1,001 Things*—political, biographical, geographical, cultural, military, and economic— that *Everyone Should Know About American History.* Harold Bloom, literary scholar and author of *The Western Canon: The Books and School of the Ages,* presents the aspiring public with an essential reading list of some 3,000 books by 850 authors, starting with the (anonymous) Sumerian epic *Gilgamesh.* Plowing through this many masterpieces, a task which Bloom himself depressingly declares "virtually impossible," would take even the nippiest and most dedicated bookworm upward of ten years.

The amount of available information, writes Richard Saul Wurman in *Information Anxiety*, now doubles every five—soon to be four—years. Over a thousand new books hit the shelves daily worldwide—125 of them American—and American printing presses roll out a daily 62.5 million newspapers. A single weekday edition of the *New York Times*—a publication that sops up an annual 346,000 tons of newsprint—provides us with more information than the average seventeenth-century citizen had to cope with in a lifetime. The hapless citizens of the Information Age have more to internalize than a scattering of nut burial sites, the scent of a childhood nestmate, or the coordinates of the odd watering hole.

Knowing That and Knowing How

H UMAN MEMORY, THAT mysterious storage bank in which we keep our 1,001 science facts, the headlines of this morning's newspaper, and the location of our galoshes, performs so many different functions that observers have designed for it a taxonomy all its own. Memory, no matter how integrated it seems to its individual owners, is not a bloblike single entity, indiscriminatingly engulfing all information in its path, but a collection of discrete operating systems, interconnected by the working brain. Keeping track of all these rapidly moving parts is no easy task. Proposed divisions and subdivisions of memory, derived from observations of subjects in clinical or laboratory studies, are so numerous that memory appears to be a psychologist's version of the mythological Hydra: a monster that whenever you manage to chop off one head sprouts two others in its place. The scientific literature lists over forty different names for different types of memory, all struggling to work their way into common usage.

Many of these categories are based on memory content and accessibility: that is, what kinds of things are stored in memory and how available are they to conscious recall? In the simplest case, multiple terminological contenders can be reduced to two: *declarative* memory, which includes both memories of past episodes from our personal lives and stores of general knowledge, and *procedural* memory, which includes our memories of learned skills. Declarative and procedural memory are terms borrowed by biologists from the electronic world of the artificial intelligence community. These first emerged in the 1970s as fighting words among computer nerds—proponents of *declarative representation* arguing that programmable knowledge was best coded as a series of discrete facts; supporters of *procedural representation* favoring programs consisting of a series of activities or procedures. A familiar example of declarative programming is the electronic psychiatrist ELIZA, which, by generating set responses to selected key words on the computer screen, cleverly mimics the real thing. Mention "mother" or "father," for example, and ELIZA will solicitously request that you TELL ME MORE ABOUT YOUR FAMILY. Robots, on the other hand, are prime examples of procedural programs, animated by sequential lists of manipulations that allow, for example, a robotic claw to lift and stack an assortment of blocks.

Declarative memory in all its many human aspects is sometimes described as a process of knowing *that.* We know *that* Columbus, for better or for worse, reached the Caribbean in 1492; we know *that* we broke a leg by falling out of a tree at the age of ten. Declarative memory, furthermore, is subject to conscious recall. Its contents are (more or less) readily accessible; given a little brow-furrowing cogitation, they can be deliberately brought to mind.

Procedural memory, in contrast, is a process of knowing *how.* We know *how* to swim, *how* to dunk a basketball, *how* to play "The Flight of the Bumblebee" on the violin. Procedural memory is what athletic coaches sometimes refer to as "muscle memory": it's what allows us, fifteen years after the fact, to hop back on a bicycle and insouciantly pedal away. Unlike declarative memory, procedural memory can be run on autopilot. As learned sequences become automatic, procedural memories are accessed without conscious thought: Once you've mastered the art of riding a bicycle, you no longer have to think about it anymore. I watched my middle son some time back, smoothly juggling three blue-and-yellow rubber balls. "How do you *do* that?" I asked enviously. Ethan paused in mid-juggle and looked puzzled. "You know," he said after a moment, "I don't think I know." Such is the nature of procedural memory. It functions nicely on its own.

Declarative memory, in turn, is generally subdivided into two parts. Its most familiar component—what most of us think of as the true essence of memory—is *episodic* memory, our personal store of reminiscences from times past. Episodic memory, explains psychologist Endel Tulving, is our own private time machine. This is the memory of reminiscent grandpas reliving World War II, the memory evoked by scrapbooks stuffed with snapshots of bygone babies, birthday parties, and summer picnics. When Sam sits down at the piano in *Casablanca* and sings "As Time Goes By" for Ingrid Bergman, he's conjuring up episodic memories. Recall your senior prom, your wedding day, or your army induction physical and you're calling upon the same. The process of nostalgic personal recollection is very different from its opposite number: the encyclopedic compilation of general information known to psychologists as *semantic* memory. Semantic memory stores the essential raw material that allows us to define, order, and operate within the world: the definitions of bat and butterfly, for example, and the awful truth about poison ivy, the meaning of the red and green lights on traffic signals, the number of pints in a quart, and the capital of Oklahoma. We access semantic memory to locate middle C on the piano keyboard; procedural memory provides the know-how for playing "Eine Kleine Nachtmusik"; and episodic memory generates images of childhood piano recitals.

The existence of separate episodic and semantic memory systems is dramatically illustrated by an amnesic patient first described by Endel Tulving and tactfully referred to in the psychiatric literature by his initials, K.C. K.C. missed a curve on his motorcycle in late October 1980, and suffered severe damage to the frontal and parietal lobes of his brain. When he came to in the hospital three days later, he was a man without a personal history. All episodic memories were gone. While K.C. cannot

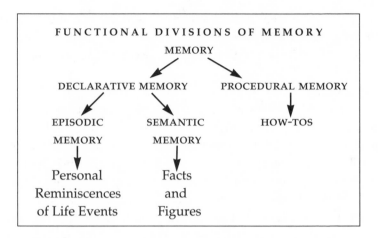

FUNCTIONAL DIVISIONS OF MEMORY

MEMORY

DECLARATIVE MEMORY   PROCEDURAL MEMORY

EPISODIC   SEMANTIC   HOW-TOS
MEMORY   MEMORY

Personal   Facts
Reminiscences   and
of Life Events   Figures

remember his past, however, his semantic memory remains intact. He knows how to play chess, though he does not recall learning how to play or remember the details of any games played in the past. He knows that his family owns a summer cottage in Ontario—he can locate it on the map—but he cannot recall what the cottage looks like or remember any incidents from all the many vacations spent there. K.C.'s memory retains impersonal facts but has purged itself of human characters and familiar scenery. His mind is a dictionary rather than a scrapbook; an instruction manual rather than an autobiography. He knows what a Christmas tree is, but remembers no Christmases; he knows that leaves turn color in the fall, but remembers no walks through the woods; he can identify a daffodil, but remembers no springs. His personal past is gone.

> *"In this life, we want nothing but Facts, sir;*
> *nothing but Facts!"*
> Charles Dickens,
> *Hard Times*

Squawk to Syntax

In SEMANTIC MEMORY we also package all the complexities and categories of language, that seminal talent that skyrocketed us so abruptly, some 1.5 million years ago in the days of *Homo erectus*, out of apedom and into humankind.

Language—a neurologically complicated can of worms—may be an innate feature of the overblown human brain. Linguist Noam Chomsky hypothesizes that a "language bioprogram" is hardwired in our mental circuitry in the same way that birds are genetically programmed for song. Language, for *Homo sapiens*, is thus as inevitable as walking upright and having opposable thumbs. Small children are greedily acquiring vocabulary words by the age of two, sometimes at the rapid rate of ten new words a day. By three, they've begun to arrange their mushrooming store of linguistic raw material into grammatical patterns: they've picked up the trick of adding "ed" to a verb to denote past tense and "s" to a noun to form a plural; and they know how to report, in logical sequence, who did what to whom on the preschool playground. All this takes place without conscious and deliberate teaching. Parents don't conjugate verbs or define the object of a sentence for their toddlers. Adults simply talk, and children—primed to master the intricacies of language—rapidly follow.

The ability to transform sensory input into symbols, symbols into sounds, and sounds into syntax is our great talent. It

shapes our behaviors, forges our social relationships, and channels the very way we think. The ability to convert sensory
impressions into symbols and sounds was an evolutionary leap
for the language-bound primate. Chimps, who use dozens of
different communicative vocalizations, are adept at it, able to
translate the sight of a leopard slinking through the bushes into
a precise warning squawk that alerts the rest of the tribe to the
nature of the approaching trouble. Both screeching chimps and
pontificating human beings package their vocalizations in
phonemes—the individual sound units that, pasted together,
make up meaningful words. Phoneme-wise, we're not all that
different from the chimps. Chimpanzees use a couple of dozen
different phonemes; English speakers use thirty-eight; and all
the world's languages together, including Xhosa, Inuit, Apache,
and !Kung, are covered by a mere two hundred. It's not sounds
that distinguish us from our primate cousins; it's syntax that
gives humans the edge in the communications game. Syntax is
grammar, the manner in which phonemes are combined to form
words, and words ordered to form sentences. Syntax is the feature that puts the adjectives after the nouns in French (*la table
rouge*) and determines the small but crucial difference in meaning between "Dog bites man" and "Man bites dog." Stringing
words into sentences astronomically increases the complexity of
the concepts that can be passed from person to person. It's our
mastery of syntax that has allowed us to progress from "Leopard!" to "To be or not to be. . . ."

> *"Then you should say what you mean," the March Hare
> went on.*
> *"I do," Alice hastily replied; "at least—at least I mean
> what I say—that's the same thing, you know."*
> *"Not the same thing a bit!" said the Hatter. "Why, you
> might just as well say that 'I see what I eat' is the same
> thing as 'I eat what I see'!"*
> Lewis Carroll,
> *Alice's Adventures in Wonderland*

> *No matter how eloquently a dog may bark, he cannot tell*
> *you that his parents were poor but honest.*
> Bertrand Russell

> *The limits of my language are the limits of my mind. All I*
> *know is what I have words for.*
> Ludwig Wittgenstein

Sensory input is repackaged by the human brain into concepts, phonemes, and words. Bite a juicy red Delicious apple, for example, and your brain is excitingly bombarded with data. In less time than it takes to chomp and chew, you register multiple sensory impressions: the glossily colorful sight of the apple, the satisfying sound of the bite, the fruity scent, the sweet taste, the feel of the cool smooth skin. Such sensations—alone or in company—activate the linguistic memory banks that spit out the word *apple,* and may then proceed, chain-reaction-style, to turn up wave after wave of associated apple memories: Adam and Eve, William Tell, Johnny Appleseed, Atalanta falling for the Golden Apples of the Hesperides, Snow White's poisoned apple, Mom's apple pie.

Wind in the Trees

WHEN ALL DOES NOT go well, however, as when stroke, acute infection, chronic disease, or catastrophic motorcycle accident lays a victim low, the tragic consequences allow scientists to peer into the tangled web of linguistic memory. Language, as evidenced by the way in which people lose it, is not stockpiled in a lump, in some single internal dictionary, but is distributed in scattered pockets across the brain. These pockets, furthermore, are variously governed by at least two different memory systems. Recent evidence suggests that our stockpiles of vocabulary words are stored as declarative memories, while our grasp of the rules of grammar is a facet of procedural memory. Words and their definitions, in other words, are treated in memory like facts and figures, discrete snippets of information embedded in the brain by rote repetition. The rules of grammar, on the other hand, are treated like physical activities, stored as procedural memories, in the same manner that we package the know-how for balancing on ice skates or paddling a canoe.

This conclusion—that your brain stores your grasp of subject and predicate in the same place as your tennis swing—is based on studies of patients with memory impairments by Michael Ullman and colleagues at Georgetown University. Patients with Alzheimer's disease, Ullman found, were particularly weak in their ability to recall irregular verbs. Knowledge of regular verb structures was relatively intact—given such verbs as *chop, jump,* and *kick,* for example, they could produce the proper past tenses: *chopped, jumped, kicked.* Given an irregular verb, however—a genre in which English is distressingly rich—Alzheimer's patients were stymied, unable to recall the correct past tenses of such unpredictable words as *dig, swim,* and *throw.* Patients with Parkinson's or Huntington's disease, in contrast, were undeterred by irregular verbs, but had problems with verbs that cooperatively follow grammatical rules. *Dug, swam,* and *threw* were easily recalled, but the "ed" endings of regular verbs such as *look* were either stutteringly repeated—"lookededed"—or left off altogether.

Alzheimer's patients are notably impaired in declarative memory—the hallmark of the disease is the progressive loss of memory for life events and general information—while Parkinson's and Huntington's patients suffer progressive diminution of the ability to perform sequential movements, of the sort stored in procedural memory. Language deficits, Ullman concluded, seem to parallel the patients' respective memory disabilities. Damage to declarative memory centers brought with it a loss of memorized vocabulary words; damage to procedural memory centers, a loss of grammatical processes.

This canny distribution of language centers does not, sad to say, ensure that we cannot be stricken dumb. There are devastating cases of total language loss—a condition physicians call global aphasia—in which sufferers simultaneously lose the ability to speak, to understand spoken language, to read, and to write. One such unfortunate was a nineteenth-century French aphasic, M. Leborgne, known in the scientific literature as "Tan," since, after a massive stroke suffered in the 1840s, *tan* was the only word he was able to say. After his death twenty language-less years later, his doctor, Paul Broca, examined his brain and identified the site of the damage, a checker-sized chunk of tissue just above the left ear. Loss of this crucial chunk, referred to today by anatomists as "Broca's area," is now known to have been only part of Tan/Leborgne's problem: total language wipeout requires simultaneous damage to many different regions of the brain. Specific lesions in Broca's area more commonly lead to deficits in expression. Such patients usually make sense, but their communications resemble bad telephone connections, where static obscures portions of the sentences. Asked what he did during spring vacation, a Broca's aphasic may stammer out a truncated string of nouns and phrases: "*Easter . . . holiday, like . . . eggs . . . many people . . . very good.*" The words are there but they can no longer be packaged for proper delivery.

In 1874, German neurologist Carl Wernicke came up with another putative language center, duly named Wernicke's area—a silver-dollar-sized site just downstream from Broca's, above and behind the left ear. Unlike the stammering Broca patients, Wernicke's aphasics are syntactically fluent, but their speech is a free-associative babble, smacking of Lewis Carroll's "Jabberwocky," often making no sense at all. One guess, based on this conjunction of deficits, is that the meaningful sense of speech is organized behind the ear in Wernicke's area, and the sequential vocalizations that emerge as functional conversation are assembled above the ear, in Broca's. At the very least, it's clear that speech is a cooperative package deal.

Some aphasics selectively lose the ability to understand spoken words. They hear sounds, but, explained one sufferer, "Language sounds like wind in the trees." They do, however, retain the ability to speak and understand written words, and so can still—with extra effort—communicate with the outside world. Some aphasics, though lacking the ability to speak, are still able to sing. Others—anomic aphasics—lose the ability to name names. Anomias may be nitpickingly specific. Such ailments are sometimes called "category deficits," since victims, often to their vast frustration, have lost the ability to assign names to certain classes or categories of objects.

Categorization—sorting observed objects and experiences into memory groups, based on perceived similarities—is one of the functions the human brain performs best. The brain, without conscious input from its owner, manages to match creatures as disparate as a Great Dane and a Chihuahua—both dogs—while differentiating them neatly from wolves, coyotes, foxes, and bobcats. Brain categories, furthermore, appear to be arranged in ever-deepening and more detailed layers, from the very general to the exquisitely specific. The excited cry "It's a bird! It's a plane! It's . . . Superman!" is a rough approximation of this process: the brain rapidly shuffles through its category of "flying things," identifying the sighted object at first by general superficial clues, then rapidly narrowing the field to pinpoint the singular soaring Kryptonian in the cape and red-and-blue suit.

Based on studies of anomic patients, researchers in recent years have pieced together some twenty different categories that act as mental storage bins in the brain. All our names for fruits and vegetables seem to be lumped together in one category—lose *canteloupe* to brain damage, and you'll also lose *kumquat, cardoon, cucumber, Brussels sprouts,* and *broccoli.* All animals are included in another category, body parts in a third. There are categories for numbers, letters, and colors—all the things you learned in nursery school—and categories for nouns, verbs, proper names, facial expressions, sounds, and emotions.

Neuroscientists Hanna and Antonio Damasio have studied an impairment called color anomia, in which patients, normal in all other ways, have lost the ability to name colors. Color anomics are not colorblind: they can both see and comprehend color. Give them a handful of paint chips and they can correctly match colored chips to appropriate objects: a green chip with grass, a yellow with a banana, a blue with the sky. But they cannot come up with the words *green, yellow, red, white,* or *blue,* or, when given the color name, cannot associate the spoken word with the correct color. The name *green* no longer has meaning.

Neuropsychologists Rosaleen McCarthy and Elizabeth Warrington of London's National Hospital for Nervous Diseases have studied a patient who suffers from animal anomia: he specifically lacks the ability to name animals. *Poodle, aardvark,* and *laughing hyena* have all vanished from his brain, though information relating to each remains. When shown a picture of a rhinoceros, for example, he answers, "Enormous, weighs over one ton, lives in Africa." Another patient has lost not only the names for animals, but for all natural entities. An organic anomic, he fumbles vainly after the names of animals, plants, fruits, and vegetables. The names for mechanical and manmade objects, however, remain. *Wombat, aspidistra, avocado,* and *okra* are out of reach; *shovel, screwdriver,* and *electric toothbrush* remain accessible.

Specific anomias, though annoying if one wants to give advice about what color not to wear in front of a bull or take the kids on an informative trip to the zoo, are, with a little ingenuity, possible to overcome. Other linguistic memory losses are harder to live with. The Damasios have studied two patients who have lost the ability to name common nouns. Both clearly understand the concepts underlying the missing words; they can describe, in roundabout fashion, items from widely diverse categories: animals, plants, buildings, vehicles, tools, human body parts. In doing so, however, they circle the elusive name like players in a game of Twenty Questions. *"It's in the middle of the face; you breathe, smell, and sneeze with it . . ."*—but neither patient can dredge up the word *nose.* Equally maddening is the predicament of patients who have lost the ability to use common verbs. Show them a picture of a man with a broom or a woman with a shovel and they can name the brandished tools and describe the task at hand—*"Trying to make the floor clean; making a hole in the garden"*—but cannot come up with an all-purpose *sweeping* or *digging.* Alfonso Caramazza and colleagues at Johns Hopkins have described a pair of patients who have lost the ability to deal with homonyms, words which look and sound alike, but have two different meanings. In sentences such as "The Arab ate the dates" versus "The cheerleader dates the football captain," both balk at the use of the word *dates* in verb form.

It's on the Tip of My Tongue

ALL OF US, AT ONE TIME or another, are temporary anomics, fumbling through our mental categories, at a loss for a word. Psychologists call these annoying instances of word evaporation "tip-of-the-tongue" phenomena. In practice, it's the sort of verbal boggle that leaves us gesturing helplessly and stammering, "It's on top of the . . . the . . . the . . . " while the name *refrigerator* lurks recalcitrantly out of reach. Sign language users are afflicted similarly; in their case such verbal stymies are known as "tip-of-the-finger" experiences. The result—a frustrated mental grope—is the same.

> "Well, at any rate it's a great comfort," she said as she stepped under the trees, "after being so hot to get into the—into the—into what?" she went on, rather surprised at not being able to think of the word. "I mean to get under the—under the—under this, you know!" putting her hand on the trunk of the tree. "What does it call itself, I wonder?"
>
> Lewis Carroll,
> *Through the Looking-Glass*

It's not surprising that we run into occasional verbal brick walls. Speech, according to Dr. Willem Levelt of the Max Planck Institute for Psycholinguistics in the Netherlands, involves a convoluted three-layer dive through memory. Levelt hypothesizes three levels of processing—musically designated the lexical, lemma, and lexeme networks—before ephemeral thought emerges as solid spoken word. At level one, the lexical network, thought is born. There you activate memory banks of information related to an observed or imagined image: its shape, sound, color, function, history. Loaded with this conceptual information but still wordless, you proceed to the next level, the lemma network, tapping into your memory for the rules of syntax and searching your immense stores of vocabulary, which may encode some tens of thousands of remembered words. Finally, at the lexeme level, you assemble the proper combination of sounds—those thirty-eight phonemes—that allows you at last to blurt out the desired word. Humans are experts at this; most of us shown, say, a picture of a beaver can produce the word *beaver* in seven-hundredths of a second.

Screwups, however, can happen at any level. The lexical network, for example, may activate conflicting conceptual memories—not only the packet of stored information for beaver, but equivalent packets for muskrat, water rat, and otter. This competition is enough to do you in: the "beaver" concept, thus diluted, is not strong enough to activate the memory of its name, stored at the next level up. You may get a flicker from the lemma network—*It's a two-syllable word; begins with a B*—but there you stick. Usually, however, you don't stick forever; most anomia is only a temporary disturbance in the force. Give it a few minutes and your brain, says psychologist Gary Dell, will "re-boot." In about 97 percent of cases, the correct lexical concept—the second time around—will win.

Ralph Waldo Emerson, the Transcendentalist philosopher known as the "sage of Concord," became increasingly forgetful in his later years. As his memory failed, he often found himself groping for the names of familiar objects, forced to refer to them as best he could in a roundabout fashion. His term for the forgotten word *umbrella:* "the thing that strangers take away."

Frequencies and Faces

Not all deficits are linguistic. Some people suffer from a condition called amusia, a musical aphasia that deprives its victims of the ability to recognize songs or melodies. Like the aphasics who hear spoken language only as meaningless noise—"wind in the trees"—amusics hear music as a series of distorted and incoherent sounds. An amusic can interpret other auditory input—spoken language, animal sounds, traffic noise—with ease, but is unable to tell Bach from the Beatles, Led Zeppelin from a Scottish bagpipe band. Neurobiologist Mark Tramo of Harvard Medical School suggests that amusia may involve some loss of linguistic circuitry. Normal human speech is not delivered in a monotone, points out Tramo, but in a variety of rising and falling frequencies known as pitch. Pitch is measured in wave cycles per second, a quantity known as hertz. Humans can produce sounds ranging in pitch from a rumbling 80 hertz to a piercing 1100, though typical frequencies used in speech range around 110 hertz for men, 220 for women, and 300 for children. Glass-shattering sopranos can hit 4350 hertz—E above the piano's top note; dogs bark at 452–1080 hertz; cats meow at 760–1520; and robins tweet at 2000–13,000. Pitch is an integral part of grammar: our voices rise in question, fall for emphasis. Since pitch is also an essential component of music, the same cellular circuits in the brain may be involved in decod-

ing both the changing frequencies of spoken words and the rising and falling notes of a violin concerto.

> *I only know two tunes. One of them is "Yankee Doodle"*
> *and the other isn't.*
> Ulysses S. Grant

An even stranger deficit is an affliction known as prosopag-
nosia, from the Greek *prosopon* (face) and *agnosis* (without
knowledge). Prosopagnosics are unable to recognize faces. Most
can tell that they're looking at *a* face and can identify separate
facial features—eyes, nose, and mouth—but *whose* face is
beyond them. They cannot recognize the visages of the much-
publicized rich and famous, the mugs of the Most Wanted, the
countenances of their own nearest and dearest, or even their
own faces reflected in the bathroom mirror. Deprived of faces,
they are forced to recognize acquaintances by subsidiary clues:
context, clothing, body build, tone of voice.

Loss of memory for faces is painful, since facial recognition
plays such a prominent part in our social lives. Even newborn
babies prefer facelike patterns—two stylized eyes, a nose, and a
mouth—to all others, and by adulthood we have squirreled
away hundreds or thousands of facial images. Face fragmenta-
tion studies, in which subjects attempt to identify individuals
from isolated segments of facial photographs, show that we
tend to zero in on eyes first, followed by mouth and nose. An
alternative series of experiments, in which subjects were asked
to write descriptions of faces seen in photographs, indicated that
the prime distinguishing facial feature is hair—a favored clue
for prosopagnosics; one patient was able to recognize Albert
Einstein from his wild white coiffure. Next best after hair were
eyes, nose, and eyebrows, followed at long remove by chin,
mouth, and cheeks. Whichever feature we light on, we're good
at deciding whether we like it or not: it takes us a mere 150 mil-

liseconds to decide that a given face is attractive, and the better looking it is, the better we'll remember it. This means that gentlemen, as Anita Loos suspected, should best remember blondes.

> *"I shouldn't know you again if we did meet,"* Humpty-Dumpty *replied in a discontented tone, giving her one of his fingers to shake: "You're so exactly like other people."*
> Lewis Carroll,
> *Through the Looking-Glass*

For prosopagnosics, faces may be gone but they are not totally forgotten. Evidence for this comes from the infamous lie detector test. Sometimes threateningly known as the Guilty Knowledge Test, this measures changes in the electrical conductivity of the skin in response to leading and potentially upsetting questions. A sudden increase in conductivity indicates a nervous, emotional, or revealingly criminal reaction. Prosopagnosics, in lieu of the guilt-inducing "Where were you on the night of the twenty-fifth?" were tested with displays of assorted photographs, some of familiar faces, others of perfect strangers. As they studied the pictures, skin conductivity repeatedly spiked in response to the familiar, this emotional response indicating that—at some level—memory of the once-known face was still intact. Based on such results, Antonio Damasio suggests that a two-part memory system must be mobilized for facial recognition. Remembered facial images are stored in one area of the brain; defining memories associated with each face in another. Perhaps, speculates Damasio, prosopagnosics have lost neither, but lack the ability to properly integrate the two.

*I remember your name perfectly but
I just can't think of your face.*
Reverend W. A. Spooner

*I never forget a face but in your case
I'll make an exception.*
Groucho Marx

Familiarity Breeds Forgetfulness

M EMORY, COMMON SENSE seems to tell us, should strengthen with repetition. Countless generations of piano teachers have told their fidgeting pupils that "practice makes perfect," and any aspiring college student will tell you that, in general, the more you study the better you'll do on the final exam. Repetition, however, is not always a mnemonic advantage. Episodic memories—our recollections of past events— cannot survive too large a dose of sameness.

What did you have for lunch last Tuesday? Unless you are a person of extraordinarily regular habits—always a green salad and a glass of Perrier—chances are you haven't the foggiest idea. The reason for this is that repeated episodic memories blend, becoming increasingly confused as more and more pile up, each, clonelike, resembling the last. Over the course of a year, remembrances of 365 separate, but approximately equal, lunches ooze indivisibly together. Episodic memories fade in the face of competition; they best retain their freshness and flavor if they are—and remain—unique. "First-time" experiences are therefore prominent survivors in all our memories: first day of school, first date, first car, first job. Newness, in memory, packs a powerful punch. By the 47th day of school or the 15th date, however, the newness has faded and memory becomes cloudy. Few of us remember, in that glittering first-time detail, our 12th dive off the high board, our 23rd trip in an airplane.

Strong emotional associations may also distinguish episodic memories, tagging them with unprecedented uniqueness. The lunch at which you received your first marriage proposal or the lunch at which your companion choked on the pastrami and had to be resuscitated by the waiter stands out from the common herd. A strong dose of joy or sorrow, anger, fear, or disgust is a powerful enhancer of memory; emotion-fraught episodes from our pasts are astonishingly well preserved.

> *I remember now as if it were yesterday the first time I ever stole a watermelon. I think it was the first time. I stole that watermelon out of a farmer's wagon while he was waiting on another customer. I carried it out to the seclusion of the lumberyard and broke it open. It was green. The greenest watermelon that was ever raised in the Mississippi Valley. When I saw it was green I was sorry and I began to reflect. Seemed to me I had done wrong.*
>
> *I thought, "Now, what ought a boy to do? What ought a right-thinking, clean-hearted, high-principled boy to do who has stolen a green watermelon? What would George Washington do?"*
>
> *I said to myself, "There is only one thing for him to do. He must restore that stolen watermelon."*
>
> *Not many boys would do that. I did. I rose up spiritually strengthened and refreshed and I carried it back and restored it to the farmer—what was left of it. And I made him give me a ripe one.*
>
> Mark Twain,
> "Caprices of Memory"

> *When your mother is ninety-nine years old, you have so many memories of her that they tend to overlap, intermingle, and blur. It is extremely difficult to single out one or two, impossible to remember any that exemplify the whole.*
>
> *It has been alleged that when I was in college, she heard that I had stayed up all night playing poker and wrote me a letter that used the word "shame" forty-two times. I do not recall this.*
>
> John McPhee,
> *"Silk Parachute"*

> *One Christmas was so like another, in those years around the sea-town corner now and out of all sound except the distant speaking of the voices I sometimes hear a moment before sleep, that I can never remember whether it snowed for six days and six nights when I was twelve or whether it snowed for twelve days and twelve nights when I was six.*
>
> Dylan Thomas,
> *A Child's Christmas in Wales*

Unlike episodic memories, semantic memories benefit from constant replay. Read *Hamlet* over and over again and your knowledge of the play will inevitably increase; flip through those flashcards several times a day and you'll solidify your memories of state capitals, multiplication facts, and irregular French verbs. One of the few systematic studies on the relative durations of episodic and semantic memories was conducted in the 1970s by psychologist Marigold Linton, who efficiently used herself and her diary as research tools. Daily, for six years, Linton recorded the events of her life—at least two per day—on dated index cards. She then gave herself monthly tests on her recall of the recorded events, finding, as time passed and the diary mushroomed, that repeated events gradually blurred over in the mind, while unique one-of-a-kind happenings survived. "I simply cannot adequately characterize," wrote Linton, "the year's two-hundredth hour in the classroom, my three-hundredth racquet match, or the one-hundredth dinner with friends." Some items, however, were vividly remembered: "I teach a new class or perform a novel demonstration; I find a new racquet partner, or we find half a boysenberry pie on the court surface; a new restaurant opens, or a special friend makes a rare visit to town." Semantic memory, in contrast, found strength in number. Linton describes a series of business trips to a distant city. Initially, the trip itself—a first-time experience—was prominent in episodic memory. With repeated visits, however, details of individual journeys began to blend. Semantic memories took the opposite turn: her knowledge of travel schedules, airport layout, and city geography, after multiple run-throughs, markedly and permanently increased. Years later she found herself still able to draw a map of the airport terminal building. An equivalent of Linton's business trips is run-of-the-mill weekly expeditions to the supermarket: repetition makes it difficult to remember individual shopping trips (episodic memories), but easier to remember the general layout of the store (semantic memories). You can't remember much about last Wednesday's boring grocery run, but you do know that the pickles are located next to the ketchup in Aisle 13.

Time-lapse photography offers odd pleasures: gaudy flowers blooming in a second, skyscrapers flinging themselves upward in half a minute. Reading someone's life in one of these huge chronicle diaries can be a little like watching it that way: you go through a year in maybe an hour or two. But the effects aren't so amusing as they are with the flower and the skyscraper. Ye gods, you ask yourself, how many times can someone have breakfast?

Thomas Mallon,
A Book of One's Own

Practice Makes Perfect

P ROCEDURAL MEMORY, like semantic memory, improves with reruns. The old musicians' joke, "How do you get to Carnegie Hall? Practice, practice, practice," is simple truth: the hardest workers are the best performers. K. Anders Ericsson of Florida State University, whose research centers on the relationship between practice and expertise, finds that the two are indivisibly intertwined. Star violinists, for example, usually start lessons by the age of five and, by graduation from the music conservatory, have racked up over 10,000 hours of practice time. (Lesser lights only put in 7,500 hours of practice, which shows.) Psychologist Herbert Simon of Carnegie-Mellon University figures it takes ten years of grueling practice to excel at anything, period. Even Mozart, the greatest musical prodigy who ever lived, had to put in his time. Though Mozart began composing at the age of four, it was only after twelve years spent painstakingly honing his craft that he began to produce his best and lasting compositions. The great piano concertos and string quartets didn't come along until Mozart was in his mid-twenties; *The Marriage of Figaro* was written at the age of 30, *Don Giovanni* at 31, and *The Magic Flute* at a doddering 35. In the interim, Mozart immersed himself in the practice of music. He composed from six in the morning far into the night—he could squeak by on a mere four hours' sleep—he wrote music at meals, at parties, and even, one story claims, while holding his wife's hand during childbirth. When Mozart died in 1791, of kidney failure aggravated by malnutrition, he left behind him six coats (five red, one white), three silver spoons, 346 books, a pool table, and his much-practiced-upon walnut piano.

The benefits of dedicated practice are not restricted to the young. Adults who stick to intensive practice regimes, claim Ericsson and Ralf Krampe of the University of Potsdam in Germany, are able to compensate for normal age-related declines in motor abilities and general reaction time, thus effectively holding their own against younger competitors. Ericsson and Krampe compared the skills of "amateur" and "expert" pianists in two different age groups: younger musicians ranged in age from 20 to 31; older pianists from 52 to 68. The amateurs—all practice skimpers—showed marked age-related differences in performance quality. Older amateurs were consistently outclassed by their younger peers. Professional musicians of both age groups, however, all dedicated practicers, performed about equally well. Constant practice may reinforce procedural memory processes, thus overcoming the declines of old age. Pianist Vladimir Horowitz, a musical superstar well into his eighties, practiced daily.

> *By nature, men are nearly all alike; by practice, they get to be wide apart.*
> Confucius

Like musical prowess, sports skills soar with endless practice. Top athletes nowadays start training at tender ages in order to log in enough practice time prior to the Olympics: young divers, gymnasts, skiers, and skaters may begin their training as early as age four. A study conducted by Anthony Kalinowski of the University of Chicago found that swimmers who reach national championship levels generally begin training at age ten; superstars who qualify for Olympic teams begin at age seven.

So are there no champions, no geniuses? Are all peak performances the result of nothing more than elbow grease? Perhaps. Michael Howe, in a December 1988 article in the *New Scientist*, argues that the ordinary person in the street has the potential for brilliance given sufficient practice and accompanying buildup of procedural memory. Howe, in support of this thesis, cites Antonio Vivaldi's orphans. Vivaldi, the eighteenth-century Italian composer, took holy orders at the age of fifteen, and soon became known as the "Red Priest," a nickname derived from a combination of his thick red curly hair and his penchant for wearing dramatic red clerical robes. As part of his priestly duties, the Red Priest spent the early 1700s as music teacher at La Pietà in Venice, a church-supported orphanage for girls. The children of La Pietà all came from culturally and economically impoverished backgrounds; many were simply abandoned as infants on the orphanage steps. The church housed, fed, and educated them, and Vivaldi taught the young orphans to sing and to play the violin. By the time they reached adolescence, writes Howe, about a third of the girls had developed stunning musical abilities. Concerts featuring them, at which they blithely performed even the most technically challenging pieces—most composed by Vivaldi himself—were famed throughout Italy. Members of the audience, who scrambled for admission, were reportedly awestruck by the girls' impressive talents. Paragons, it seems, may be made, not born.

> *Training is everything. The peach was once a bitter almond; cauliflower is nothing but a cabbage with a college education.*
> Mark Twain,
> *Pudd'nhead Wilson*

Practice also makes perfect, according to psychologist and Nobel laureate Herbert Simon, in the playing of chess. Chess champions learn their art by repeatedly replaying celebrated chess games of the past, halting the action at each step to practice predicting the proper move. Given enough of this, experts develop bulging memory stores of chess positions, to the point where they can play (and win) entire games when blindfolded. Or even multiple games: the world record for blindfolded chess playing, according to the *Guinness Book of World Records,* is held by one George Koltanowski who, at the Fairmont Hotel in San Francisco on December 13, 1960, took on fifty-six opponents simultaneously. He beat fifty and tied six.

> *There are 3 billion possible ways chess players can play the first four moves in a game.*
> Stephen Strauss,
> *The Sizesaurus*

The Magic Number Seven

DECLARATIVE AND PROCEDURAL, episodic and semantic, are divisions of memory based on content, each distinguished from the others by the kind of information the memory system contains. Other subsets of memory are less academic. Some are based simply on staying power and size. Musical notes and chess rules—as well as your Social Security number, your father-in-law's birthday, the colors of the rainbow, and the way to get to Omaha—first enter your memory through a short-lived holding pen. This is traditionally called short-term memory, because your awareness of the information contained in it is short—in most cases, only a few minutes long. Look up your accountant's or pediatrician's telephone number and hold it in mind on the way to the phone and you've effectively used your short-term memory. Forget the number fifteen minutes later and have to look it up all over again, and that, regrettably, is short-term memory, too. Information in all its many forms passes through short-term memory, en route to either long-term storage or oblivion.

Short-term memory, in effect, is an airlock in the brain, a holding zone where newly acquired information kicks its heels, awaiting assignment to its final destination. The airlock is easily punctured; short-term memory is readily disrupted. This is the memory that fails after a whack on the side of the head, which is why victims of concussion, staggering to their feet after a header onto icy concrete, ask, "Where am I?" Pleasant distractions also wipe short-term memory clean, which is why sly parents are able to lure toddlers away from mud puddles with offers of cherry lollipops. This feature of short-term memory, so useful as a parenting tool, can also backfire. Most people, at one time or another, have felt information delicately balanced in short-term memory dissolve upon interruption. An unexpected knock at the door and that about-to-be-written-down sentence kicks the bucket. Samuel Taylor Coleridge's much-vilified person from Porlock may not so much have dislodged a poetic dream as disrupted short-term memory.

Short-term memory has a sharply limited storage capacity. In the 1950s, George Miller of Harvard University attempted to assess exactly how much it took to fill it up by giving experimental subjects lists of numbers or words to peruse, then immediately asking them to recall as much as possible of what they had just seen. This how-much-can-you-cram-in-a-suitcase approach is the central theme of Miller's landmark paper, "The Magic Number Seven, Plus or Minus Two." Seven separate items, it seems, are about all that most of us can cram into short-term memory at a time, though a few of us can up the ante to nine or ten. Further investigation showed that the brain routinely cheats: the magical seven does not necessarily refer pristinely to individual items, but to blocks or *chunks* of information. Chunking is a creative mental packaging technique that allows us to stuff a (relatively) large amount of information into a relatively small space. Take the following string of numbers: 1 0 6 6 1 4 9 2 1 7 7 6 2 0 0 1. Taken a digit at a time it adds up to sixteen individual items: a little too much for the average short-term memory. Chunked, however, it's a breeze. (Try 1066-1492-1776-2001.) Chunking enables us to remember Social Security numbers, telephone numbers—even interminable overseas varieties, complete with country codes—and the spelling of words like *Mississippi* and *sesquipedelian*, which feats we accomplish chunk by chunk, syllable by syllable. Children generally learn the alphabet in chunks, which is why so many preschoolers make LMNOP sound like a single word. Chess players chunk when they remember patterns—organized groups—of chess pieces on the board. Experts remember positions based on alignments of pieces in real games: *"Aha! This resembles Von Scheve versus Teichman, Berlin, 1907!"* Without logical pattern, they become confused; chess masters are no better than the rest of us at remembering boards full of randomly placed chess pieces.

> *Each thought has a size, and most are about three feet tall, with the level of complexity of a lawnmower engine, or a cigarette lighter, or those tubes of toothpaste that, by mingling several hidden pastes and gels, create a pleasantly striped product.*
> Nicholson Baker,
> *The Size of Thoughts*

While the magical number seven is ubiquitous, it's not written in stone. Psychologist K. Anders Ericsson found that, with determined practice, test subjects could break the seven barrier. After 50 hours of drill in memorizing increasingly lengthy strings of random digits, Carnegie-Mellon college students managed to remember 20-number sequences after a single hearing. One particularly dedicated trainee—James Staszewski, a business major—put in 400 hours of practice and acquired the ability to memorize a string of 102. Even this feat, however, appears to consist of a heroic exercise in chunking. S.F., a student of "average" memory abilities, learned, after 230 hours of practice, to remember a list of up to 79 random digits, read to him at one-second intervals. An analysis of his accomplishment showed how he managed it: S.F., a runner, chunked the numbers into 3- or 4-digit groups and translated them into running times. The sequence 3492, for example, was remembered as "3 minutes and 49.2 seconds, near world-record mile time." This technique, known as mnemonic association, is a means of linking brand-new information with old, familiar data stored in long-term memory, thus boosting recall power. The boost, investigators concluded, represented an increase in the size of numerical chunks, rather than an increase in the capacity of short-term memory itself. Once mastery of random digit sequences had been achieved, S.F. was switched to random sequences of letters of the alphabet. Deprived of his running-time mnemonic, his short-term memory capacity was six.

> *The man who thinks over his experiences most and*
> *weaves them into systematic relations with each other will*
> *be the one with the best memory.*
> William James

102 RANDOM NUMBERS

```
1 7 4 9 3 2 0 8 9 4 9 6 8 4 3 9 3 9 2 6 9
8 9 6 4 3 8 9 6 3 4 5 6 8 3 9 7 5 0 0 7 5
2 8 4 8 6 8 3 6 7 8 9 5 6 4 5 6 2 7 5 8 4
9 6 6 7 7 7 9 4 3 2 1 1 5 7 0 4 0 0 9 4 5
6 3 3 3 6 7 4 5 6 7 3 0 1 7 3 4
```

Eidetikers

For a lucky few, performances like S.F.'s seem to come painlessly. Such privileged persons—about one in a million of us, by one estimation—are eidetikers, possessors of *eidetic* or photographic memories. Eidetic comes from the Greek *eidos*—image—and images are just what the true eidetiker sees, visualizations persisting in precise detail after the original image itself is gone. An eidetiker can briefly study a picture or printed page and then, against a neutral surface, precisely conjure up its image and describe it as though reading it off a cue card. Eidetic memories are more common in children than in adults. Some studies suggest that 50 percent of children under ten are eidetikers. Ten seems to be the cutoff point; eidetic ability drops off thereafter and young teenagers, by the age of fourteen, are eidetically over the hill, showing no greater incidence of photographic memory than is found in the general population.

Rudyard Kipling's Kim—pushing fourteen—lacked it, and so, in the turn-of-the-century novel named after him, lost the famous Jewel Game to a ten-year-old, still presumably in his eidetic prime. Kim, at the time, was honing his observational skills, practicing to become a spy. In this exotic contest, a handful of precious stones was thrown out on a copper tray. Kim and his opponent studied them—"One look is enough for *me*," boasted the younger child—and the objects were then covered with a paper, while the boys recited from memory the list of what lay beneath. The game, which ended in Kim's resounding defeat, inspired a generation of children to play imitative "Kim games" in which a scattering of small objects is assembled, the players are given a short time to study them, then the objects are covered and the players try to identify as many as possible from memory. In such trials, eidetikers—like Kim's small nemesis—invariably win.

"There are under that paper five blue stones—one big, one smaller, and three small," said Kim, all in haste. "There are four green stones, and one with a hole in it; there is one yellow stone that I can see through, and one like a pipe-stem. There are two red stones, and— and— I made the count fifteen, but two I have forgotten. No! Give me time. One was of ivory, little and brownish; and— and— give me time . . ."

"Hear my count!" the child burst in, trilling with laughter. "First, are two flawed sapphires—one of two ruttees and one of four as I should judge. The four-ruttee sapphire is chipped at the edge. There is one Turkestan turquoise, plain with black veins, and there are two inscribed—one with a Name of God in gilt, and the other being cracked across, for it came out of an old ring, I cannot read. We have now all five blue stones. Four flawed emeralds there are, but one is drilled in two places, and one is a little carven . . .

"There is one piece of old greenish pipe amber, and a cut topaz from Europe. There is one ruby of Burma, of two ruttees, without a flaw, and there is a balas-ruby, flawed, of two ruttees. There is a carved ivory from China representing a rat sucking an egg; and there is last—ah ha!—a ball of crystal as big as a bean set in gold leaf."

He clapped his hands at the close.

Rudyard Kipling,
Kim

Studies performed by psychologist Ralph Haber at the University of Rochester in the 1960s, however, did not find America's elementary schools to be filled—or even half-filled—with eidetically talented potential spies. Haber screened five hundred children, aged seven to eleven, for eidetic image retention. Each child was shown a picture—a favorite, from *Alice's Adventures in Wonderland*, showed Alice at the foot of a tree, chatting with the self-satisfied Cheshire Cat—and was allowed to study it for thirty seconds. Then the picture was removed and the children were asked to shift their gaze to a plain gray card and describe any lasting image that they could see. Strongly eidetic children, of which there were twenty, only 4 percent of the total sample, saw vivid and persistent pictures, from which they were able to count the stripes on the Cat's tail, the leaves on the flower stems, and the number of branches on the tree. The young eidetikers were also able to recall photographs in enough detail to allow them to count the stripes on zebras and to spell out—letter by letter, forward or backward—unfamiliar foreign words on pictured street signs.

Even more challenging assessments of eidetic memory employ computer-generated stereograms. These are paired pictures which, to most of us, look like gobbledegook: Jackson Pollock–like patterns of random dots. When viewed through a stereoscope, one picture seen through the right eye, the other through the left, the patterns superimpose and a three-dimensional figure emerges from the spot-spattered murk. Eidetikers, however, without a stereoscope, can manage this all on their own. One particularly talented subject, a Harvard artist known to science simply as Elizabeth, can study paired 10,000-dot images for one minute each, one with the right eye, then, after a ten-second break, the second with the left. She then mentally superimposes the two patterns, thus revealing an elevated image—a feat that would be impossible without a "photographic" memory of the original stereograms. Elizabeth's ability is definitive proof, according to excited investigators, for the existence of eidetic imagery. Elizabeth can also combine patterns of colored squares, filtered through either green or red light, to produce a mentally projected grid of mixed colors—red, blue, purple, red-brown, gray, yellow, green—in the proper hues, saturations, and intensities.

Ordinary persons, given the proper visual cues, can experience an optical illusion called the motion after-effect. Originally known as the "waterfall illusion," this effect was first described in a British philosophy journal in 1834 by a Mr. R. Adams. Stare steadily at a moving object such as a cascading waterfall, wrote Mr. Adams, and then quickly shift your gaze to a nearby stationary object, such as a boulder or a tree. The rock or tree will momentarily appear to rise magically upward, in a direction opposite to that of the falling water. Mr. Adams's outdoor illusion can be reproduced in the living room or laboratory with a pair of black-and-white-patterned spirals. In these experiments, one spiral is rotated such that it appears to contract, tornado-style, inward. After subjects have stared at it woozily for a brief period, they are told to switch their gaze to the center of an adjacent stationary spiral. When they do so, the stationary spiral appears to expand outward, moving in the opposite direction from its inward-spinning twin. Elizabeth was able to reproduce this visual trick on her own, using eidetic imagery. First she studied a stationary spiral, forming, in memory, an eidetic image. Then she stared at an inward-spinning spiral for two minutes. Finally she turned her eyes to a square of blank black velvet and conjured up her remembered image of the stationary spiral, which appeared illusorily to expand.

MR. ADAMS'S MAGIC WATERFALL

Just why the waterfall illusion works was recently revealed by Roger Tootell and colleagues at Massachusetts General Hospital. Tootell's volunteers were asked to stare at a moving pattern of outwardly expanding concentric rings of the sort seen when a pebble plops into the middle of a pond. When the movement was stopped, all subjects experienced a waterfall-style illusion: the rings appeared to reverse direction and move inward.

Throughout this experience, the volunteers' brains were scanned using magnetic resonance imaging. The MRI scans showed that as the volunteers stared at the moving rings, a specific portion of the visual cortex of the brain, which analyzes visual information transmitted from the eyes, became active. This particular portion of the visual cortex, known as V5, is packed with nerve cells sensitive to motion. When outward ring motion stopped and the volunteers experienced the illusory inward reversal, V5, already active, became even more so. Tootell explains this extra spurt as the result of cellular bullying. Nerve cells activated by movement in one direction—say, outward-spinning rings—deliberately inhibit neighboring nerve cells ordinarily activated by movement in the opposite direction. When outward movement stops and the outward-sensitive cells shut off, the inward-sensitive cells break loose. Released at last from inhibition, they erupt into an excited burst of activity. This sudden activation of the inward-motion-sensing cells gives the illusory sense of actually seeing inward movement.

The Blackboard of the Mind

WHILE EIDETIC MEMORIES are rare, all of us proudly possess "working memory," the versatile faculty of mind that neurobiologist Patricia Goldman-Rakic dubs "the most significant achievement of human evolution." Working memory is a newfangled and more complex entity that, in current research circles, enlarges upon the earlier and simpler concept of short-term memory. Working memory is the behind-the-scenes machinery that allows us to make rapid associations between brand-new input and previously stored information; using it, we are able to ponder, contemplate, and manipulate data. Some investigators call it the "blackboard of the mind." Others compare it to random access memory (RAM) computer chips, which hold data pulled from "long-term memory" on a computer hard drive or CD-ROM. In working memory, we can combine recent input with stored data from the past, juggling, dissecting, and resynthesizing both in order to solve problems or to generate complete new ideas. The Theory of Relativity and the structure of the benzene ring emerged from the cranking wheels of working memory; as did Shakespeare's sonnets, Euclid's geometry, British common law, and the Declaration of Independence. So, if you were lucky, did the solution to last Sunday's *New York Times* crossword puzzle. Goldman-Rakic explains that working memory is the "mental glue" that links a train of thought coherently through time, allowing us to work our way from point A (say, a five-letter word for "winter wear") to point B (parka).

Researcher Alan Baddeley hypothesizes a three-part sub-structure to working memory. In Baddeley's model, a bossy "central executive" coordinates input from a pair of Dilbert-style subservient systems, dampingly referred to as "slaves." The central executive is the memory feature that allows us to keep two (or more) things in mind at once, to juggle multiple mental activities. Under the guidance of a vigilant central executive, we can manage to talk shop on the telephone with a business associate, add oregano to the spaghetti sauce for supper, and keep a weather eye on the baby, all at the same time. Baddeley proposes that central executive malfunction may be a major component of Alzheimer's disease. Alzheimer's patients, it appears, unlike most of the rest of us, can handle only one mental task at a time. Baddeley gave a group of Alzheimer's subjects a pair of simple tests. One was visual—patients were asked to track a spot of light moving across a screen; the other verbal—patients were asked to listen to a series of short sentences and then repeat the last word of each. The Alzheimer's sufferers could manage each task separately. When asked to handle light and sentences simultaneously, however, their performances abruptly deteriorated. Normal subjects, in contrast, had no problem managing both tasks at the same time—an accomplishment that requires the support of working memory's central executive.

Working memory's "slave" systems, in Baddeley's model, include the solid-sounding (but theoretical) "visuospatial sketch pad" and the "phonological loop." The sketch pad is the mental system with which we manipulate images and patterns. Picture an object, diagram, or map in your mind—conjure up the *Mona Lisa*, the borders of North Dakota, or the alignment of pieces in a backgammon game—and you're scribbling on your visuospatial sketch pad. The phonological loop, Baddeley explains, is the verbal element of short-term memory. We use it to store and mull over words. Vocabulary passes through the loop en route to permanent storage: with it, you process new words in your own and foreign languages. Lose your loop and you'll never learn Latvian, Swahili, or the names of the Mighty Morphin Power Rangers. The loop also functions in subvocal repetition, the technique with which we forcibly maintain verbal material in memory for short periods by muttering it over and over again to ourselves. This incessant rehearsal is the common method for preserving telephone numbers in that sensitive gap between directory and dial, and for remembering the road directions you just got when, hopelessly lost, you finally broke down and asked the clerk at the 7-Eleven. (*Turn right, go over the bridge, take the second left. Turn right, go over the bridge, take the second left.*)

Pad and loop functions of working memory have been teased apart in the laboratory with the same sort of double-pronged tasks used to study the role of the central executive in Alzheimer's patients. Paired visuospatial tasks were found to conflict with each other—subjects were unable, for example, to simultaneously track moving spots of light and analyze moves in a chess game—but a visuospatial task did not interfere with a concomitant verbal task. Paired verbal tasks similarly conflicted with each other—it's nearly impossible to learn a word list while simultaneously repeating a series of nonsense syllables—but a verbal task did not impede a visuospatial task. Since visuospatial sketch pad and phonological loop operate as separate functions, you should be able to play checkers while reciting poetry—but not effectively participate in two competing conversations at a cocktail party. The latter is not only good manners, it's a built-in limitation of working memory.

Schizophrenia, a devastating mental disorder characterized by bizarre and disconnected thought patterns, may involve a defect in working memory. Some evidence for this derives from the euphoniously named Stroop task, a psychological test in which subjects are asked to read aloud the names of colors printed in different colors of ink. Normal subjects perform best when the color's name and the color of the ink it is printed with match—a green GREEN, for example, or a red RED. Reading rates characteristically slow when name and ink color clash: a red GREEN or a purple GREEN apparently induces a brief, but time-consuming, mental double take. Psychologist Carmi Schooler and coworkers at the National Institute of Mental Health in Bethesda, Maryland, used a version of the Stroop task to compare normal and schizophrenic subjects. In one sample experiment, test takers were shown a computer screen upon which color names appeared, blandly printed in white, for periods of 150 milliseconds, followed by a restful 150-millisecond display of blank screen. Rectangles of matching or clashing color were then shown for up to three seconds; participants were asked to name aloud the color of the pictured rectangle. The brief blank pause between color name and colored rectangle was no help to normal subjects: when word and color were at odds, their color-naming speed markedly slowed. The pause, however, was a plus for schizophrenics. Given the 150-millisecond break, schizophrenics read color names of clashing colors just as rapidly as the names of color matches. The results suggested to the researchers a defect in working memory: during the pause, they hypothesized, schizophrenics were unable to hold the initial color name in working memory. Eliminated from the mind, it was no longer available to interfere with subsequent color-naming tasks. In normal subjects, however, working memory determinedly held on to the word—say, *red*—throughout the pause period; its persistent presence interfered with the subjects' ability to name a subsequently displayed rectangle clashingly colored green.

The Stuff of Dreams

EVEN IN THE MOST normal of persons, new information entering short-term or working memory walks a risky road. Within minutes, forgettable data are unceremoniously eliminated from the brain, and memorable survivors are selected for transfer into permanent storage. This transfer appears to be a prolonged process, occupying weeks, months, or—in some cases—even years. The upshot is that, with the march of time, memories gradually become tougher, more ingrained, increasingly difficult to dislodge. This transformation, from the will-o'-the-wisps of short-term memory to the solidities of long-term storage, is called memory consolidation. Just how long this takes is often assessed after the fact in the clinic, based on the experiences of patients who have suffered memory loss. Persons with retrograde amnesia have lost the memory of events that happened before they suffered their "amnestic event," the medical term that covers a multitude of amnesia-inducing disasters, from hellacious head injury to electroconvulsive shock therapy. Collision, convulsion, and disease can all produce the same effect. Retrograde amnesiacs form new memories normally—all current memory systems are up and go—but the pre-disaster past is a blank. Usually, however, it is an uneven blank. The most recent memories invariably are the most thoroughly gone. Events of last week or last month are irretrievably erased, never to return. Events of the last two or three years may be wiped out, or at least scrambled and confused; even memories four years old or more may wobble, emerging as partially intact, ragged remnants of what they once were. The further back in time one goes, however, the more memories stabilize. The older the memory, the better it holds its ground. You may, post-bump, have lost the events of last week, but chances are good you'll still remember your first tricycle. The relative susceptibility of memories to trauma indicates just how far along in the consolidation process that memory is. The newer the memory, the weaker it is, and the less chance it has for survival. In the event of mental shipwreck, it's these fragile passengers that don't make it into the lifeboats.

Memory consolidation, like digestion, doesn't take conscious effort on our part. In fact, some psychologists believe we do it in our sleep. A crucial period here appears to be REM (rapid eye movement), a sleep stage characterized by a back-and-forth darting of the eyes under closed lids, irregular breathing, and increased heartbeat. This is the phase of sleep that so worried Hamlet, the time of night in which we dream. Researchers Avi Karni and Dov Sagi at Israel's Weizmann Institute believe they have evidence linking REM sleep to memory. Karni and Sagi trained volunteers in a procedural memory task, teaching them to recognize patterns hidden in images flashed on a computer screen. The test subjects were then either allowed to get a good night's sleep, or were repeatedly awakened, some during REM, some during non-REM sleep, by the annoying ringing of a bell. The next morning all were retested on the previous day's memory task. Undisturbed sleepers and those awakened during non-REM sleep showed marked improvement in test performance; subjects jolted awake while dreaming—deprived of REM sleep—not only showed no improvement in test scores but actually backslid, performing as though they had never been trained at all.

The physiology of sleep was first elucidated in the 1950s, using electroencephalogram (EEG) recordings to spy on the mental workings of those in the land of Nod. Results showed that we enter sleep through an introductory hypnogagic state—a brief period of groggily disconnected thought, familiar to those caught drifting off in the midst of a post-lunch business meeting—followed by a plunge into deep or slow-wave sleep, so named for the pattern of large low-frequency brain waves detected during it by EEG. Slow-wave sleep is punctuated by periods of REM, the first occurring about an hour and a half into the night's rest, with three to four more spaced at shorter intervals. The night's final bout of REM, usually about thirty minutes long, clicks in just before awakening; it's from this period that dreams are most likely to be remembered.

Rats, on the other hand, unlike us, don't seem to need dreams to remember. Instead rat memory is peacefully consolidated during slow-wave sleep. Researchers Matthew Wilson of MIT and Bruce McNaughton of the University of Arizona surgically implanted test rats with microelectrodes, inserted into the hippocampus, a portion of the brain believed to be involved in spatial memory. The rats—wearing homecoming queen–style crowns of embedded wire—were then taught to run a maze. As they navigated the twists and turns of the maze, the implanted electrodes recorded specific patterns of activity in the hippocampus, patterns that represented learning and memory formation. For several nights thereafter, as the rats snored in slow-wave sleep, their brains continually replayed the maze-running patterns, repeating them over and over. The activity patterns ran much faster in deep sleep than during the initial learning episode; Wilson and McNaughton guessed that this repetitive fast-forwarding was an efficient means of consolidating memory. Activity patterns generated in REM sleep, in contrast, bore no relationship to those generated during previous learning experiences. Rat REM, however, did have an impact on slow-wave sleep. Over time, the patterns of electrical activity during deep sleep began to slow, fade, and peter out. After an episode of REM, the deep-sleep patterns snapped back, reinvigorated and restored to fresh levels of speed and intensity. Perhaps, hypothesizes McNaughton, REM sleep somehow functions to refurbish the brain's deep-sleep "playback" equipment, in the same manner that head-cleaning optimizes the performance of the family VCR.

Jonathan Winson of Rockefeller University points out that all mammals dream, with the glaring exception of the echidna, or spiny anteater, a primitive egg-laying mammal (formally a monotreme) native to Australia, Tasmania, and New Guinea. The dreamlessness of the echidna suggests to Winson that the REM phase of sleep first popped up about 140 million years ago, at the evolutionary juncture where the marsupial and placental mammals first branched off from the ancient monotreme line. Dreaming may thus represent an evolutionary advance in memory processing, a new and improved means of memory consolidation for the up-and-coming denizens of the Cretaceous period.

Animals, some research suggests, spend their dream time consolidating memories of recently learned survival skills. In the 1950s, researchers at UCLA discovered a new form of brain wave—a regular pattern called a theta rhythm—emanating from the hippocampi of rabbits. Once psychologists knew what to look for, theta rhythms were identified in a range of animal species, including moles, shrews, cats, and rats. In the waking hours, the distinctive theta rhythms seemed to appear when animals were responding to new stimuli or honing their survival behaviors. Rabbits, nervously scanning their surroundings for predators, generate theta rhythms, as do hunting cats and exploring rats. During sleep, identical theta rhythms resurface during episodes of REM, suggesting that the original theta experiences are being replayed and transferred into long-term memory. When theta rhythms were blocked, spatial memories in exploring rats promptly disappeared.

Other dream observers are less convinced of REM's memory-consolidating role. Some believe that dreams are simply meaningless babble, the brain's vain nighttime attempt to piece random flickers of electrical activity into some semblance of a coherent story. Dreams in which we appear naked playing the piccolo in a subway car full of blue apes are thus explicable as the hit-or-miss activation of miscellaneous memory banks, which the brain, a stickler for order, fuses as best it can into a related whole. James Horne, author of *Why We Sleep*, suggests that dreams are idle recreation, the brain's way of killing time during the dull sensation-deprived downtime of sleep. Dreams, says Horne, may be the "cinema of the mind," an anti-boredom device akin to the deliberate daydreaming we indulge in while squirming in our seats during less-than-enlivening lectures, seminars, or sermons. Francis Crick and Graeme Mitchison see dreaming as serious business, but propose that REM sleep, rather than processing memories we want to keep, disposes of memories that we want to throw away. The tremendous amount of information that we sop up each day puts us in continual risk of overload, Crick and Mitchison hypothesize, and leads to the accumulation, due to sheer overcramming, of false associations and distracting "parasitic thoughts." The brain thus must purge itself nightly of all this trash, dreaming away bizarre images and unwanted interconnections. We don't dream to remember, insist Crick and Mitchison, we dream to forget.

> *Dreams are surely difficult, confusing, and not everything in them is brought to pass for mankind.*
> Homer

> *"Many's the long night I've dreamed of cheese —toasted, mostly."*
> Robert Louis Stevenson,
> *Treasure Island*

Jeanne and Eva

MEMORIES, DREAMILY OR NO, once consolidated are said to have been transferred into long-term storage. Once safely stashed in long-term memory—the brain's version of a safe-deposit box—memories have the potential to last as long as we do, which is the closest the mind comes to permanence. Some personal memories indomitably pass the century mark. Jeanne Calment of France, who died in August 1997, at the age of 122, was the last living person to have met Vincent Van Gogh, an event that took place at a garden party over 100 years ago in Arles. She was thirteen at the time, and refused an introduction on the grounds that the great man was "very ugly, ungracious, impolite, and not well." Other stubbornly ineradicable memories last nearly as long. Sadie and Bessie Delany, the 103- and 101-year-old stars of their joint memoir, *Having Our Say*, remembered hearing, as young girls, their father's stories of life in slavery. Eva Hart, over a span of 84 years, remembered with chilling clarity the sinking of the *Titanic*. The then seven-year-old Eva—who died in 1996, at age 91—and her mother were two of the 705 passengers who survived the sinking of the White Star Line's "unsinkable ship" on April 13, 1912; her father and 1,500 other passengers and crew members were drowned. "I saw that ship sink," Ms. Hart said in one of the last interviews of her life. "I never closed my eyes. I didn't sleep at all. I saw it, I heard it, and nobody could possibly forget it."

The Ghost in the Machine

So WHERE AND HOW are such lifelong memories stored in the brain? It's a question that both absorbs and puzzles modern neuroscientists, who are, at least, one up on scientists of previous centuries, many of whom doubted that the brain had much to do with memory at all. The ancient Greeks, usually so astute, insisted that higher mental functions took place in the heart, a belief we perpetuate today when we speak of heartache, heartbreak, and heartfelt emotions, all of which are generated unromantically between the ears. Galen, the second-century Greek physician who spent his career attempting to probe the mysteries of human anatomy without actually dissecting anybody—he was particularly good on muscles, having spent time in sports medicine as adviser to the gladiatorial school in Pergamum— believed that thought was centered in the cerebrospinal fluid. By the Renaissance, scholars had moved headward, assigning such mental functions as reason, memory, and imagination to the brain's ventricles, a scientific choice on par with forgoing the doughnut in favor of the hole. The ventricles are, in fact, holes: a collection of four large cavities located at the center of each of the brain's two cerebral hemispheres, in the midbrain, and in the brain stem. (Shakespeare, who seems to have been scientifically literate, seventeenth-century-style, subscribed to this idea: Holofernes, the fast-talking schoolmaster in *Love's*

Labour's Lost, babbles of the "forms, figures, shapes, objects, ideas, apprehensions, motions, resolutions . . . begot in the ventricle of memory.")

René Descartes, the seventeenth-century French philosopher and mathematician, favored the pineal gland as the crucial organ, the seat of mind and thought. The pineal gland, in Descartes's scheme, did not generate thought; it simply served as handy housing for the mind or soul. The Cartesian mind was believed to be wholly separate from the brain, an independent and ethereal little being akin to the vaporous ghosts that scoot across the screen in Universal's *Casper.* When Descartes thought (and therefore was), he did so through the medium of "subtle, volatile, invisible, and immaterial animal spirits"—what British philosopher Gilbert Ryle called the spiritual "ghost" in the bodily "machine." While much of Descartes's thinking—for example, his mathematical system of graphing by coordinates, a watered-down version of which most of us use today when frantically searching for H-9 on a road map—proved valuable, the pineal hypothesis was doomed to fall by the neurobiological wayside.

The pineal gland, named for its presumptive resemblance to a pinecone, is an organ about the size of a blueberry, nestled deep in the interior of the brain between the two cerebral hemispheres. Rather than encasing our souls, it appears to regulate our body clocks, largely through the production of a hormone called melatonin. Like bats, cats, owls, and astronomers, melatonin is active after dark: its production cranks up at bedtime and winds down at dawn, allowing us to fall asleep on cue and wake up, reasonably perky, at breakfast time.

Descartes's own pineal gland, by a strange quirk of fate, ended up in Sweden. At the age of fifty-three, he accepted a lucrative invitation from Queen Christina: room, board, and a generous salary in exchange for instructing the Swedish court in philosophy. The queen, an intellectual go-getter and indefatigable early riser, demanded personal philosophy lessons at the uncongenial hour of 5 A.M. Descartes, by nature a late sleeper, exhausted himself trekking to and from the royal apartments in the frigid predawn and caught pneumonia and died. His body was reverently returned to his native France, inexplicably without the head, including brain and pineal gland. Descartes's skull (empty) eventually ended up in the hands of the Swedish chemist Berzelius who, in 1824, discovered the element silicon, thus inadvertently paving the way for the twentieth-century's Information Age. Berzelius, with a fine sense of propriety, sent the skull back to France, into the keeping of the anatomist Georges Cuvier. It finally ended up, restored to its proper body, in the Pantheon in Paris.

Descartes was a prime contender in what has come to be known as the mind/body problem: that is, is there an ethereal mind or soul apart from the lumpy realities of biology, or is all that we are—personalities, beliefs, emotions, memories—explicable by complex neuronal circuitry? It's a question with a lot of touchy implications, to which straight answers have never been wholly welcome. In 1746, Julien Offray de la Mettrie, a somewhat injudiciously direct French army physician, wrote a book called *Histoire naturelle de l'âme* (The Natural History of the Soul) in which he announced that brain is all we've got; the ugly convoluted ball of tissue between the ears is the sole generator of the human mind. The idea was poorly received: de la Mettrie was kicked out of the military and the French Parliament ordered all copies of his book burned. He relocated—hastily—to Holland where, undeterred, he wrote the whole thing over again under the title *L'Homme-machine* (Man, A Machine). The Dutch, outraged in turn, ordered all copies burned; de la Mettrie, still touting the supremacy of the brain, ended up in Prussia under the protection of Frederick II, who had a reputation as a freethinker.

Man is only man at the surface. Remove his skin, dissect,
and immediately you come to machinery.
Paul Valéry

You're nothing but a pack of neurons.
Francis Crick,
The Astonishing Hypothesis

What Is It Like to Be a Bat?

THE IDEA THAT ALL we are is brain is, to the bulk of humanity, inherently off-putting. Poet W. E. Henley, fervently thanking whatever gods may be for his unconquerable soul, was certainly not contemplating cranial anatomy; nor was William Wordsworth who, in "Intimations of Immortality," described the soul as arriving on earth neck-and-neck with the body, but from a different realm altogether, trailing clouds of glory from heaven. The majority of neuroscientists today, a determinedly unromantic band, subscribe more or less to the "astonishing hypothesis" described by Nobel laureate Francis Crick: "'You,' your joys and your sorrows, your memories and your ambitions, your sense of personal identity and free will, are in fact no more than the behavior of a vast assembly of nerve cells and their associated molecules." In other words, the "me" that most of us so clearly perceive as peering out at the world through our eyes from some sequestered internal vantage point is simply a construct in time, the on-going product of sensory input and complex nervous-system response.

Just *how* the brain generates the unique and individual mind is a matter of intense debate. The precise delineation of the transition from point A—the biology of the brain—to point B—personhood—remains a scientific sticking point. Some philosophers doubt that such a delineation is even possible. The solution to the mind/body problem may remain forever out of reach. Thomas Nagel, in his essay "What Is It Like to Be a Bat?," points out that some levels of experience are closed to us, impenetrably unknowable. It is possible, explains Nagel, for scientists to elucidate every physical and physiological detail of the bat, but still impossible to share a bat's subjective experience—that is, to know what it is really like to be a bat, flittering through the summer night sky, hot on the trail of mosquitoes. "How do you know," writes Nagel, "that red things don't look to your friend the way yellow things look to you? Of course if you ask him how a fire engine looks, he'll say it looks red, like blood, and not yellow, like a dandelion; but that's because he, like you, uses the word 'red' for the color that blood and fire engines look to him, *whatever* it is. Maybe it's what you call yellow, or what you call blue, or maybe it's a color experience you've never had, and can't even imagine." It's not difficult to imagine a future in which neuroscientists have traced all the physical events that occur in the brain when we bite an apple or watch a glorious sunset, but we may never be able to communicate the subjective aspects of the experience. Does an apple taste the same to you as it does to me? Do we see the same pinks and purples in the setting sun?

> *If I had to make a bet I would say that the mind is a ghost*
> *from God that comes from the sky and lives in the brain.*
> Jimmy Breslin,
> *I Want to Thank My Brain for Remembering Me*

A Quick Trip Through the Brain

THE brain, since the days of the ancient Greeks, has come into its own, revealing to the inquiring psychiatrist and surgeon layer upon layer of functional and physical complexities. Structurally, the human brain is a reflection of its evolutionary journey through time. Nature, thriftily, has preserved the earliest and most primitive brain structures, progressively enlarging and adding to them as needed in the evolutionary struggle for survival. Bygone brain models still exist within our own—somewhat as though, if such a thing were possible, the engine of Henry Ford's original Model T still chugged away indomitably beneath the larger and more powerful fittings of the modern automobile. The brain's most ancient component is the primitive brain stem, bulging off the top of the spinal column, all that remains to us of the primeval reptilian brain. The brain stem, the dull kid on the mental block, concerns itself mostly with the absolute fundamentals of life, such as breathing and heartbeat, falling asleep, and waking up. Just behind the brain stem perches the cerebellum ("little brain"), which looks much like a small grubby cauliflower. The cerebellum processes input from muscles and joints to control balance, body position, and movement: usually it enables you to walk and chew gum at the same time. The cerebellum also appears to be the site of procedural memory; it's here that you store your Rollerblading skills, your tennis serve, and your balletic *grand jeté*.

Perched on top of the brain stem is the limbic system, sometimes called the "old mammalian brain" because it showed up
first in the evolution of mammals. The limbic system consists of
a collection of organs roughly in the center of the brain, all surrounding the yellow olfactory bulb that interprets signals
wafted brainward from the nose. (The pre-1950s name for the
limbic system was rhinencephalon, which means "nose-" or
"smell-brain.") The limbic system is best known for its starring
role in the generation of emotions, predominately those heavy-
duty responses having to do with survival. Students of neurobi-
ology urbanely group these behaviors together as the Four F's:
feeding, fighting, fleeing, and—you got it—sex. A jolt of electrical juice delivered to the limbic system through implanted
microelectrodes sends the recipient into fizzing emotional
overload. A peaceful household pussycat may turn into a
snarling, hissing virago or a cowering lump of terror; a zapped
rat may viciously attack its cage mates. Or it may become a
tuned-out pleasure addict: in one series of experiments, microelectrodes in a pleasure-producing center of rats' limbic systems
were connected to a stimulating lever. The rats, once they discovered the thrill associated with lever-pressing, became
hooked; they neglected food, drink, sex, and sleep in favor of the
lever, and in some cases continued pounding away, enraptured,
until they fell over from exhaustion.

Organs that make up this passionately volatile system
include the hippocampus, of which each of us has two, located
just above the ears and about an inch and a half toward the
middle of the head. The name comes from the Latin for "seahorse," because its fat little curl reminded some early neu-
roanatomist of a seahorse's tail. Many structures in the brain
have such descriptive Latinate names, derived from far-out
chance resemblances, assigned in much the same manner that
homesick and womanless French explorers looked up at
Wyoming's immense pointed mountains and longingly dubbed
them the Grand Tetons. The hippocampus appears to function
in learning and memory: hippocampal electrical patterns

recorded in Bruce McNaughton's sleeping rats, for example, reflected the process of learning the way through a maze and the subsequent consolidation of the newly acquired memory.

Neurobiologist Gary Lynch proposes that the hippocampus plays a multifaceted and elaborate role in human memory. Among the several hippocampal hats is what Lynch calls "recency memory," a remembered time tag for experience. Recency memory supplies information about how much time has passed since you've seen someone or done something, enabling you to determine, upon meeting an old college roommate, that you haven't seen him in ten years, or, upon running into the next-door neighbor at the mailbox, that you last saw her yesterday morning. A second suggested hippocampal function is summed up by the cynical T-shirt slogan "Been there, done that": this scratch-pad-style memory stashes, for short periods of time, information about where you've been and what you've done. This is the memory that you access to locate your car in the shopping mall parking lot, to remember when the pie comes out of the oven, or to identify the waitress who should be bringing you your check. Finally, the hippocampus deals in the memory of logical expectations, that is, the memory of what general form a given event sequence should take. A trip to the library, for example, does not ordinarily involve somersaulting clerks in clown costumes; a visit to the farm does not usually involve an encounter with elephants and giraffes. This hippocampal ability to make an instantaneous assessment—"All is not right with the world"—may have been immeasurably valuable in the early days of evolution, when the strange and unexpected was, more likely than not, dangerous or deadly.

Other limbic residents include the amygdala (named for its resemblance to an almond), the mammillary bodies (look like tiny breasts), the cingulate gyrus (looks like a ridged belt), and the thalamus, hypothalamus, and pituitary gland. The Chiclet-sized hypothalamus is a powerful middleman in the brain, communicating emotional signals, via hormones, to the pea-sized pituitary gland, which passes the information on to the rest of the body. The horrified all-over *thunk* of fear experienced when your car spins out of control on a patch of highway ice or a bear is sighted lumbering hungrily toward your campsite is the limbic system in action, excitedly preparing for battle or quick getaway. The limbic system also, like a persistently humming motor, maintains bodily homeostasis, constantly adjusting such essential functions as body temperature, blood pressure, heart rate, and blood sugar level. Persons plunged into a prolonged coma are kept alive in part by the indefatigable limbic system, gamely plugging along.

The limbic system communicates with the rest of the brain by way of the thalamus—from the Greek for "inner room" or "bridal chamber"—which sits essentially in the middle of the brain. As its position implies, the thalamus functions as a sort of cranial Grand Central Station. All sensory input passes through it en route to the cerebral cortex. It is also connected, through the fibers of the reticular activating system, to the brain stem, which is what keeps the brain awake and functioning even when we're not. The thalamus also functions in selective attention, which allows us to zero in on various aspects of the world about us— or, in daydreaming, meditating, or just plain thinking, to focus on the world inside. A disruption in thalamic circuitry may be the root of attention-related learning problems such as Attention Deficit Disorder (ADD) or wholesale withdrawal conditions such as autism.

Surrounding the thalamus and the rest of the limbic system is the monstrous cerebrum, a corrugated, melon-sized mass that comprises two-thirds of the brain. The cerebrum, as far as neuroscience goes, is largely unknown territory. Most of our personal memories are stored here, among its near-incalculable numbers of brain cells. The cerebrum is split into two not-quite-equal halves (the right side is wider), each controlling movement and receiving sensory input from the opposite side of the body. The right brain thus oversees the left half of the body, and vice versa. Cerebral halves (hemispheres) are connected by a thick belt of nerve fibers—some three hundred million in all—

called the corpus callosum, which allows us, among other things, to let our left hands know what our right hands are doing. Right and left hemispheres are not slavish mirror images of each other, but have physical quirks and intellectual abilities all their own. The left brain, for example, specializes in language abilities; the right brain in visual-spatial skills. Writers and stand-up comics tend to be left-brained; painters, sculptors, and architects, right-brained.

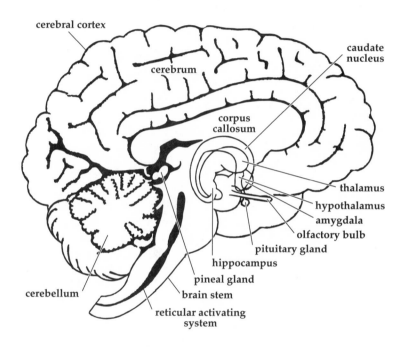

The surface of the cerebrum, which contains a good 70 percent of our brain cells, is called the cerebral cortex, from the Latin for "bark" or "rind." The cortex is wrinkled and folded into a series of distinctive ridges and fissures (in Latin, *gyri* and *sulci*); without this crumpling, it would be too large to squash into our skulls. Unfolded, the human cerebral cortex would be about the size of a small bath towel. (The cortex of the chimpanzee, our next-brightest primate relative, is about the size of a sheet of typing paper; that of the rat, the size of a postage stamp.) The human cortex would make a lousy bath towel, however, because it's thin—generally no more than an eighth of an inch thick. What we see, looking down upon it, is what is popularly known as "gray matter," though in real life it tends more toward rusty pink. Gray matter—what Agatha Christie's mustachioed detective Hercule Poirot referred to fondly as his "little gray cells"—consists of the cell bodies of the brain cells. The underlying white matter—the wiring of the brain—consists of long tentacular processes extending out from these cell bodies, known as axons.

The Superb Cerebrum

Each cerebral hemisphere is roughly divided into four lobes. The occipital lobes, directly at the back of the head, house the visual cortex, where input from the eyes is analyzed and synthesized, allowing us to see. Beauty, rather than in the eye of the beholder, lives in the occipital lobes, and a bad enough bash on the back of the head can cause total blindness. Arching over the top of the head—about where, if one were so inclined, one would perch a propeller beanie—are the parietal lobes. Encoded in strips across the parietal lobes are a pair of topographical maps corresponding to the parts of the body. One strip—the motor cortex—governs movement; its partner—the somatosensory cortex—processes incoming information about such external experiences as touch, pressure, and position. (Get a back rub and you feel it via the somatosensory cortex.) All body parts, as represented in the motor and somatosensory cortices, are not created equal: the more sensitive a body bit is, or the more capable of intricate and specialized movement, the more space it gets on the surface of the brain. Hence lips, tongue, hands, and genitals—all high on the human sensitivity list—get the lion's share of the available cortical space; shoulderblades and toes get short shrift. The cortical maps of cats and rats show analogous patterns, devoting a lot of space to whiskers—in the rat, each separate whisker has its own special segment of brain surface, reserving only stingy cortical snippets for the less sensitive paws.

The frontal lobes, looming just behind the forehead, are the biggest of the cerebral four, and evolutionarily the newest. Frontal cortex in human beings accounts for 29 percent of total brain surface, as compared to 17 percent in the chimpanzee, 3.5 percent in the cat, and practically nothing in the rat. The frontal lobes are the closest thing the brain has to a central executive; with the frontal lobes, we plan ahead, establish goals, and make decisions. The frontal lobes allow us to cope with the ups and downs of daily life, adapting to endlessly altering contingencies—what to do if we miss the bus, or how to respond when, having hiked halfway up Mount Washington, an unexpected thunderstorm rolls in.

The importance of the frontal lobes—hitherto an underappreciated portion of brain anatomy—was impressively demonstrated by the famous case of Phineas Gage, a twenty-five-year-old foreman on the Rutland & Burlington Railroad, who, one summer day in 1848, lost his in a freak accident. Gage met his frontal doom in the shape of a three-and-a-half-foot-long iron rod, used to tamp charges of black powder in place prior to blowing holes in rock, a necessary prelude to creating a level bed on which to lay new railroad track through Vermont's notoriously unlevel mountains. Gage's fatal tamp, that hot September afternoon, set off the charge prematurely, producing a shattering explosion and propelling the rod, like an inch-wide iron rocket, through Gage's left cheek and out the top of his skull. The victim, incredibly, not only lived but apparently never lost consciousness. His appalled crew transported him by oxcart to the nearest town—Cavendish—where, propped up on the hotel veranda, he was given cold lemonade. A local doctor treated the wound and Gage spent two months in bed, after which he was pronounced more or less cured.

Less, sad to say, was the operative word. The destruction of his frontal lobes left Gage an irrevocably damaged man. Prior to his encounter with the tamping rod, Gage had been a shrewd and able businessman, ambitious, hardworking, and much admired by both his employers and employees. Post-accident, however, his entire personality changed. Those who knew him protested, puzzled, that "Gage was no longer Gage." He became impatient, restless, and profane, incapable of functioning socially—women were warned to stay away from him—or of making logical decisions for the future. Intelligence, memory, and language all remained; responsibility, social competence, and the ability to set and fulfill reasonable goals were gone. Gage drifted hopelessly from place to place and job to job— among them a stint with P. T. Barnum's Museum in New York and a brief period as a stagecoach driver in Argentina—and finally ended up in California, where he died at the age of thirty-eight. The tamping rod was buried with him. It was unearthed five years later: both tamping rod and Phineas Gage's skull are now at the Warren Medical Museum of Harvard Medical College in Boston, Massachusetts.

Despite this awful warning, surgeons in the first half of the twentieth century set about deliberately creating analogues of Gage. The technique they used is called prefrontal lobotomy, a frighteningly imprecise surgical procedure first practiced in 1935 by a Portuguese psychiatrist named Egas Moniz who, for this landmark accomplishment, eventually won the Nobel Prize. Prefrontal lobotomy—the operation that played such a climactic role in Ken Kesey's *One Flew Over the Cuckoo's Nest*—involves slicing the nerve fibers connecting the prefrontal cortex (the front end of the frontal lobes) to the rest of the brain. (Walter Freeman, the surgeon who introduced the lobotomy to the United States in 1936, is said to have performed the act with a gold icepick.) Patients undergoing it woke up drained of personality; they became docile zombies, apathetic, uncaring, and shallow, Gage-like shells of their former selves.

Personality does not lie wholly in the frontal lobes. Equally important to our sense of self are the temporal lobes, positioned on either side of the head, just over the ears. (The name *temporal*, as in "having to do with time," comes from the location of these lobes over the temples, which is where Father Time tends first to turn hair gray.) The temporal lobes include the auditory cortex—a quarter-sized chunk of tissue necessary for processing input from the ears—and play an essential role in the transfer of information from short-term into long-term memory. It's through this role in memory that the temporal lobes contribute to our existence as unique human beings. Without them, the past dissolves and vanishes before our eyes, and we live in a meaningless and eternal present, unable to connect ourselves to what we've done and where we've been.

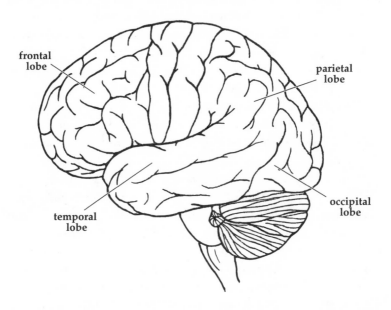

As the frontal lobes made their presence known through Phineas Gage, the temporal lobes also have a human representative: one of psychiatry's most-studied patients, a neurologically famous gentleman from Connecticut known as H. (for Henry) M. On September 1, 1953, H.M. underwent an operation for epilepsy, in which the surgeon—armed with a rotary drill, a pair of metal spatulas, and a silver straw—removed a fist-sized hunk of his brain, including, from both right and left hemispheres, the hippocampus, the amygdala, and the inner surface of the temporal lobe. From that moment, for H.M., time stood still.

Most of us, at one point or another in our swiftly passing lives, have wished that Time's winged chariot would squeal to a dead stop—or, at the very least, slow down for a while. The price for stopping time, however, as evidenced by patients such as H.M., is personal devastation. H.M.'s condition is technically known as anterograde amnesia, the inability to remember events that have happened since the onset of his amnesic condition. The most common form of anterograde amnesia is probably alcoholic blackout, in which, after sufficient intake of rum, scotch, or champagne—the amnestic event—memory is obliterated for a period of time. Dorothy Parker's short story "You Were Perfectly Fine," in which a horribly penitent young man learns of his behavior the night before, is a tale of alcoholic anterograde amnesia.

"So I sang," he said. "That must have been a treat. I sang."

"Don't you remember?" she said. "You just sang one song after another. Everybody in the place was listening. They loved it. Only you kept insisting that you wanted to sing some song about some kind of fusiliers or something, and everybody kept shushing you . . ."

"Didn't I eat any dinner?" he said.

"Oh, not a thing," she said. "Every time the waiter would offer you something, you'd give it right back to him because you said that he was your long-lost brother, changed in the cradle by a gypsy band, and that anything you had was his. You had him simply roaring at you."

"I bet I did," he said. "I bet I was comical. Soci-

ety's Pet, I must have been. And what happened
then, after my overwhelming success with the
waiter?"

Alcoholic anterograde amnesia, of the sort brought on by a
sensational night on the town, is temporary: the normal flow of
memory resumes as the effects of the party wear off. H.M.'s
anterograde amnesia, however, is permanent. His memories are
intact through the summer of 1953, but there they end: H.M.
remembers his birthday, but not his present age; he recognizes
photographs of Alf Landon and Calvin Coolidge, but does not
know the name of the present president of the United States. He
cannot recall the Kennedy assassination or the moon landing—
shown pictures of astronauts, he refers to them as "rocketeers."
He cannot remember the deaths of his parents. He cannot hold
the plot of a television show in mind from beginning to end—
interrupt the action with a commercial, and H.M. forgets all that
has gone before. Enter into a conversation with H.M., leave the
room briefly, and upon your return, he will have forgotten who
you are. Life has no continuity for H.M.; the thread of his being
was chopped off short over forty years ago. "Every moment," he
once told a team of interviewing doctors, "is like a waking
dream."

Not all of H.M.'s memory-forming abilities, however, are
lost. While he can no longer store episodic or semantic
memories—he can't remember what he had for breakfast or
memorize a list of random words—he can still acquire new
procedural memories. H.M. has learned, for example, how to
mirror-draw; that is, to reproduce a drawing while watching
only the reflection of his hand in a mirror, an upside-down-
and-backward performance that, though crazy-making on first
try, improves steadily with practice. He has also mastered the
Tower of Hanoi puzzle, an infamous peg-and-block affair
much beloved by testing psychologists, in which blocks of various sizes must be moved from peg one to peg three according
to a simple set of rules. The minimum number of Tower-

solving moves is 31, a score that H.M. attained after several training sessions. H.M.'s new skills were acquired without conscious knowledge—presented with the Tower of Hanoi puzzle, he cannot remember ever having seen the thing before—but his skillful performance proves that his procedural memory is in fine shape. He simply doesn't realize that it's there.

Butterflies and Building Blocks

THE HUMAN BRAIN, up close, is an impressively massive snarl of biological circuitry. Sliced and laid out under the microscope, it resembles a vast spiderweb, a seemingly endless conglomeration of interwoven fibers. Early biologists, naturally enough, assumed that this network was all of a piece, each fiber physically running into the next like interlocking pipes in household plumbing. The first scientist to get a good close-up peek at the constituents of the brain was probably the Italian anatomist Camillo Golgi, whose secret, a staining solution that turned the cells a natty black against a purply-rose sunset-colored background, is said to have been discovered by mistake when his cleaning lady chucked a sample of brain tissue into a waste bucket full of silver salts. Golgi's silver was put to better use a few years later by a Spanish shoemaker's-apprentice-turned-physician, Santiago Ramón y Cajal. By cunning applications of Golgi's silver, Cajal managed to map out many of the connections of the nervous system, demonstrating that the vines and tendrils of the brain were not all interlinked like some gargantuan neural blackberry bush, but instead consisted of almost-but-not-quite-touching individual cells, formally dubbed neurons. Cajal made elaborate pen-and-ink drawings of his discoveries, and assigned them romantically descriptive names redolent of Victorian drawing rooms: chandelier cells, basket cells, stellate neurons. Golgi, who persistently upheld the interlocked-pipe, or syncytial, view of the brain, shared the Nobel Prize in medicine in 1906 with Cajal, who vociferously disagreed. The ill-matched pair are said to have spoken to each other only once, an exchange of curt and insincere congratulatory sentences at the Swedish awards ceremony.

Time—though not soon enough for the crucial acceptance speech—eventually vindicated Cajal. It is now known that as the brain functions, information flickers through convoluted networks of separate, but communicating, neurons. Cajal poetically referred to these cells as "the mysterious butterflies of the soul"; modern biology textbooks prosaically call them "the building blocks of the brain." Block-shaped, however, they're not: unlike the average cell—a rather characterless blob of protoplasm—the neuron is an anatomical knockout. Neurons display a creative mix of shapes and sizes—some resemble fan coral, others cheerleaders' pom-poms, Koosh balls, exploding stars, or frizzled spiders—but all are variations on a single theme. Each consists of a pyramidal cell body, the control center for daily cellular operations, and a single long information-transmitting extension known as the axon. Flaring out from the cell body is a frizzy halo of fibers called dendrites, from the Greek for "tree," because they reminded some early neurobiologist of the top of one. The axon similarly terminates in a spray of minuscule fibers, each ending in a tiny bulb, known as a synaptic button.

The synapse that caused Cajal and Golgi so much mutual professional hostility is the contact point between cells, the junction where the terminal fibers of the axon of one neuron meet the dendrites on the cell body of the next. Between axon and dendrite is a minuscule gap called the synaptic cleft. As clefts go, this one isn't much—it measures about 20 nanometers across, which translates to an infinitesimal 8/10,000,000 of an inch—but it's across this crucial cleft that chemical transmitters drift, forging the connections, axon to dendrite, neuron to neuron, that form the complex circuitry of the brain.

Frogs' Legs and Frankenstein

INFORMATION FLOW THROUGH the neuronal network is both electrical and chemical. The nerve impulse—the town crier of the cell—is electrical, fizzing along the length of the axon in much the same manner, writes one neurobiologist, that a flame travels along the fuse of a firecracker. This fizz, depending on the size and structure of the axon, moves at anywhere from one to 200 miles per hour; that is, from the top speed of the three-toed sloth to that of the floored Maserati, and it packs measurable, if not spectacular, electrical punch. Cartoonists are on the right track when they suspend a switched-on electric lightbulb over a character's head to represent the birth of a bright idea. Hook up a handful of human neurons and you'll generate as much voltage as a D-cell battery—enough to illuminate a flashlight bulb, or to allow interested medical specialists to map your brain waves by recording an electroencephalogram. (The South American eel, in humbling contrast, can mobilize its specialized neurons to generate a spectacular 600 volts of electricity, enough to stun a horse.)

Eels aside, the average axon, electrically speaking, isn't much as a conductor. Current zips through copper wire en route to your bedside reading lamp at close to the speed of light, over a million times faster than the feeble buzz ambling through your nervous system. This buzz, such as it is, was first deduced in

1771 in the laboratory of Luigi Galvani, the Italian scientist whose name survives in *galvanometer,* an instrument that detects and measures electrical current, and in the verb *to galvanize,* which is what happens to us when we are suddenly shocked by events (say, sticking a screwdriver into an electrical outlet or stepping on a bumblebee) into unprecedented levels of activity. The eighteenth century, scientifically, was a galvanic period in its own right. Pieter van Musschenbroek of Leyden invented the Leyden jar, a gallon-sized glass jug capable of storing a considerable electrical charge; and gleeful experimenters were delightedly using the new source of electricity to kill chickens, ignite glasses of wine at parties, punch holes through stacks of paper, ring bells, and once—for the edification of Louis XV at the Palace of Versailles—to deliver a simultaneous shock to 148 grenadiers, causing them all to yell and jump, with military precision, at the same time. In Berlin, an electrophile named Christian Friedrich Ludolff dramatically set a container of sulfuric ether on fire with a spark drawn from the sword of a court cavalier; and in America, Ben Franklin, whose "electrical bottle" and accompanying apparatus were built for him by a Philadelphia silversmith (using in the process one of the cannonballs stockpiled by the city for defense against the French), managed—in a fine spirit of scientific inquiry—to electrocute a chicken, a turkey, and nearly himself. Franklin also devised an electrically powered "curious Machine" that played tunes upon eight musical bells, an artificial spider that when charged could be made to spring up and down, and a booby-trapped portrait of George II: unsuspecting admirers who simultaneously seized the picture frame and the king's gilt crown received, electrically, a "terrible blow."

Galvani, a physiologist and lecturer at the University of Bologna, seems to have taken electricity in a more serious vein. His laboratory, on the cutting edge of eighteenth-century electrical technology, was well supplied with Leyden jars, one of which he employed in his landmark experiment. He applied a charge to the muscles of dissected frogs' legs—passing through the laboratory, one story claims, en route to the Galvani family soup kettle—and found that the electrical jolt caused the muscles to jerk and twitch. This portentous twitch led Galvani to develop his theory of "animal electricity": muscle cells, he hypothesized, must generate a charge of their own in order to contract. Galvani's grand idea—though somewhat wrong—remains with us: fictional mad scientists, since the days of Mary Shelley's Dr. Frankenstein in 1818, have been galvanically animating their creations with gargantuan jolts of electricity.

The animal electricity that flickers through our nerve—not muscle—cells is far subtler stuff than the potentially lethal zap administered by the average Leyden jar. The electrical impulse, called an action potential, that moves down the length of the nerve cell's axon is generated by the busy movement of charged particles (ions) across the axon's encasing membrane. Cells are fairly stubborn about swallowing or spitting out ions. In fact, such particles can only get in and out of cells through specific channels in the cell membrane, tiny pores that ordinarily stay firmly shut. This seal between cell interior and outside world means that cell innards may contain very different kinds and concentrations of ingredients than are found in the outside environment. In the resting nerve cell—just lolling about, beach-bunny style, doing next to nothing—there are many more negatively charged potassium ions inside the cell than outside, and a lot more positively charged sodium ions outside than in. This unequal balance of power—sodium out, potassium in—abruptly reverses itself when an electrical impulse starts. Pores in the membrane flip open like manhole covers; sodium ions swarm into the cell. Pack enough sodium into an axon and you boost the voltage by as much as a tenth of a volt, from the ordinarily restful -70 millivolts to a startled +30. This voltage change, the basis of the nerve impulse, vanishes almost as quickly as it appears, lasting a fleeting thousandth of a second in any one spot. Potassium channels, spurred into action by the sodium invaders, fling open, pulling more negative potassium into the cell; sodium channels, satisfied that they've done their duty, close down. Equilibrium is gradually restored.

The nerve impulse meanwhile moves fuselike down the axon, sequentially snapping ion channels open and closed, until it reaches the very end. There, at the terminus of the axon—in lieu of a bang and a shower of sparks—the electrical impulse stimulates the release of a shower of chemical transmitter molecules. There are many, perhaps hundreds, of different kinds of chemical transmitters, all small organic molecules, each capable of setting off a different response in the contacted cell. Examples include glutamate, acetylcholine, norepinephrine, serotonin— too much of which appears to be correlated to aggression in humans and animals—and dopamine, too little of which is associated with the symptoms of Parkinson's disease. Transmitters accumulate in little bubblelike vesicles at the synaptic button and are spit out into the synaptic cleft in response to an electrical goose from the axon. (It's at this point that the botulinum toxin—the poison produced by bacteria found in improperly bottled pickles and bulging cans of corn—exerts its lethal effect. Botulinum toxin blocks neurotransmitter release, thus grinding nerve impulse transmission to a halt, and bringing on an often-fatal paralysis.) Neurotransmitter molecules, by the thousand, then drift across the gap, a journey of less than a millisecond, and stick to specific receptors on the dendrites of the next neuron in line. Some neurotransmitters—party animals among biochemicals—have an excitatory effect, setting off a new electrical impulse, headed down another axon and yet another, conducting information through a complex pathway that eventually, with greater or lesser efficiency, culminates in a muscle twitch or surfaces to consciousness as the date of the Louisiana Purchase, the recipe for apple dumplings, or the elusive identity of that woman in blue at the office Christmas party. Others are inhibitory: their interaction with dendritic receptors has the damping effect of a cold shower, bringing all action discouragingly to a halt. Since each neuron simultaneously receives inputs from many neuronal neighbors, it's the final sum of all these excitatory and inhibitory effects that ultimately determines what happens next. If inhibitory inputs outnumber excitations, the impulse—thwarted—stops. If excitatory inputs triumph, the impulse continues. The brain runs—at least in part—on arithmetic.

A Galaxy of Neurons

THE BRAIN CONTAINS some 100 billion neurons, as many as there are stars in the Milky Way Galaxy, twenty times as many as there are human beings on Planet Earth. A sliver of cerebral cortex the size of a Rice Krispie contains about one million neurons. Each is capable of making 10,000 or so synaptic contacts with its neighbors, which makes for a staggering total of 10^{15} possible cell-to-cell connections per brain. This number, which mathematicians refer to reverently as a quintillion, is of such awesome enormity as to ensure that none of us need ever run out of mental storage space. (Just to count to it, at the rate of one number per second, would take 30 million years.) In addition to the electrically jittery neurons, the brain also contains a second—and bigger—class of cells known to neurobiologists as glial cells, from the Greek word for glue. There are about ten glial cells for every neuron, for a grand total of one trillion: glial cells make up about nine-tenths of the cells in the brain. Dogma to date has held that the glial cells are the brain's equivalent of styrofoam peanuts: mere packing material, filling up what would otherwise be an awful lot of empty space. More recent evidence, however, gives all this cellular glue a more impressive role. Glial cells appear in part to act as neuronal nannies, producing health-food-like substances called neurotrophic factors that keep neurons hale and hearty. This, in itself, is no minor task: deprived of neurotrophic factors, neurons shrivel up and die, taking our memories, emotions, rational thinking processes, and motor control along with them. Glial cells, furthermore, may play a more active role in the brain than that of slavish worker to neuronal queen. Glial cells, like neurons, both produce and pick up neurotransmitters, according to the research of Stephen Smith and colleagues at Yale and Stanford, suggesting that they are capable of communicating. If glial cells as well as neurons can form message-carrying networks, the communicatory capacity of the brain may be even more astronomical than previously imagined.

Even without the help of those one trillion potentially active glial cells, we could, one estimate holds, pack away 1,000 new bits of information a second, from birth to ripe old age, and still have used only a fraction of our total brain capacity. Others boost the tally, calculating that the accumulated memories of an average human lifetime would occupy 10^{17} (100,000,000,000,000,000) bits of information—which means that the contents of the average human brain could be packed onto a mere 20 million CD-ROM computer discs. That's 500 times more information than is contained in the entire collection of the Library of Congress, equivalent to some 7.5 trillion densely packed pages of text.

> *And still they gaz'd and still the wonder grew,*
> *That one small head could carry all he knew.*
> Oliver Goldsmith

> *The Brain—is wider than the sky—*
> *For—put them side by side—*
> *The one the other will contain*
> *With ease—and You—beside—*
> Emily Dickinson

Why such a massive brain? One theory, according to evolutionary biologists, has to do with cold weather: an ancient shift in world climate patterns, beginning some 40 to 50 million years ago, presented nascent humankind with a battery of new environmental challenges, thus favoring the survival of individuals with increasingly larger brains. Neurobiologist William Calvin suggests, more specifically, that our big brains may be offshoots of the development of hunting skills. The selective pressures that encouraged early hominids to acquire the ability to aim, throw, and accurately bean a running rabbit with a rock may, simultaneously, have given us improved muscle-sequencing and visuospatial skills, brain lateralization into right and left hemispheres, and even, eventually, the capacity for sophisticated language. Perhaps "'throwing genes,'" writes Calvin, "are little more than bigger-brain genes." Or our hefty brains may have blossomed in response to the demands of developing human culture. The necessity for cooperation among early tribespeople in battling off predators and killing large game animals—you couldn't nab a mammoth on your own—may have fostered enhanced allotments of communications and problem-solving skills and, concomitantly, bigger brains.

Memory, for millennia, has been a trump card in the evolutionary struggle for survival. Those who best recalled the locations of food and water, the appearance of poisonous versus nonpoisonous berries, and the most successful strategies for avoiding danger had a biological edge over their foggier-minded competitors: their chances for survival and opportunities for reproduction were markedly boosted. Thus memory—an eternal plus—has been conserved over countless evolutionary generations.

Reduce, Reduce

THE MIND-BOGGLING VASTNESS and versatility of human memory have confounded researchers for decades. How to begin to analyze an organ the size of a small cabbage that manages to store and manipulate 100 quadrillion scraps of information? The attempt to solve the mysteries of the working brain seems akin to Napoleon's attempt to capture Moscow: a classical exercise in biting off more than one can possibly chew.

> *We don't know one-millionth of one percent about anything.*
> Thomas Edison

> *If the brain was so simple we could understand it, we would be so simple that we couldn't.*
> Lyall Watson

A traditional means of tackling a problem of grandiose proportions is to pare it down to its simplest possible pieces, a scientific approach formally known as reductionism. Reductionists believe (or hope) that all wholes are ultimately describable as the sums of parts, even though some wholes—the human brain is a classic example—possess stupendous emergent properties that are not exhibited by their individual components. (Brain cells don't think; brains do.) Still, reductionism, historically, has often worked. Chemists are able to explain all matter, from gold bricks to gasoline, as the shuffle of a mere 110 (or so) basic elements; physicists are fast boiling life, the universe, and everything down to a handful of fundamental forces and particles. Investigators of memory, accordingly, aim for the lowest mental common denominator, attempting to solve their massive intracranial puzzle by studying the smallest recollections, formed by the simplest thinkers.

> *Simplify, simplify.*
> Henry David Thoreau

The simplest forms of learning are those in which the learner links cause and effect in memory—the sort of mental leap our distant ancestors took in registering that suspicious rustle in the grass = saber-toothed tiger. The first to study such elementary acts of learning in the laboratory was the Russian experimental psychologist Ivan Pavlov who, in the early years of the twentieth century, trained dogs, our best friends, to drool at the sound of a bell. He accomplished this by repeatedly ringing a bell at dinnertime; eventually, in anticipation of imminent food, the dogs would salivate at the sound of the bell alone. This process is known as classical conditioning. It traditionally involves pairing an ordinarily innocuous event like the ringing of a bell (the "conditioned stimulus") with an irresistible treat. This reward—usually food—is known as the "unconditioned stimulus." Present these repeatedly in tandem and the conditionee learns to associate the conditioned stimulus—the bell—with the presentation of goodies, and to respond to it accordingly. Due to the exigencies of various experiments, however, not all researchers are able to maintain this jolly Santa

Claus approach to learning. The unconditioned stimulus can also take the form of abrupt unpleasantness. In lieu of reward, the conditioned stimulus may be paired with unexpected nastiness—for example, a sharp electric shock. Pull this dual stunt a few times and the hapless conditionee soon learns to respond frenziedly to an initial mild signal: shock-conditioned laboratory rats, at the sound of a tone, learned to scramble frantically onto ledges; conditioned goldfish, at a blink of light, to hurl themselves hastily over barriers.

Pavlov's hungry puppies provided support for the ideas of John Watson, the American professor who founded the school of behavioral psychology. All human behaviors, argued Watson, could be explained by a series of conditioning events, a matter of learned responses to perceived punishments or rewards. Aldous Huxley populated his *Brave New World* with such conditionees. New World babies, raised in State Conditioning Centers and destined to be factory workers, were channeled toward their chosen futures by lambasting them with shrieking alarm bells and electric shocks whenever they crawled toward roses or books. "They'll grow up with what the psychologists used to call an 'instinctive' hatred of books and flowers," Huxley's behaviorist Director explains. "Reflexes unalterably conditioned. They'll be safe from books and botany all their lives."

While most psychologists now agree that the countless complexities of human life cannot be accounted for by simple conditioning, the phenomenon has nonetheless proved invaluable to experimenters delving into the workings of the mind. The ability to pair two sensory events and to store the association for future recall is ubiquitous, even displayed by the most simple-minded denizens of the animal kingdom. Bees, for example, possess minuscule brains, a cubic-millimeter-sized pinpoint of neurons, smaller than the bee's bulging compound eyes. Still, with the help of cleverly positioned dishes of honey, bees have been taught to differentiate among a battery of colors. Set the honey out repeatedly on a mat of blue cardboard and, researchers discovered, the bees soon make a beeline for blue, determinedly preferring it over alternative offerings on gray, black, or white cardboard. (Bees do have some ingrained color preferences: it's easiest to train them to approach royal purple, the all-time bee favorite, followed in order by blue, ultraviolet, green, and orange.) Once educated, bees tenaciously retain information: even after a five-month time-out for hibernation, they still remember the colors of their former food sites. Similarly, fruit flies, with barely enough mental armament to zero in on a mushy banana, can be taught to avoid or approach odors; octopi, with the help of a rewarding snack of crab, can learn to distinguish among simple geometric patterns; rats, mice, and hamsters, properly encouraged, can learn to negotiate mazes; pigeons, bribed with food pellets, can learn to peck sequences of colored buttons.

The rationale behind reductionist research—other than the diehard inquisitiveness that Rudyard Kipling, who attributed it to the Elephant's Child, dubbed "satiable curtiosity"—is that many traits and features in the grand scheme of evolution are conserved. Nature, never wasteful, tries to hang on to a good thing. Thus simple solutions to problems in lower life forms are not eliminated willy-nilly, but are enhanced, multiplied, and built upon to take on more challenging functions as we move up the evolutionary scale. The biological click within the brain that reminds the bee that blue = a spoonful of sugar may be—given some hundreds of millions of years of development and diversification—the same cellular fizz that for us conjures up the words to "Yellow Submarine." The no-frills memory mechanism of the worm, the fruit fly, and the bee may prove to be the basic building block of our own far more sophisticated mental machinery.

Worm Running

O NE OF THE FIRST simple-minded thinkers to make an impact in the mysterious milieu of memory study was the worm. The name synonymous with "worm" in the experimentally booming 1950s and 1960s was James McConnell, a psychologist at the University of Michigan, whose work revolved around the planarian. Planaria (in the plural) are tiny freshwater flatworms usually found lurking under rocks in streambeds, from which they can be lured out by baiting their pool with a strip of raw beefsteak. Most measure about a quarter of an inch in length, but real monsters may reach as much as half an inch. All are hermaphrodites, possessed simultaneously of both male and female sex organs; each worm also possesses a pair of light-sensing eyespots, pigmented so as to appear endearingly crossed, and a very rudimentary "brain"—a dual lump of clustered nerve cells in the head.

Planaria admittedly are no mental giants, but under McConnell's tutelage they became star performers in a series of attention-grabbing investigations purporting to show that established memories existed in a form that could be passed from subject to subject. Memory, in short, was edible. Though it now sounds like the stuff of supermarket tabloids (EAT CALCULUS!) the premise behind the work was straight-facedly serious. Memories, it was hypothesized, were stored as molecules—

most likely short-chain proteins—which were synthesized in response to experience in much the same way that the immune system manufactures antibody molecules in response to bacterial infections. The brain, over time, should thus accumulate immense quantities of these molecules—a different protein, perhaps, for each recollection.

McConnell's worms were initially taught to cringe at the sight of light—in somewhat the same manner that humans squinch up and retreat under the blanket when the bedside lamp is suddenly flipped on in the middle of the night—by repeatedly exposing them to a beam of light, then administering a nasty electric shock. After multiple rounds of this treatment, the worms, understandably nervous, cringed expectantly at the sight of light alone. Once the light lesson had been mastered, McConnell diced up his newly accomplished worms and fed the resultant gruel—planaria are notoriously unpicky eaters—to their untutored relatives. The relatives (the "naive" worms), now presumably full of memory molecules, seemed to have absorbed knowledge along with dinner: when tested, they were found to cringe on cue at the sight of light, just like their educated predecessors. McConnell published his results under such titles as "Memory Transfer through Cannibalism in Planarians," and the worms soon proved popular and outlandish enough to merit a journal all their own. Titled *The Worm Runner's Digest* (an "Informal Journal of Comparative Psychology") with the portrait of a perky planarian on the cover, it was published from 1958 to 1979.

In the 1970s, Georges Ungar at Houston's Baylor College of Medicine attempted a series of worm-style experiments with rats. Rats, whose sleazy reputations derive in part from their shadow-lurking behavior, are largely nocturnal, preferring the dark to the daylight. Ungar trained his rats out of their natural shady inclinations by delivering a jolt of electricity every time an animal edged into the darkened portions of its cage, thus eventually developing a class of determinedly pro-light, anti-dark rats. He then homogenized the brains of the trained rats and injected the extract into normal animals. The normal rats promptly became scared of the dark. From the brains of some 4,000 dark-avoidance trained animals, Ungar eventually managed to isolate the meat of the matter: a small but significant protein molecule, which he dubbed scotophobin, from the Greek *skotos*, meaning "darkness," and *phobos*, meaning "fear of." More memory proteins followed. Ungar next came up with anelatin, isolated from the brains of rats trained to respond to the sound of an electric bell, and chromodiopsin, isolated from the combined brains of 10,000 goldfish, painstakingly taught to distinguish between the colors blue and green.

Memory proteins, for a twenty-year span or so—overlapping the advent of the Beatles, love-ins, and Woodstock (the original)—were a hot topic among neurobiologists. At one point even *Time* magazine leaped on the bandwagon, with a Swiftian suggestion for the recycling of aged college professors; they should be used, *Time* proposed, as a source of brain extract, to be injected into freshmen, thus, via memory transfer, bypassing four expensive years of taxing mental effort. To the relief of octogenarian professors worldwide, however, early memory transfer experiments proved largely unrepeatable. A letter to the journal *Science* in 1966 reported the joint failures of 23 frustrated investigators to demonstrate memory transfer at all; and a tally of transfer studies compiled in 1970 announced at best a data tie: 133 studies for transfer; 115 against; and 15 sitting inconclusively on the fence. Memory molecules thereafter faded slowly, like old soldiers, from public view, to take their place with such fringe phenomena as corn field circles, healing crystals, and UFO abductions. Finally the cult of edible memory remained alive only in the Pacific Islands, among the cannibals of New Guinea, who believed that one could absorb the attributes of friends, relatives, and admirable enemies planaria-style, by consuming their brains. This ill-starred custom was unfortunately most effective at transferring not character traits or memories, but a debilitating disease, kuru. Kuru, which slowly destroys the central nervous system, became increasingly rampant among brain-eating tribespersons, eventually attracting the attention of Carleton Gadjusek who, for elucidating its bizarre cause and abominable effects, won the Nobel Prize in 1976.

> *A mental life cannot be reduced to molecules.*
> Israel Rosenfield

Spinach for the Synapse

THE HUMAN BRAIN, for all its chemical diversity, simply doesn't contain enough proteins to account for the immensity of human memory. Investigators, after two decades of observing worm eat worm, turned their attention away from putative proteins and toward the structure of the nerve cell itself—specifically toward the synapse, that glitzy little junction between brain cells where a message, mediated by a spray of neurotransmitter molecules, leaps insouciantly from the axonal terminal of one neuron to the receptive dendrite of the next. Perhaps learning, the hypothesis ran, strengthened certain synapses, making them jumpier and more active, in the same manner that scarfing down a can of spinach invigorates Popeye. The originator of the idea that memory lay in a high-powered synapse was psychologist Donald O. Hebb, born in Chester, a fishing village on the coast of Nova Scotia, in 1904. He came from a family of doctors (both parents, two brothers, and his sister), but Hebb himself, the odd person out, studied English in college, with the intention of becoming a novelist. To support himself pre-publication, he taught school, farmed (with a team of horses) on the west Canadian prairie, and almost got a job as a deckhand on a slow boat to China—novelists need exotic experience—before ending up in graduate school in the psychology department of McGill University in Montreal.

Hebb's career in psychology was long and varied. He was one of the first psychologists to foresee Flipper, suggesting—after observation of their elaborate social behavior—that porpoises were just as smart as chimpanzees. He studied the outer limits of boredom by clapping human volunteers into sensory deprivation booths (nobody lasted so much as a week) and investigated the effects of environment on intelligence, designing experiments to support his contention that animals raised in enriched atmospheres would have an intellectual head start, allowing them to go straight to the head of the class at maturity. In one instance, Hebb's entire psychology department participated: litters of purebred Scottie puppies were divided into two groups, members of the first to be raised in the homes of members of the teaching staff and lavished with rubber balls, carpet slippers, and attention; members of the second to be raised in Spartan laboratory cages. Results were annoyingly inconclusive: Hebb's own experimental Scottie, Henry, despite determined enrichment, passed from confused puppyhood—he continually got lost and had to be retrieved from the local dog pound—to backward adulthood. Mazes baffled Henry. In the final performance tests, the cage-raised laboratory Scotties beat him hands down.

Henry's owner is best known, however, for his insight into the physical basis of memory. Hebb's hypothesis revolves around the aforementioned synapse. Memory, Hebb proposed, takes place when neural cells are activated. This activation—the firing of an electrical impulse—leads to a strengthening of synaptic connections, in the same manner that repeated exercise builds biceps. Turn on a whole interlinked network of cells—as occurs, say, when you sit down to memorize the Gettysburg Address—and you simultaneously beef up a whole battery of synapses. This intensified array is called a cell assembly and is, the hypothesis claims, the biological basis of short-term memory. Translating the Address into long-term storage form is trickier, requiring actual anatomical changes in the neuronal pathways. Once these form, the pathway is permanently strengthened, and the Address, all 267 words of it, is locked in memory, thus allowing you years hence to recite it to your grandchildren at family reunions.

Savvy Slugs

Nobody, of course, wants to be told that they think like a slug, but science—a great equalizer—shows that when it comes to memory we just may be brothers and sisters under the skin. A number of laboratories, notably those of Eric Kandel at Columbia University and Daniel Alkon at the National Institutes of Health, have used large shell-less marine snails—sea slugs—as models for the study of memory formation. A popular slug among these is *Aplysia californica*, a blobbish animal commonly known as the California sea hare from the paired bunny-ear–like protuberances on its head. The sea hare, a splotchy purple-and-potato-brown creature about the size of a guinea pig, is the ugly stepsister of its kind; the sea snails, by and large, are invertebrate beauties. (Among them is the Haitian jewel snail, a ruffled turquoise-blue, orange, and cream, an example of molluscan pulchritude so spectacular that the Haitians have immortalized it on a postage stamp.) Charles Darwin, newly aboard the *Beagle* and deathly seasick, noticed *Aplysia* in the waters off the island of Saint Jago: they are, he wrote, "a dirty yellowish color, veined with purple," and when annoyed they spew out a cloud of concealing purplish fluid in the same spirit that the upset octopus secretes ink. Grabbed, they sting, and they must taste awful, says the *Audubon Encyclopedia of Animal Life*, because almost nothing will eat them.

The chief advantage of *Aplysia*, from a neurobiological point

of view, is its tiny and readily analyzable mind. While the average *Homo sapiens* boasts a skull filled with 100 billion neurons,
and the average bumblebee brain features 950,000, the slug, as it
slogs from seaweed patch to seaweed patch, is powered—like
the diminutive fruit fly—by a mere 20,000 nerve cells. Some of
the slug's 20,000, furthermore, are huge—in some instances,
large enough to be seen with the naked eye—and, for added
effect, they're orange. Perspicacious researchers, armed with
microelectrodes, have managed to isolate individual cells that
function during certain slug learning episodes. Learning, slug-
style, is no great feat of scholastic achievement, but *Aplysia*, like
the rest of us, can sense, grasp, and remember.

This is not, for the laboratory slug, a wholly pleasant
experience: *Aplysia* does not like to be poked in the siphon, the
organ that sucks oxygen-laden water over the slug's breathing
apparatus, the gill. Prod the siphon and the slug will suspiciously haul in its gill, concealing it under a protective flap of
tissue called the mantle: move number one in the slug's battery
of self-defensive maneuvers. The slug can be lulled out of this
precautionary withdrawal with repeated prods: enough pokes
and the slug gets used to the stimulus, shrugging it off as one of
the givens of daily life. Once the slug ceases to withdraw its gill
upon prod, it is said to have become habituated—that is, accustomed to the stimulus to the point of ignoring it, which is what
happens to us when, after an initial moment of startled attention, we cease to hear the steady roar of the air conditioner, the
ongoing squeals of the street traffic, or the interminable rattle of
rain on the living-room roof.

The flip side of habituation is less relaxing. In sensitization,
the response to a stimulus is not soothingly reduced, but galvanically enhanced. In *Aplysia*, this occurs when the siphon
poke—delivered in the laboratory by a calibrated squirt of water
from a WaterPik—is rudely paired with an electrical shock to
the tail. A few rounds of this and the horrified slug soon figures
out that a squirt on the siphon means all hell is about to break
loose in the rear. It responds to a squirt by whipping siphon and

gill under cover, battening down the hatches for impending disaster.

So what goes on in *Aplysia*'s juicy orange nerve cells when such memories form? Habituation and sensitization—the damped-down or enhanced response to a stimulus—have their roots in the behaviors of individual nerve cells. The neural wiring diagram of a slug is straightforwardly simple. In this case, sensory neurons in the siphon are linked, each via a single synapse, to motor neurons controlling the movement of the gill. Squirt the siphon and an electrical impulse shudders down the axon of the sensory neuron. This electrical blip can be sensed by delicately implanted microelectrodes; amplified, it stutters through laboratory loudspeakers as a cereal-like snap, crackle, and pop, nerve impulses translated into sound. At the synapse, the impulse—like a pin bursting a bevy of microscopic balloons—causes membranous bubbles stuffed with neuro-transmitter molecules to spit their contents into the synaptic cleft. The neurotransmitter spray spatters the dendrites of the next neuron in line—the motor neuron—and sets off a second electrical impulse, which stimulates movement: in the case of the squirted slug, the protective yanking in of siphon and gill. Translate habituation and sensitization into cellular terms and you find that the explanation is chemical. The laid-back habitu-ated neuron spills very little neuron into the synaptic cleft, so lit-tle that the motor neuron ignores it altogether; the hysterical sensitized neuron spills a flood, kicking the motor neuron into overdrive. Learning, as Donald Hebb predicted, increases the strength of the synapse.

The Rats with the Most Toys

THERE'S MORE TO memory, though—even slug memory—than an extra splurt of neurotransmitter molecules. This brief strengthening, researchers guess, is just a prelude to the main event: transfer into long-term permanent storage. Permanent storage implies—somewhere, somehow—permanent change, a change long-lasting enough to allow such long-lived individuals as Jeanne Calment to cast her mind back 107 years to her close encounter with Vincent van Gogh or Eva Hart to call up an 84-year-old recollection of the sinking of the *Titanic*. The brain changes forever with the formation of long-term memories. A meeting with a great painter—even if, as the young Jeanne did, one finds him a social dud—or participation in an awe-inspiring historical tragedy leaves physical tracks behind. As we remember, brain topography alters: new dendrites sprout and branch, new connections form and strengthen.

In the 1960s, Mark Rosenzweig and colleagues at the University of California at Berkeley set out to document such change in the brains of rats. Rosenzweig's rats were divided into two groups. Group one, dubbed the bright rats, were raised in an environment rich in mind-broadening luxuries—rotating wheels, swings, ramps, ladders, and toys—plus the companionship of other like-minded rats and the frequent attention of concerned human researchers. Their unlucky counterparts, the dull rats, were raised in leaden isolation, ignored by all about them, and provided with nothing for amusement other than a food dish. At the conclusion of the experiment, both the pampered "enriched" rats and their "impoverished" litter mates came to the same bad end: all were killed, and their brains analyzed, weighed, and measured. When the results were in, it was clear that those who died with the most toys won. The cerebral cortices of the enriched animals were considerably thicker than those of the deprived group. Bright rats had fatter brains.

Subsequent experiments confirmed the original results and showed where the nitty-gritty of the difference lay. The enriched rats, after a lush life of friends and mind-expanding manipulatives, had 20 percent more dendritic branching—the stuff of neuronal connections—than did their unstimulated brothers and sisters. Even better, the effect was not confined solely to the very young. Staid middle-aged rats exposed to the toys-and-playground environment similarly sprouted a new crop of dendrites.

Fred Gage and coworkers at the Salk Institute for Biological Studies in La Jolla, California, found that enriched mice, here supplied with intriguing paper and plastic tubes, a multidoored fiber tunnel, and a creative assortment of nesting materials, developed enriched hippocampi. These lucky rodents were found to have on average 40,000 more neurons in their hippocampal tissue than their Spartanly reared peers, an impressive increase of 25 percent. The hippocampus, which functions in learning and memory, seems to function even better if bigger: the enriched mice performed superlatively on memory-challenging maze tests.

Michael Merzenich at the University of California at San Francisco has also demonstrated how day-to-day activities alter the topography of the brain. Merzenich trained owl monkeys to rotate a disk using only the three middle fingers of one hand. The monkeys, solemnly spinning, worked at this task for an hour a day for three months, by the end of which time they had performed thousands of three-fingered disk turns. Merzenich then examined the somatosensory regions of their cerebral cortices, where sensory input from the fingers is registered. In the disk-rotating monkeys, the area of the cortex keyed to the three middle fingers was enlarged, at the expense of the areas devoted to the neglected little finger and thumb. The brain had rearranged itself in response to learning, altered with feed-in from the outside world. A similar effect is seen in amputees— the region of the cortex devoted to the vanished limb dwindles, while compensatory areas expand—and in users of Braille, whose increased finger sensitivity shows up as increased territory on the map of the brain.

Experience, clearly, shapes the brain; and our brains, given the uniqueness of each and every life, are thus as individual as our fingerprints. "At fifty," wrote George Orwell in his manuscript notebook, "everyone has the face he deserves." The same, it seems, can be said of the stuff inside the skull.

Permanent Ink

Precisely *how* experience sets its fingerprints upon the brain remains a matter of debate. One candidate for the mental equivalent of permanent ink is a phenomenon known as LTP, originally described in 1973 by Terje Lømo and Timothy Bliss, then working together, with numerous rabbits, in Oslo. LTP is an acronym for "long-term potentiation," a descriptive, if somewhat linguistically infelicitous, condition first observed in the hippocampus of the rabbit brain. When rabbits' brains were implanted with microelectrodes and repeatedly stimulated with a tingling train of electrical impulses, the strength of the stimulated synapses increased sharply. This enhanced synaptic strength was remarkably durable, stubbornly persisting for periods of up to four months. The duration and location of LTP—in the hippocampus, a crucial memory-processing region of the brain—led researchers to conclude hopefully that this might be, at last, the long-sought source of long-term memory.

LTP, biochemically dissected, proved a surprise for neurobiologists who, for comfortable decades, had believed information transmission in the brain to be unidirectional—axon to dendrite to axon to dendrite—like the one-way flow of electricity through a string of Christmas tree lights or of water through a garden hose. LTP, rather than trucking resolutely forward, establishes and maintains itself by backtracking. The interconnected cell assemblies in the hippocampus communicate with one another by means of a neurotransmitter called glutamate. Under the influence of an electrical impulse, glutamate molecules spray from the tip of the axon of a transmitting (pre-synaptic) neuron into the synaptic cleft, drift across the gap, and bind, like jigsaw puzzle pieces snapping into place, to receptors on the dendrites of the receiving (post-synaptic) neuron. Unlike jigsaw puzzles, however, in which each piece so annoyingly has only one proper place to fit, glutamate molecules have a choice. It now appears that there are many different kinds of receptors for glutamate on the receiving cell membrane. Prominent among these are the NMDA receptors, named for their ability to bind an arcane chemical called N-methyl-D-aspartate, an act which they never ordinarily perform in real life. A second class, non-NMDA receptors, not only don't bind NMDA, but couldn't even if they wanted to.

NMDA receptors usually play a poor second fiddle to their non-NMDA competitors—and through no fault of their own; usually they are kept firmly plugged by interfering magnesium ions such that nothing can stick to them. When LTP is initiated, however, magnesium pops off like a champagne cork, and the NMDA receptor is open for business. With NMDA receptors in the running, more receptors are available to bind more glutamate molecules, a wealth of interactions that makes for a more and more excited post-synaptic neuron. As in the case of the squirted slugs, the more neurotransmitter, the bigger the buzz. All this excitement causes a channel to open up in the NMDA receptor through which calcium pours into the cell. Calcium—so essential in the building of strong bones and teeth, to say nothing of sta-lactites, seashells, and eggshells—has the effect of an intracellular four-alarm fire, setting off a flurry of biochemical events. Among these is the release of a factor from the receiving post-synaptic cell that feeds back to the transmitting pre-synaptic cell and causes it to release even more neurotransmitter. In effect, it's as if the very act of turning on a Christmas tree light sent a message backward to the wall socket yelling for more electricity, which in turn causes the light to burn more and more brightly.

This backward-leaking mystery factor—officially called a retrograde messenger—may be, compared to most neurological biochemicals, embarrassingly simple. There's some evidence that LTP's retrograde messenger is nitric oxide, a short-lived gas whose chemical formula is a resounding NO. Nitric oxide (NO) in nature is created out of thin air by passing bolts of lightning and is generated here on earth by combustion: hence it figures in the unpleasant chemical pantheon that makes up such unnatural stuff as acid rain and smog. Inhaled in any quantity, nitric oxide is downright nasty: like carbon monoxide, it is poisonous, binding suffocatingly to the oxygen-toting hemoglobin of red blood cells. It also—as if that were not enough—rapidly reacts with oxygen and water to produce nitric acid, which is burningly painful. Ordinarily it's a gas to avoid. In small controlled doses, however, it's another story. Nitroglycerin and analogs, the magical little pills that relieve the pain of angina, do so by the grace of nitric oxide: its release causes constricted blood vessels to dilate, thus dropping blood pressure. In the body, naturally secreted nitric oxide relaxes the muscles of the stomach, allowing it to expand and making possible the consumption of enormous Thanksgiving dinners, and dilates the arteries supplying blood to the penis, allowing erection and the accompanying perpetuation of the species. (Rats, pharmacologically prevented from manufacturing nitric oxide, become impotent.) In the brain, nitric oxide appears to play an equally impressive role. Turn on the NMDA receptors of a post-synaptic neuron, researchers have found, and one of the results is the release of nitric oxide. Block nitric oxide release and you wipe out LTP.

Another candidate for retrograde messenger is a second unappealing gas: hydrogen sulfide, the volatile compound that gives rotten eggs their distinctively dreadful odor and boiled cabbage its off-putting bouquet. Like nitric oxide, hydrogen sulfide appears to enhance connections between brain cells that strengthen during LTP. Memory, if not outright poisonous, may invariably be accompanied by a minuscule whiff of skunk.

While LTP has been demonstrated in immobilized rabbits

and in slices of brain floating eerily in petri dishes, proof for its essential involvement in memory necessarily involves showing that without it we lapse into leaden forgetfulness. Some evidence that LTP is indeed the right stuff comes from Richard Morris at the University of Edinburgh, whose memory model is based on rats paddling through murky pools of milky water. The pool is a Morris water maze: it contains a submerged platform, invisible due to the opacity of the milk, which the swimming rat must first find by trial and error, then locate through memory, using learned spatial cues. Normal rats manage this quite well; after an initial trial period of frantic paddling, they learn to make directly for the location of land. Rats treated with a drug called APV (aminophosphonovaleric acid), however, paddle indefinitely unless they stumble upon the hidden platform by sheer dumb luck. APV disables the crucial NMDA receptors on the post-synaptic membrane, thus blocking LTP. The LTP-less rats aren't totally brainless—show them an island poking above the milky waves and they'll make a rat-line for it—but, in the absence of LTP, they simply cannot remember the position of a hidden platform.

The work of Nobel Prize–winner Susumu Tonegawa and colleagues at the Massachusetts Institute of Technology pushes rodent memory one step further. Tonegawa's group has produced a strain of "knockout" mice—not, as the name suggests, a woozy population of miniature boxing victims, but a group of animals deprived of a single gene. In Tonegawa's mice, the gene essential for the manufacture of the NMDA receptor in the cells of the hippocampus has been "knocked out." The NMDA receptor–less mice are memory morons. No amount of hidden cheese can tempt them to learn the layout of even the most straightforward maze; they are simply unable to remember. Deprived of NMDA receptors, they are incapable of increasing the strength of synapses: their brain cells, jogged with repeated pulses of electricity, are unable to register LTP. You can lead a knockout mouse through mazes, but you can't make it learn.

Rutabaga, Radish, and Dunce

A FOUR-MONTH BOUT OF LTP, while impressive, does not a lifetime's worth of memory make. For solidly permanent storage to take place, DNA has to enter the act: gene activation, with subsequent new protein synthesis, must bring about physical changes in the structure of the involved nerve cells. The process by which ephemeral short-term memories are converted into unshakable long-term memories has been partially clarified through studies of a collection of mutant fruit flies, each deficient in a specific step of the memory acquisition and storage process. Some of the memory mutants are mildly absent-minded, others are pathologically vague, and at least one enviable group is mentally enhanced, displaying fly-style megamemories. The fruit (or vinegar) fly, *Drosophila melanogaster*, is the minuscule pest found swarming around mushy bananas, dissolving peaches, and other fruit that has unmistakably passed its prime. Fruit flies, due to such food-foraging behaviors (they're not interested in the fruit *per se*, but in the yeasts that sprout on its softening skin), are notably interested in odors. The scent of banana oil, for example, is a perennial fruit fly favorite; some fruit flies, perversely, adore the scent of citronella; and Mediterranean fruit flies—bane of California fruit growers—are said to be mad for the smell of kerosene. The flies' ability to sniff out and store remembrances of scents past has enabled scientists to get a fly's-eye view of long-term memory.

To provide their tiny subjects with analyzable memories, researchers first trap flies—who sniff with sensory organs on the tips of their feet—in small training chambers, the inner walls of which are coated with electrifiable copper grid. The flies are then exposed to two different scents, each in turn wafted zephyrlike through the test chamber on currents of air. Tim Tully and colleagues at Cold Spring Harbor Laboratory, New York, train their flies on octanol, which smells spicily of black licorice, and methylcyclohexanol, which smells of sweaty socks. During exposure to the first scent, the flies are given a rousing electric shock; during exposure to the second, they are allowed to smell serenely in peace, like Ferdinand the Bull savoring his flowers. Post-training, the flies are transferred to a T-shaped maze, one arm of which is scented with the shock-paired odor, the other with the benign odor. Bright flies—usually about 90 percent of the total population—head for the benign odor; forgetful flies bumble toward the shock-paired odor or remain undecided, dithering about at the maze entrance.

Fly memory, investigators explain, proceeds, like human memory, through sequential stages. Initially flies form short-term memories, fleeting remembrances that last only a few minutes. If all goes well, these are transformed to "middle-term" memories, capable of surviving for several hours. Both short- and middle-term memories are slippery: they can be dislodged, in human beings, by such insults to the system as a blow to the head, a violent electrical shock, or general anesthesia. In flies, researchers find that early-stage memories can be wiped out by "cold shock": place the flies in a test tube and dunk the tube in ice water; within minutes the chilled flies crumple unconscious to the bottom of the tube. Warmed, the flies pop up again with no physical ill effects—except that they have lost their short- and middle-term memories. As time between training and ice-water bath increases, however, the memory eradication effect disappears. If the ice-water treatment is delayed for three hours post-training, the flies revive with their odor memories stubbornly intact. This relatively durable stage of memory has been dubbed "anesthesia-resistant memory" (ARM), and researchers once believed that it was the necessary prelude to—or early form of—full-fledged permanent long-term memory (LTM).

Normal flies, barring a dip in the ice-water bath, proceed painlessly through the memory sequence, eventually achieving long-term memory. Mutant flies, however, have a rockier row to hoe. Researchers at Cold Spring Harbor Laboratory, at Caltech, and at the Massachusetts Institute of Technology have identified flies with genetic mutations at several different steps in this memory sequence. In each case, the mutation—like a dam across a river—blocks memory activity downstream. A mutation in middle-term memory, for example, as occurs in a forgetful fly fittingly called *amnesiac,* blocks acquisition of the later long-term memory, but has no effect on the preceding short-term memory. Flies with a mutation insensitively known as *dunce,* blocked at an earlier stage of the memory sequence, are even more forgetful than amnesiac. *Dunces,* though properly responsive to smells and electric shocks, are simply unable to learn from experience. They, and the similarly vague victims of a mutation called *rutabaga,* both suffer from obstructions in short-term memory. Minutes after odor training, their miniature minds are once again clean slates; placed in the T maze, *dunces* and *rutabagas* behave like untrained control flies, as likely as not to buzz blithely off in the wrong direction.

While *dunce, rutabaga,* and *amnesiac* were straightforwardly dumb, a mutant fly known as *radish* posed a more challenging problem. Memory in *radish* is blocked further down the line, at the level of anesthesia-resistant memory (ARM), which—in normal flies—develops about three hours after initial licorice/sweaty socks training. *Radish,* the traditional memory model predicts, should have a bleak long-term future: a block in ARM should also disrupt the final stage of long-term memory formation (LTM). Such, however, according to Tim Tully and associates, is not the case. *Radish* flies have normal long-term memories. ARM, rather than a prerequisite for long-term memory, appears to be a separate system, an offshoot of middle-term memory. The key, explains Tully, lies in the training schedule. Flies—just like the rest of us—learn best after multiple training sessions, regularly interspersed with rest periods. Following such a relaxed training series, both normal flies and *radish* mutants demonstrate stable long-term memories. If training occurs in a single prolonged session, however—called "massed" training, the fly equivalent of all-night cramming for an exam—normal flies acquired anesthesia-resistant but not long-term memory, and *radish* flies developed no late-stage memories at all.

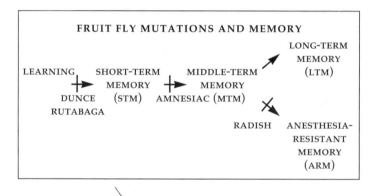

The biochemical roots of the troubles of these forgetful fruit flies have recently been identified. *Dunce* and *rutabaga* have defects in the metabolism of a cellular chemical called cyclic AMP, a ubiquitous molecule that acts as a messenger boy within cells, turning on or off various intracellular processes—including those required for the establishment of middle- and long-term memories. (The caffeine in your morning jolt of java ups cyclic AMP; so, astronomically, does cholera toxin, which, in doing so, brings on life-threatening diarrhea.) The *radish* mutation, however, is a more puzzling kettle of fish. Why can it form long-term memories after spaced training sessions, but no anesthesia-resistant memories after massed training? Tully and coworkers guess that the answer lies in functional differences between the two forms of later-stage memory. Anesthesia-resistant memories, it appears, can be established thriftily, using those materials that the participating cells already have on hand. Long-term memories, in contrast, only form after the cellular equivalent of a shopping spree: LTM requires the synthesis of new proteins. For such synthesis to occur, cells seem to require crucial intervals of rest. Perhaps during those intertraining recess periods, Tully and colleagues hypothesize, some factors become active that set the stage for memory-building protein synthesis. All work and no play in *radish* flies is the coup de grace for long-term memory.

CREB and the Absentminded Professor

THE ANSWER TO THE mystery of *radish* may lie in a class of molecules called CREBs, a name that is a somewhat convoluted acronym for "cyclic AMP-responsive element-binding protein." CREBs are transcription factors; that is, they participate in the activation of genes on strands of DNA, which in turn direct the manufacture of necessary new proteins. Eric Kandel, of sea slug fame, explains that CREB in *Aplysia* manifests itself in at least two different forms. CREB1, an activator molecule, enhances protein synthesis and promotes the establishment of long-term memory. CREB2, an inhibitor, turns the whole thing off. (Perhaps, jokes Kandel, the Shass Pollak—the Hebrew scholars famed for their massive verbatim memories of the Talmud—are high producers of CREB1; while absentminded professors are oversupplied with CREB2.)

Fruit flies, similarly, possess both Jekyll and Hyde versions of CREB. Jerry Yin and Tim Tully have identified a fly with a mega-memory, able to learn in a single trial what takes an ordinary fly ten. This superfly appears to owe its talents to CREB: it synthesizes the activator form of the molecule in abnormally high amounts. Its opposite number, a memory midget, overproduces the inhibitor form of CREB: these flies possess normal short-term, middle-term, and anesthesia-resistant memories, but are unable to transfer any information into long-term memory.

The CREB-controlled memories of slugs and flies are not wholly unique. Mice—whose genetic makeup is more similar to that of human beings than most of us care to admit—also depend on CREB for long-term remembrance of things past. Alcino Silva and Roussoudan Bourtchuladze of Cold Spring Harbor Laboratory have studied a population of mutant mice deficient in the activator form of CREB. The CREB-less mice are chronically forgetful. Taught to locate a sunken platform in the Morris milky water maze, they perform expertly for thirty minutes or so; then, as middle-term memory fades, they forget where they're going. Lacking the ability to form long-term memories, CREB-less mice are doomed to mental oblivion.

Praying Mantises and Pecking Chicks

If CYCLIC AMP AND CREB1 do their duty, the end result is a burst of protein synthesis, producing new compounds which, tacked on and inserted here and there, change the shape of nerve cells. The link between new protein synthesis and long-term memory has been known to science since the 1960s. It was first demonstrated in the ever-popular white rat, by researchers Wesley Dingman and Michael Sporn, who trained rats to negotiate a water maze, then injected their damp subjects with 8-azaguanine, a drug that blocks protein synthesis. Rats injected just before training soon forgot all they learned, but rats injected at progressively longer intervals after training retained increasingly more information, until finally a point was reached at which the drug had no effect. Long-term memory was fully established and the rats remained aquatically savvy.

Neurophysiologists have also shown a link between new protein synthesis and long-term memory formation in less common experimental animals: the goldfish and the praying mantis. Goldfish, taught to hop over a barrier in the middle of their tank in order to avoid an electric shock, forget to do so if injected with a drug that blocks protein synthesis; drugged fish simply hang around naively in harm's way, unmindful of the inevitable zap. Praying mantises, studied in 1980 by Klaus Jaffé at the Centro Biofísica y Bioquímica in Caracas, were similarly rendered forgetful by protein synthesis inhibition. Mantises, unlike goldfish, were apparently uncooperative—even hostile—test subjects and had to be restrained during experimental procedures in a device known as a "mantis-holder," a block of wood to which the annoyed mantis was stuck with adhesive tape. In addition to this insect version of the straitjacket, the mantises also suffered the indignity of having a tiny copper wire with a bead of wax on the end glued to their foreheads: insects wearing this foolish-looking bauble, Jaffé explained, showed better retention than headdress-free mantises. The taped, glued, and wax-decked mantises were positioned behind a glass wall, through which they were shown a tantalizingly out-of-reach rotating black star. The mantis, identifying the star as food, would strike at it hungrily with its forelegs. After repeated futile episodes, however, even the dullest mantis eventually cottoned to the fact that the star was unattainable, and the number of attacks sharply dropped off. Inject a newly trained mantis with protein synthesis inhibitor, however, and the luckless bug goes right back to square one: forgetting the lessons of the past, it once again begins to reach for the unreachable star. New permanent memories, it seems, require new permanent proteins.

One possible result of this flurry of protein production comes from the work of Steven Rose and colleagues at the Open University in London. Rose's neurobiological career has centered on studies of memory in the chick, that fuzzy little denizen of farmyards and Easter baskets. Chicks are precocial birds, which means that within minutes of hatching, they're up and running, ready to fend for themselves in a hostile world of chicken hawks and foxes. (Their opposite numbers, altricial birds, are born helpless, naked, shrieking, and totally dependent on their doting parents.) Rose trains day-old chicks to peck or not to peck, by dangling before them on the end of a wire handle shiny chrome beads coated with either plain water or an evil-tasting liquid called methylanthranilate. A tinge of methylanthranilate is what puts the grape flavor in soda and cough syrup; on its own, it's yellow and bitter and chicks hate it. One peck is plenty; methylanthranilate-trained chicks refuse to have anything more to do with chrome beads. They have formed and stored a memory of gustatory awfulness: bead = bad news. Rose then injects his chicks with a radioactive sugar, which sticks in the brain in regions that are most active, and finally, Red Queen–style, chops off their heads and searches their brain tissue for traces of memory. Sections from active portions of the chick brain, sliced and stained, show that in chicks with newly established memories, neuronal shapes had changed. Ordinarily the branches of the frizzled crown of dendrites that tops each neuron are studded with tiny spines, like the thorns on the branches of a rosebush. Under the electron microscope, at magnifications at which a paperclip would be the size of a football field, it's possible—if you are a graduate student with the patience of Job—to count the spines on each dendritic branch. Counted, it turned out that memory sprouts a thicket of thorns. Trained chicks, with memories of methylanthranilate on their minds, had 60 percent more dendritic spines than their plain-water-fed mates. Long-term memory may write its signature across the brain in sticky spikes of protein.

Memory in Quantumland

THE IDEA THAT memory, mind, and all our fondest thoughts result from patterns of electrical blips and chemical spills passing among the cells of the brain is known as the neural connectionist hypothesis. This is the current favorite these days among neurobiologists and cognitive philosophers, but it doesn't fill the bill for everyone. A bevy of physicists, following the lead of Oxford physicist/mathematician Roger Penrose, famed for his work on the geometry of tiling patterns, suggest that the building blocks of memory may be even smaller than imagined, the result of subatomic flip-flops known as quantum effects. In the Wonderland-like world of the quantum, everything exists only as a series of unresolved probabilities, called a wave function, which, upon measurement or observation, solidifies decisively into reality. Physicists traditionally explain this phenomenon using the example of Erwin Schroedinger's cat. The hapless theoretical cat is placed, by ailurophobic theoretical physicists, in a box along with a source of a lethally poisonous gas, which can only be released upon the random decay of a radioactive atom. As long as that box is shut tight, quantum theorists argue, the cat is neither alive nor dead, but caught in a limbo of undecided probabilities—a tenuous lady-or-tiger situation that cannot be resolved as long as the box remains enigmatically closed. Once you open the box and peek, however, the wave function collapses and one of the probabilities becomes real. The cat, once observed, either sits up and meows or keels over.

The human mind, some theorists argue, similarly acts like a quantum cat: it exists as an array of unresolved decision-making possibilities that suddenly collapse into a single reality when one forms a conscious stream of thought. Stuart Hameroff at the University of Arizona feels that he has identified the potential cellular site where such quantum waffling may occur in the brain. Cells—including the brain's billions of neurons—are filled with microtubules, stiff little protein rods arranged in a latticelike scaffolding, the closest thing a cell has to a supportive inner skeleton. Microtubules aren't simple sticks, like tiny toothpicks: each has a complex substructure, consisting of thirteen taffylike twisted molecules of a protein called tubulin. Segments of these tubulin strands, Hameroff explains, can be made to vibrate rapidly in response to subtle atomic shifts; and the individual vibrations may reach such a pitch that they merge into a coordinated tremor that shimmers down the outer surface of each microtubule like the spiraling stripe on a barber pole. The atomic shifts that set the initial ripples off, Hameroff further proposes, are quantum events, single electron flip-flops that, like a series of toppling dominoes, add up to a coherently propagated wave. This coherent wave could, like Morse code, act as an information-transmitting source within cells—which suggests that the microtubules might be a network within a network, a smaller and subtler level of neural processing. Perhaps, says Hameroff, thought is produced when enough microtubules vibrate in synchrony, reaching some certain critical threshold. Memories may be preserved as unique microtubular wave patterns, permanently "frozen" standing waves on the microtubule surfaces.

Eliminating the Impossible

Quantum flip-flop is too far out for most neurobiologists, who argue that tiny microtubular wave effects would be drowned out by the—comparatively—deafening chatter and static of the brain's greater electrical activity, in the same manner that the feeble light from a kitchen match is swamped by the glare from a bolt of lightning. They turn instead from the atomically infinitesimal to the anatomically large, searching for sites of memory storage not within individual cells, but in the whole brain. Among the earliest seekers of such macro-memory sites was neurobiologist Karl Lashley, who embarked upon his life's work when, as a seventeen-year-old laboratory assistant in 1907, he came upon a series of microscopic sections of frog's brain in the trash. Lashley fished them out and, then and there, with the unsinkable optimism of the young, decided to piece together the connections of the preserved brain, definitively figuring out how a frog works—a project somewhat akin to disassembling your grandfather's pocketwatch to see how it keeps time, only to find more minuscule wheels, cogs, screws, springs, and gadgets than you had ever thought possible. Leaving behind the not-quite-yet-deciphered frog, Lashley, now with a doctorate under his belt, moved on to the rat. His aim was to localize specific rat behaviors to specific sites in the brain, identifying for each a physical memory path or trace, an elusive entity for which he adopted the term *engram*. He tracked the engram through the cerebrum using a technique formally known as ablation, which means, in cold truth, chopping out defined chunks of a rat's central nervous system and then observing the animal to see which behaviors, if any, disappear. He spent years training his rats to run mazes, then excising slices of cerebral cortex and sending the lesioned rats back into the maze again in hope that at some point they would forget all they knew, thus allowing him to pinpoint the site of memory in the rat brain. The rats, stubbornly, didn't forget. Even reduced to neurological colanders, they managed to stagger and lurch through the intricacies of the maze—a feat that led Lashley, in dismal summation of his career in 1950, to write: "I sometimes feel, in reviewing the evidence on the localization of the memory trace, that the necessary conclusion is that learning is just not possible." Memory, Lashley concluded, was simultaneously everywhere and nowhere, like God. Embellished for publication, this became known as the "doctrine of equipotentiality"—that is, no part of the brain is more important than any other in the maintenance of memory.

Lashley's argument, for all this simplistic boiling down of data, was far from naive. The brain, clearly, is highly organized and astoundingly complex: no modern neurobiologist views its two hemispheres, four lobes, and other major and minor subdivisions as interchangeably homogeneous, like an undifferentiated bowl of oatmeal. The behavior of Lashley's rats merely added another puzzling layer to the already complicated whole. Individual memories, the ablation experiments seemed to show, were not localized to specific single plugs of cranial tissue. Instead, they appeared to be diffuse, coordinated functions, relying perhaps on the overall activity of the entire brain.

Survival of the Fittest

For Gerald Edelman, the scattered pattern of memory in the brain reflects a wildly variable conglomeration of neuronal "maps," each a triumphant survivor in a Darwinian struggle for dominance. Edelman, the recipient of a Nobel Prize in 1972 for his work on the chemical structure of antibody molecules, hypothesizes that memory is in many ways analogous to the immune system. Each human body is poised to battle disease with an army of some two trillion white blood cells—lymphocytes—each of which, on its surface, carries specific receptors capable of recognizing specific foreign antigens. When antigens, notably such undesirables as bacteria, viruses, and ragweed pollen, hit the bloodstream, sooner or later each makes contact with its matching receptor on the surface of a vigilant lymphocyte. Once contact occurs, the alerted lymphocyte rapidly divides, and its progeny proceed to spew out a host of antigen-grabbing antibody molecules. This protective barrage, pumped out at a rate of 2,000 antibody molecules per minute, is what ultimately cures us of chicken pox, flu, and the infuriating common cold. Each of us possesses, from birth, an immensely varied population of lymphocytes, collectively capable of recognizing millions of equally varied antigens. Not all lymphocytes multiply and manufacture antibodies, however; only certain cellular candidates are selected for reproductive stardom, based on the body's exposure to particular kinds of antigens. The eradication of smallpox dooms those lymphocytes carrying a smallpox-recognizing receptor to a life of solitary oblivion.

Edelman's hypothesis suggests that in the same manner that an invading *Streptococcus* selects a few deserving lymphocytes from a vast white blood cell population, an incoming memory—represented by an array of sensory data and perceptions—may select a few appropriate cell groups from multitudinous preexisting neuronal cell assemblies. The simultaneous stimulation of these chosen few assemblies leads to a strengthening of interassembly connections, creating an enhanced network referred to as a "neuronal map." The astonishing variability among human brains—the quality that allows the same basic organ to accommodate the memories and skills of an acrobat, an architect, a hunter-gatherer, and a financier—may result from this "neural Darwinism." Though each of us starts out with approximately the same biological equipment, as each brain is exposed to different external stimuli, different neuronal maps are selected and promoted to positions of power.

PET and MRI

I F ,   A S   N E U R A L   D A R W I N I S M   implies, the brain catches memories like measles, it may be possible to watch the process in action. In recent years, a battery of new sensitive scanning techniques has allowed investigators, with the aid of computer imaging, to trace thought springing kangaroolike through the tissues of the human brain. Brain activity (or lack thereof) is translated on the computer screen into color-coded maps: lollipop swirls of red, blue, and green, highlighted with splashes and dabs of orange and yellow.

These modern scanning systems take advantage of the gluttonous need of brain cells for energy. As nerve networks become active, they become piggish consumers of fuel, in the form of oxygen and sugar. Fuel requirements in the brain are high: when the straw-headed Scarecrow in *The Wizard of Oz* begs for a brain, he is letting himself in for a most demanding organ. The brain accounts for only 2 percent of body weight, but sops up 15 percent of our blood supply and 25 percent of all inhaled oxygen. (The only animal that outdoes humans in cranial energy-guzzling is the elephant nose fish, a foot-long denizen—much of it nose—of the lakes and rivers of western and central Africa. It channels over 50 percent of its total body oxygen to its brain.)

In positron emission tomography (PET), the best known of the brain-imaging systems, patients are injected with radiolabeled molecules and then scanned with a ring of sensitive detectors that respond to emitted gamma rays. The radiolabeled molecules are quickly and specifically snapped up by working hungry nerve cells: radioactive hot spots in the brain indicate active sites where thought, memory, and emotion occur. Most of the brilliantly colored slices and sections of brains pictured these days in the scientific literature are the results of PET scans.

A second technique, functional magnetic resonance imaging (MRI), uses a powerful magnetic field to align atomic nuclei in the brain. These nuclei swivel and line up in response to magnetic pull in the same manner that iron filings snap into ordered arrays under magnetic influence. The aligned nuclei are then beamed with pulses of radio waves, which causes them, at certain frequencies, to resonate. This atomic quiver indicates the concentrations of various elements in different portions of the brain, allowing scientists to measure activity-revealing changes in oxygen uptake and blood flow. MRI can be hard on the scannees: patients must lie motionless, encased in the scanning apparatus for prolonged periods—an experience that one MRI critic compares to being trapped in a thermos bottle. While some patients find this lullingly peaceful, others find it claustrophobically threatening. About 10 percent of MRI subjects, according to the *Journal of the American Medical Association*, turn tail and run.

> *Nowhere has anybody seen the mind. They can see on one of the magic machines the dead brain cells that wreck a leg. But not the mind.*
> Jimmy Breslin,
> *I Want to Thank My Brain for Remembering Me*

Brain-imaging techniques have given us some of our best guesses to date as to how human memory is organized and where it sits in the mysterious innards of our heads. Some aspects of memory are clearly localized to specific home bases in the brain. The colorful blips and blobs that represent the imaged brains of patients with anomias show distinctively positioned clusters of ominous dark spots: holes where memory used to be. Persons unable to use verbs, for example, all appear to have lesions in the same area: a tiny pocket of the cerebral cortex a few inches back of the forehead, not far from the motor strip where physical movement originates. Noun-deficient patients—those who have lost their memories for the names of animals, plants, or manmade tools—show a sprinkling of dark blobs in a precise region of the temporal lobe. Alexics— persons who have lost the ability to read—show damage in a specific bit of cortex well back of the ear, just behind Wernicke's speech area.

Episodic memories, in contrast, are more diversified: the brain, it seems, prefers to keep its remembered eggs in many different baskets. PET scan studies suggest that the left side of the prefrontal cortex is the prime mover in the acquisition of new information, while the right specializes in later recall. Recall of specific incidents, furthermore, is not brought about by the tidy turn-on of one discrete plug of tissue, but involves the coordinated activation of areas across the brain. Normal subjects, asked to conjure up specific memories—to recall, for example, the Christmas they got a puppy, or the day they broke an ankle while bungee-jumping—show unique patterns of brain activity scattered eclectically about right temporal and frontal cortices, the limbic system, including the hippocampus and amygdala, and the cerebellum. The cortex, with its vast multiplicity of storage sites, depends on input and feedback from its many companion systems. Cortical connections to the amygdala, for example, call up the emotional associations of a given memory: the warm rush of nostalgia experienced when the orchestra plays your song or the nasty chill that runs down your spine at the sight of a tarantula. Different emotional sets affect, in turn, the makeup of the switched-on cortical areas. Reproduce something dreadful from your past—or even experience vicarious awfulness by viewing the shower scene in *Psycho* or that horrid episode in *The Godfather* where the horse's head is gruesomely discovered in a bed—and one battery of brain areas will become active; think happy thoughts and you'll energize another. Focus on a face and activity will flash between visual cortex and prefrontal lobes; then, recognition accomplished, will shoot to the amygdala for a feed-in of feelings. The features of Grandma, Simon Legree, or the Big Bad Wolf, processed by the limbic system, come with respective emotional doses of affection, loathing, and fear. Memories, rather than single notes, are complex chords—even entire symphonies.

Functional MRI studies of working memory reveal a similarly complex mental choreography. In studies by Susan Courtney at the Laboratory of Brain and Cognition at the National Institutes of Health and Jonathan D. Cohen at Carnegie Mellon, volunteers were monitored during tasks that involved assimilating, storing, and coordinating information—all functions of memory's "blackboard of the mind." Subjects, for example, were presented with a face-matching exercise: a picture of a face was shown on a computer screen, followed by an eight-second pause, and then another picture. The subjects signaled a match by pressing a button. As they studied and compared the pictured faces, active sites in the brain flickered on and off. Areas in the back of the brain became active during the initial observation period; areas in the frontal cortex turned on during storage and recall phases.

THE SYMPHONY OF MEMORY, WITH SNAKE

1. You see, coiled in the grass beside the back porch, a colored tubelike object.

2. The shape is registered at the back of your brain, in the visual cortex of the occipital lobe, which promptly relays the image to your frontal cortex for identification. The frontal cortex, matching image to memory, produces a rapid ID: "Snake!"

3. The information flashes to your limbic system, reaching the hippocampus, which assesses the situation and tells you that something is wrong here—you've never seen a snake in the backyard before—and the emotional amygdala. The amygdala, all too aware of your terror of snakes, communicates with the hypothalamus and pituitary gland, releasing the battery of internal chemicals associated with fear.

4. A message from the motor cortex shoots to the spinal cord, which sends excited instructions to your muscles: "Jump back!"

5. Even as you leap, heart pounding, subsequent cues from the visual cortex direct your prefrontal areas to alternative memory categories, reidentifying the snake as the homely garden hose.

Memory is like a piece of music—it has lots of different parts that come together to create the whole.
Marcus Raichle

The Blind Men and the Elephant

If MEMORY, AS visualized by brain scans, exists as a scattering of isolated components, how do these fragments coalesce to generate coherent conscious thought or integrated recollections? While memory seems to be strewn about the brain like grains of sand on the beach, scientists believe there is an organizational method to this distributive madness. Neuroscientist Antonio Damasio suggests that the brain possesses a system of "convergence zones"—master command centers that contain the operating instructions for reassembling the disjointed components of individual memories into coherent wholes. Memories, according to this organizational model, are stored as dissected snippets, each piece stashed near the area of the cortex where the relevant sensory impression first entered the brain. "Elephant," for example, is packaged as an array of separate attributes: shape, size, color, smell, sound. The brain, in fact, may function much like the old tale about the blind men and the elephant, in which six blind men, each feeling a different portion of an elephant, come to very different conclusions about what the animal looks like. The man patting the elephant's side pronounces it to be very like a wall; the man stroking the elephant's leg protests that the elephant is very like a tree; and so on through tusk, trunk, ear, and tail. Depending on the content of their sensory input, separate cortical memory storage areas similarly perceive the elephant differently—very like a wall, tree, rope, or snake. These features, each represented by an enhanced network of nerve cells, are linked to produce on recall a complete picture of an elephant. Linkage doesn't necessarily stop there, but may then proceed through higher and higher levels of processing. The scattered bits of *elephant* may connect to a battery of increasingly widespread associations: to the waterholes of Africa, the teak forests of India, Hannibal's trek over the Alps, P. T. Barnum's Jumbo, mammoths and mastodons, ivory billiard balls, Bomba the Jungle Boy, and, eventually, pink elephants, white elephant sales, elephant garlic, and elephantiasis.

The beauty of this model, according to psychologist Larry Squire, is that, like memory itself, it can operate in two directions. The brain can use a whole elephant—excitingly glimpsed at the zoo—to mobilize a coordinated network of elephant associations (even unearthing that cute little elephant song you learned forty years ago in kindergarten); or it can proceed from any one of elephant memory's component parts—the sight of wrinkled gray fabric, for example, vaguely reminiscent of elephant skin—to assemble a memory of the entire animal.

"It's a poor sort of memory that only works backward,"
said the Queen.
Lewis Carroll,
Through the Looking-Glass

To Put Humpty-Dumpty Together Again

THE MYSTERIOUS MEANS by which all the Humpty-Dumpty-like shards of memory are patched together into an integrated whole is referred to by neuroscientists as the "binding problem." How are all the individual fragments of *elephant*, for example, twinkling about the cerebral cortex like the localized pinpoints of light on an electric map, instantaneously fused to produce a complete trunk-to-tail animal? One possible solution to the binding problem is simply timing. If several separate brain sites are activated simultaneously, their temporal association—the fact that they all happen to be turned on at once—may be sufficient impetus for the mind to merge their disparate outputs into a single image. It's somewhat like the situations of those random assortments of people—the journalist's cherished cross-section of humanity—thrown together by fatal timing in the face of natural disaster. Everyone who just happened to step into the elevator at the moment of the East Coast blackout in 1965 was bonded by timing into a memorable shared experience. The crucial tie that binds such simultaneously active brain sites together—according to such researchers as Nobel Prize–winner Francis Crick, Christof Koch, and Rodolfo Llinás—may be a wave of electrical activity emanating from the intralaminar nucleus, a life preserver–shaped ring of cells in the thalamus, smack in the center of the head. When the brain is wide awake, the cells of the intralaminar nucleus fire in a steady drumlike rhythm, at a frequency of 40 cycles per second. This 40-cps wave sweeps like radar across the surface of the cerebral cortex every 12.5 thousandths of a second, detecting as it passes any regions of electrically active cells in its path. These cortical patches of cellular activity—each representing one aspect of a forming or established memory—may be synchronized by the passing wave, pulled together into a coordinated lockstep that is perceived as a single mental image.

Precisely how such biological phenomena as strengthened synapses and nerve assemblies, newly sprouting neurons, and intracranial radar sweeps interact to generate the intricate immensities of human memory is still to be seen. For all the wealth of scientific speculation, exactly how we remember what we remember remains a not-quite-solved mystery. Most of us, however, ostrich-style, don't concern ourselves much with the technicalities of how we remember as long as memory holds its own. We worry when we begin to forget.

> *There is something fascinating about science. One gets such wholesale returns of conjecture out of such trifling investments of fact.*
> Mark Twain

> *The capacity to leap across mountains of information to land lightly on the wrong side represents the highest of human endowments.*
> Lewis Thomas

ABSENTMINDED

On Friday morning there was always extra activity
Around the Buxton farmhouse.
That was the day Alfred and his wife went to town
Carrying their butter and eggs and perhaps some
    vegetables.
They'd come back around five with the wagon-box
Well filled with all the things their large family
    demanded.
Almeda spent her time with her sister
While Alfred took care of the day's business.
Alfred was large, good-natured, and very forgetful.
The older children often made fun of his
    absentmindedness
And he usually joined in.
Almeda wasn't endowed with much sense of humor
And she viewed her husband's failures to remember
As something to be borne—but not in silence.
She was systematic and methodical in all her work
And she tried in vain to train the children in her ways.
So the good times the family had together often left
    Almeda out.
One Friday Almeda had handed Alfred an unusually long
    list
When they started out from the house.
And she recalled to his mind that there had been times
When even with her carefully prepared lists
He'd come home with important things missing.
Alfred started home around three that afternoon.
He'd got rid of all his produce and he'd done all his
    errands.
He was smiling over a story the miller had told him
As he drove out of the village and along the river.
Gradually a feeling that he had forgotten something

Crept into his mind.
Unable to get rid of it he finally pulled Almeda's list
Out of his pocket and spread it on his knee.
He couldn't think of a thing he'd missed
So he put it back and settled down in the seat.
As the horses began the long steady climb into the hills
He hummed a little tune over and over
Matching the tone with the crickets' fiddling.
As he got nearer home the feeling that he'd forgotten
  something
Began to annoy him again.
He stopped the team and taking his list he checked over
  the bundles
Which were in boxes back of him and on the seat beside
  him.
Finding everything there he clucked to the horses.
As he drove into the yard the three younger children,
Just home from school, hurried down the home lane to
  meet him.
As he drew near they stopped and looked.
Suddenly they were silent.
Then in a subdued chorus they asked:
"Where's Ma?"

Walter Hard

FORGETTING

I've a grand memory for forgetting, David.

ROBERT LOUIS STEVENSON

The Videotape of the Mind

As PUZZLING AS HOW and why we remember is the flip side of the coin: why, how—or even if—we forget. Some claim that we never forget at all; the memories are in there all right, but have become tantalizingly inaccessible. The inaccessible but lurkingly present memory is the root of Sigmund Freud's theory of repression. Painful or unpleasant memories are not lost but hustled out of sight—swept like dustballs under the mental rug—where, though they may occasionally surface as odd lumps in our psyches, they remain hidden from conscious awareness.

Freud hypothesized two different forms of such memory burial. The first, which he called *Unterdrückung* (suppressing), is a conscious process of shoving a difficulty aside to deal with later—the kind of mental sidelining Scarlett O'Hara used when, abandoned by Rhett Butler ("Frankly, my dear, I don't give a damn"), she squared her shoulders and said, "I won't think about it now . . . I'll go crazy if I think about losing him now. I'll think about it tomorrow, at Tara." This is suppression, a temporary stopgap measure, and the tormenting squashed-down memory can, in theory, be unearthed at will, whenever its possessor feels equal to tackling it. The second—*Verdrängung* (ousting)—takes burial a step further, permanently banishing the hateful memory from the mind. This process of locking a mental door on the unthinkable and flinging away the key seems to be common in traumatized children, and recoveries of such ousted memories are presently having a field day in courts of law.

> *In mental life nothing which has once been formed can perish.*
> Sigmund Freud

> *Each person is at each moment capable of remembering all that has happened to him and of perceiving everything that is happening everywhere in the universe.*
> Aldous Huxley

Seemingly direct evidence for the ineradicable and ever-present memory came from the famous studies of Wilder Penfield, a Canadian neurosurgeon specializing in patients afflicted with focal epilepsy. Epilepsy—the affliction Hippocrates called "the sacred disease"—is an electrical storm in the brain, originating at some localized focal point and spreading across the cerebral cortex, tidal wave–style, in a surge of static that ends in seizure. Depending on where the focal point is located, seizures may be instigated or accompanied by specific sensations. One patient's seizures, apparently originating near the auditory cortex, were set off by the bong of London's Bow Bells. Other epilepsies, with focal points in or near the visual cortex, are triggered by spatial patterns, such as the crosshatched mesh of a screen door or the repetitive diagonal lines of herringbone tweed. Seizures are sometimes accompanied by visual or auditory hallucinations—Saint Paul's gripping experience on the road to Damascus is thus medically suspect—or by certain smells, such as a piercing odor of burning rubber.

Epilepsy can often be cured or alleviated by finding and eradicating this focal trigger tissue, cutting off seizures at their roots. Patients remain fully awake during the surgical procedure, alert and able to respond as the surgeon explores their cerebral cortices with stimulating electrodes, attempting to pinpoint the crucial origination site. In some cases, Penfield's exploratory electrical zaps elicited startling results, conjuring up what appeared to be past memories. Patients described brief cinematic flickers of experience: "I hear someone talking . . . I think it was about a restaurant or something." "My mother is telling my brother he has got his coat on backward. I can just hear them." "I just heard one of my children speaking." "Now I hear people laughing—my friends in South Africa." And, from a less happy patient, "There they go, yelling at me again, stop them!" Several patients heard music, selections ranging from "White Christmas," "Hush-a-Bye Baby," and "You'll Never Know" to excerpts from the musical *Guys and Dolls* and an intimidating classical piece titled "The War March of the Priests." Penfield guessed that these impressions were snippets of real life, permanently preserved like pressed flowers, and localized to specific sites on the brain's cortical surface. Once the right spot was stimulated, the stored memory popped up again, clear as the day when it was originally laid down.

Subsequent researchers have come up with alternative explanations for the Penfield patients' "memories." Many of the elicited recollections, rather than crisp replays of real events, were fuzzy and dreamlike; and localization of the impressions, more closely studied, wasn't as precise as had first appeared. Sometimes different images emerged from stimulation of the same site; sometimes stimulation of widely separated sites turned up the same remembered image. The vast majority of Penfield's patients (480 out of 520), despite determined electrical prodding, never produced any memories at all, and of the 40 who did, half explained apologetically that just that type of ectoplasmic hallucination habitually accompanied their epileptic seizures. Penfield, however, believed that his elicited remembrances proved that memory is like a tape recorder—better yet, a videotape—upon which all life experiences are stored in sequence, never to be erased. Modern neurologists suspect that the Penfield memories were more ephemeral, such stuff as dreams are made of rather than genuine recollections. Most likely they were the result of tiny hallucination-inducing seizures.

Memoryless Memory

W HILE DR. PENFIELD MAY not have uncovered hidden memories, the unconscious—what some researchers oxymoronically call "memoryless memory"—reveals its sneaky self in other ways. The unconscious is a notoriously weaselly concept, difficult to pin down under the fluorescent lights of the laboratory. Still, enough measurable evidence has surfaced that experimental psychologists, coming down firmly on their chosen side of the fence, recently pronounced its existence "no longer questionable." Definitive demonstrations of the unconscious are hard to come by; most subjects are unable to display theirs at will for the edification of investigators. Items packaged in the unconscious, after all, are just that: out of conscious reach, cagily shuffled out of sight like the traditional skeleton in the family closet. Some tests, however, do seem to show that they're still there.

One indication that the unconscious actually exists is the so-called false fame effect. All of us, it seems, are susceptible to the insidious deceptions of false fame. This memory twist is the specialty of psychologist Larry Jacoby, whose experiments potentially fulfill the hopeful dictum of artist Andy Warhol: "In the future, everyone will be famous for fifteen minutes." Jacoby gave volunteers a list of names to read: an eclectic mix of the famous, the not-so-famous, and obscurely nondescript hoi polloi. After a period of time, his subjects were given a second list of names—a combination of new names and names from the original list—and asked to identify which belonged to the famous. The test takers consistently identified the names from the earlier list—famous or no—as those belonging to famous people. Even subjects to whom the original list had been read while they were zonked under anesthetic fell for false fame: they too identified the early-list names—even those of total nobodies—as famous. The conclusion drawn was that an unconscious sense of familiarity led to the false fame identifications. The volunteers, invisibly aware that they had heard the names before, used this unconscious familiarity to breed misconceptions. "Memory," wrote Dr. Jacoby, "can automatically influence the interpretation of later events"—without, the implication is, registering at any point in the conscious mind.

Harvard psychologist Daniel Schacter describes a phenomenon known as "priming," in which the unconscious mind appears to impinge upon conscious thought. In Schacter's studies, test subjects were given lists of random words to study—for example, *assassin, octopus, avocado, mystery, sheriff,* and *climate.* Then, writes Schacter, "imagine that you go about your business for an hour and then return to take a couple of tests. First I show you a series of words and ask whether you remember seeing any of them on the earlier list: *twilight, assassin, dinosaur,* and *mystery.* Presumably you had little difficulty here. Next I tell you that I am going to show you some words with missing letters. Your job is to fill in the blanks as best you can: ch– – – –nk, o–t– –us, –og–y– – –, and –l–m–te. You probably had a hard time coming up with a correct answer for two of the word fragments (*chipmunk* and *bogeyman*). But with the other two fragments, the correct answers probably jumped out at you." Your triumphant performance with *octopus* and *climate* and your sad failure with *chipmunk* and *bogeyman* are the result of unconscious memory in action: you have been successfully primed.

Priming may account for many such covert operations of memory. The response of surgical patients to suggestions made while they were under anesthesia, for example, indicates unconscious learning. Anesthetized patients, told optimistically by the medical staff that their operations have gone well and rapid recovery is expected, woke up in notably better frames of mind and spent less postoperative time in the hospital than did their suggestion-neglected peers—even though they had no conscious memories of hearing conversation during surgery. Unwitting plagiarism, that bugbear of horrified authors, may also result from priming, Schacter suggests, as may unrecognized or unsuspected racial and sexual prejudices. Consider the old riddle about the injured child who is rushed to the hospital by his father, only to have the emergency room doctor exclaim, "Oh no! It's my son!" If the explanation isn't instantly apparent—the doctor is the child's mother—perhaps you are a victim of priming, burdened with unconscious stereotypic conceptions of traditional gender roles.

When my first book was new a friend of mine said to me, "The dedication is very neat."

Yes, I said, I thought it was.

My friend said, "I always admired it, even before I saw it in The Innocents Abroad."

I naturally said, "What do you mean? Where did you ever see it before?"

"Well, I saw it first some years ago as Doctor Holmes's dedication to his Songs in Many Keys."

Of course my first impulse was to prepare this man's remains for burial. But upon reflection I said I would reprieve him for a moment or two and give him a chance to prove his assertion if he could.

We stepped into a bookstore, and he did prove it. I had really stolen that dedication almost word for word. I could not imagine how this curious thing had happened . . .

However, I thought the thing out and solved the mystery. Two years before, I had been laid up a couple of weeks in the Sandwich Islands and had read and re-read Doctor

> *Holmes's poems till my mental reservoir was filled up with*
> *them to the brim. The dedication lay on the top, and handy,*
> *so by and by I unconsciously stole it. Perhaps I uncon-*
> *sciously stole the rest of the volume too, for many people*
> *have told me that my book was pretty poetical in one way*
> *or another.*
>
> Mark Twain,
> "Innocent Plagiarism"

Amnesic patients, whose conscious memories for studied word lists are severely impaired, often show normal priming effects—that is, even though they can't remember ever having seen the original word lists, their performance on fill-in-the-blank tests is still filled with inspired "best guesses," presumably based on the previously viewed information. Tested amnesics come up with *octopus* and *climate* as readily as normal volunteers do.

Schacter and colleague Peter Graf have coined a new term for such forms of surreptitious learning: *implicit* memory. Implicit memory includes the many undercover activities of the mind: false fame, priming, and procedural memories, exemplified by the ability of amnesic patients to learn new skills without conscious (explicit) recollection of the learning experience. H.M.'s steady improvement in mirror writing and his performance on the Tower of Hanoi puzzle, for example, are tributes to the power of implicit memory.

Another window on the unconscious is the bizarre phenomenon first described by Lawrence Weiskrantz known confusingly as "blindsight." Certain patients who have been blinded due to damage to the brain's visual cortex retain the unconscious ability to see. These people have no conscious awareness of sight. Their world is dark; in all ways they are functionally blind. On vision tests, however, they perform remarkably well. They are 80 percent accurate at locating positions of lights flashed on the wall; they can select designated geometric shapes on picture cards. One woman, asked to choose between pictures of an intact house and a burning one ("Which would you rather live in?"), invariably chose the undamaged house, insisting throughout that her choices were pure guesswork. At some unconscious level, however, the blind brain still saw.

Monsters in the Lime Tea

Unconscious memories, storehouses of real but inaccessible data, may lie at the root of hunches, intuition, lucky guesses, and nasty premonitions. The crucial word here, and a bone of contention these days among warring lawyers, is "real." What we dredge up from the dark depths of the unconscious, with or without professional help, may—or may not—be. Repressed memories, shunted firmly off-line for decades, may burst back into consciousness, one theory holds, if activated by the right trigger. In the popular press, such memories are horrific: tales of murder and rape, childhood sexual abuse, gruesome satanic cults, and alien abduction. Buried memories are not invariably hideous; some quite blameless experiences, writes Marcel Proust, may simply "lie dormant so long that they go beyond the power of conscious recall." In *Du Côté de chez Swann*, the first of the fifteen volumes of Proust's massive autobiographical novel, *Remembrance of Things Past*, a single munch of madeleine cake soaked in hot lime tea triggers the retrieval of a long-lost childhood memory:

> Straightaway, like the backdrop on a stage, the large, old house facing the street appeared to me, seen from the back garden where my parents had their own cottage. And with the house I saw the town, the Square where I was sent to play before

lunch, the streets where I often ran errands, the good ways to go in the fine weather. And just like the Japanese game where you soak little bits of paper in a bowl of water, and watch them unfold, take shape and colour and grow into flowers, houses, and recognisable people, so now all the flowers in our garden, the waterlilies of Vivonne, the good village folk and their cottages, the church, the whole of Combray and the country round, everything which has shape and solidity, town and gardens, all came out of my cup of tea.

Unfortunately what often bubbles out of our cups of lime tea is far fouler stuff. One January afternoon in 1989, Eileen Franklin Lipsker's five-year-old daughter, Jessica, sitting on the floor drawing pictures of princesses, looked up at her mother to ask a question, lifting her blue eyes and turning her small neck at an angle that triggered a memory twenty years old. Eileen, in that shocked instant, recalled the rape and murder—by beating over the head with a rock—of her best friend, eight-year-old Susan Nason, by George Franklin, Eileen's father. Franklin, on the strength of his daughter's emergent memory, was brought to trial in 1993.

For Gary Baker, a cell biologist working on memory in fruit flies, memory rebirth was a slower process, a mental awakening beginning years ago when, at the age of thirty, he took up scuba diving. The experience brought back childhood nightmares and a vague terrifying memory of nearly drowning. "When you're underwater and you look up, there's a silver surface to the water," he told psychiatrist Lenore Terr. "That's what I remembered." Scary or no, Gary became increasingly addicted to diving—he is now, says a friend, one of the greatest river divers in the world—and increasingly subject to the frightening pressures of slowly emerging memories. Eventually that eerie glimpse of the silver surface above the diving pool brought back total recall of years of childhood abuse, including, at the age of three or four, being flung into an irrigation ditch by his mother and left to struggle underwater, panic-stricken, until she relented and pulled him out.

> *Memory is the thing you forget with.*
> Alexander Chase

While some of the monsters in the tarpits of memory are horribly real, others may be fantastic constructs of the fertile human mind. Some psychiatric techniques, such as hypnotherapy and visualization—in which patients are simply told to imagine experiences without considering whether they actually happened or not—tend to make the suggestible brain even more so, enabling careless therapists to implant "memories" of wholly fictitious events. Richard Ofshe at the University of California at Berkeley casts a cold eye on the credibility of recovered memories, citing the case of Paul Ingram, a deputy sheriff from a small town in Washington. In 1988, Ingram's two daughters, then aged eighteen and twenty-two, attended a lecture on sexual molestation at a religious retreat. Memories triggered there led them to accuse their father of sexual abuse and produced a lurid harvest of sensational stories for the media featuring satanic rituals, human sacrifice, sexual intercourse with animals, and rape. Ingram, appalled, initially denied all charges. Later, however, with the aid of police officers, a minister, and a psychologist, he began to see pictures in his mind that seemed to confirm the girls' descriptions. When Ofshe arrived on the scene as a consultant for the prosecution, Ingram was convinced of his own guilt. Ofshe, skeptical, suspected a strong element of suggestion and distortion. He asked Ingram to confirm the reality of a fake incident in which Ingram had supposedly forced his son and daughter to have sex. Ingram was unable to remember this imaginary episode until he returned to his cell to "pray on the image" as instructed by his pastor. Soon a memory emerged: Ingram admitted his guilt and cranked out yet another confession, a three-page statement packed with vivid detail. This demonstration of the malleability of memory, in company with the lack of any corroborative evidence, Ofshe pointed out, rendered the entire case suspect. Ingram nonetheless pleaded guilty to six counts of third-degree rape and was sentenced to twenty years in prison. He now believes his recovered "memories" to have been investigator-induced fantasies.

Aliens in the Bedroom

THE OUTER LIMITS of remembrance of things false may be the experiences of those thousands of Americans who claim to have been abducted by aliens. Following the lead of abductee Whitley Strieber, who came out of the extraterrestrial closet in 1987 with the publication of his alien-encounter book, *Communion*, most victims report some variation on the same theme: a nighttime kidnapping by short skinny gray aliens with immense, lens-shaped black eyes, translocation to a spaceship full of medical examination tables, and subjection to some form of unpleasant surgery, usually including extraction of ova or sperm and implantation of a nasal (tracking?) device. Barring acceptance of these tales at face value, scientists have sought other explanations for these memories of uncanny experiences. Even fantasized memories, most reasoning goes, must form around some core event, some seed crystal of suggestion. Some researchers propose that in the case of alien abduction memories, the starting point may be the phenomenon known as sleep paralysis. During REM sleep, as humans lie dreaming, they also lie paralyzed: motor functions are deeply suppressed, which is what normally keeps us from walking (or worse) in our sleep. (Cats with brain lesions that abolish this sleep-linked paralysis dramatically act out their dreams, running across the floor, jumping in the air, and pouncing upon invisible dreamworld mice.) Usually REM-phase sleepers are really down and out;

people immersed in REM are most difficult to wake up, and it's during REM that you're most likely to sleep through the ordinarily arousing buzz of the alarm clock or blurt of the telephone. Sometimes, however, we wake up—or partially wake up—while muscle paralysis persists, a spooky sensation sometimes accompanied by the feeling that someone or something is trying to crush, choke, or smother us. About 20 percent of people at one time or another have consciously experienced sleep paralysis, large enough numbers such that, according to psychologist Susan Blackmore, persistent superstitions have grown up around the condition. The incubi and succubi of the Middle Ages, for example, who moved in to seduce their limp victims in the dead of night, may have been invented by temporarily paralyzed, but vaguely conscious, sleepers. Alien abduction—scary little creatures sidling into the bedroom while you lie there helpless as a wet noodle—may be the twentieth-century equivalent of the lascivious medieval demon.

Neuroscientist Michael Persinger of Laurentian University in Ontario argues that alien abduction experiences may be linked to high "temporal lobe lability"—the tendency of the brain's temporal lobes to erupt into spates of high electrical activity, detectable as a series of explosive stutters on an EEG. This electrical chatter in the temporal lobes, claims Persinger, may be related to a whole battery of mystical activities: out-of-body experiences, hallucinations, feelings of floating or flying, déjà vu. Furthermore the magnetic fields generated by earthquakes are sufficient to set off temporal lobe firing, which may explain why Californians are more subject to psychic phenomena than the rest of us. (Whitley Strieber, however, hails from geologically stable upstate New York.)

Memories of alien abduction, however illogical they seem in the cold light of day, are hard to satisfactorily explain away. Memories closer to home are similarly slippery. Some 9,500 families, all members of the Philadelphia-based False Memory Syndrome Foundation, insist, outraged, that their grown children's accusations of sexual abuse are sheer fantasy, joint creations of suggestible minds and overzealous therapists. Some researchers agree. Traumatic experiences, they point out, are if anything only too well remembered: witness Vietnam veterans, still afflicted decades later by harrowing flashbacks and post-traumatic stress syndrome, and the painfully persistent memories of Holocaust survivors. The twenty-six Chowchilla, California, children, kidnapped from a school bus in the summer of 1976 and buried alive in a truck trailer in an abandoned quarry, remembered their terrifying experience clearly, both immediately after the event and five years later.

Psychologist Elizabeth Loftus, an expert on the ingrained inaccuracies of human memory, argues that while some people may indeed temporarily forget and later retrieve memories of bygone abuse, there is little scientific evidence to support a memory mechanism that totally blanks out recollections of severe trauma. Some memories—notably luridly newsworthy accounts of satanic carouses and tales of past lives led in medieval Japan, ancient Rome, and biblical Bethlehem—are only recovered after intensive therapy, which again casts doubts on therapeutic retrieval techniques. Most famous of such past-life experiences is that of Virginia Murrow who, when hypnotized at a party in 1952, produced a story of an earlier existence as a nineteenth-century Irishwoman named Bridey Murphy. Her detailed revelations, complete with names, dates, and family tree, all delivered in a thick Irish brogue, created a sensation, and eventually generated both a best-selling book and a movie. The original hypnotist (and author of the book) was a local businessman with an avid interest in amateur hypnosis and reincarnation, which of itself is suggestibly suspicious. Virginia/Bridey's memories were never verified, and Murrow refused to repeat hypnotic sessions for interested experts.

"Almost every factor we know that increases susceptibility to suggestion is typical of memory-recovery therapy," says cognitive psychologist D. Stephen Lindsay of the University of

Victoria, Canada. Hypnosis—a notoriously tricky technique—is particularly under the gun these days; members of the British False Memory Society point out that in Great Britain all it takes to become a practicing hypnotherapist is a twelve-lesson correspondence course.

THE SIX LIVES OF GENERAL PATTON

General George Patton, under hypnosis, produced memories of six previous existences, all military and male:

1. A prehistoric warrior who "battled for fresh mammoth"
2. A Greek hoplite who fought the Persians under King Cyrus
3. A soldier of Alexander the Great
4. A legionnaire with Julius Caesar in Gaul
5. An English knight during the Hundred Years' War
6. A French marshal under the emperor Napoleon

How to Hide a Memory

THE ISSUE WITH doubting psychologists is not the existence of childhood sexual abuse, but that of absolute memory oblivion—what Richard Ofshe calls "robust repression," a memory burial so deep and final that large-scale trauma is effectively eliminated from the mind. People do, nonetheless, seem to forget. A national survey conducted under the direction of Diane Elliott of the UCLA School of Medicine found that while most survivors of trauma—60 percent—be it childhood sexual abuse, military combat, street violence, or natural disaster, clearly remembered their experiences, 40 percent suffered periods of total or partial amnesia. Most of the forgetful reported eventual spontaneous return of their memories, usually triggered by some prompting event: a story in the news, a television program, a dream or nightmare, or a similar repeat encounter. A study by Linda Williams of the University of New Hampshire, generally accepted as the most convincing support for the reality of repressed memories to date, produced similar forgetfulness figures. Williams interviewed 129 adult women who, according to their hospital records, had been treated for sexual abuse as children. About a third of the interviewees had no memory of the abusive experience, and another 16 percent reported a period of amnesia, followed by memory recovery.

Psychiatrist Lenore Terr bridges the gap between the traumatic extremes of memory—blindingly persistent recall and total forgetfulness—by hypothesizing two distinct types of childhood trauma victims. Type I victims, explains Terr, are the survivors of uniquely disastrous onetime traumas, such as the Chowchilla kidnapping; Type I traumatic memories are usually vivid and intact. Type II victims, in contrast, have been subjected to repeated ("multiple-event") abuse and often have forgotten their painful experiences. Forgetfulness, for Type II victims, is a mental survival mechanism. "Holes in the memory are created by defensive operations," writes Terr, "such as the very common defense of repression."

A possible biological mechanism for the repression of hideous memories comes from the work of Michela Gallagher at the University of North Carolina. Scared rats, Gallagher discovered, remember their frightening experiences better when norepinephrine—a red-alert-associated neurotransmitter released during episodes of stress—is spewed out by the neurons of the amygdala, that almond-shaped denizen of the limbic system that functions, along with the hippocampus, in the storage of memories. Scary memories are weakened, however, by the release of naturally occurring morphinelike molecules called endorphins. Endorphins are our own natural painkillers: long-distance runners produce a lot of them; so do anorexics, schizophrenics, and profound meditators, all of whom are toughly impervious to pain. Endorphin levels are also elevated in hibernating hamsters, enrapt concertgoers, and alcohol imbibers—the emotional thrill you get upon hearing your favorite sonata or guitar riff, or the rosy glow that hits as you tackle that third glass of Chardonnay is due to a soupçon of imitation morphine in the brain. The role of endorphins is not confined to such physiological frivolities as giving us a nice buzz at the neighborhood brewery; these compounds are also secreted in times of trouble, to protect us from shock, pain, and severe distress. Their ability to block memory storage may be an aspect of this protective mechanism. Endorphins may provide victims of repeated abuse with an emotional escape hatch by eradicating trauma from the mind.

The falsity or truth—with attendant consequences—of buried memories continues to plague courts of law. Richard Ofshe, citing cases such as Paul Ingram's, urges that only pre-therapy memories be treated as potentially true, and the American Medical Association has cautiously followed his lead. "The use of recovered memories," now states the AMA, "is fraught with problems of potential misapplication." The true nature of the questionable memories that stymie lawyers and therapists, however, may eventually be determined by objective analysis. Daniel Schacter recently demonstrated that list-learners, under proper experimental conditions, can be jockeyed into generating false memories. Subjects who were read lists of related words—*sharp, point, prick,* and *pin,* for example—were found, in subsequent tests, to mistakenly identify additional related words (*needle, pain*) as items on the original list. When the subjects were given PET scans during the test periods, it became clear that only the memory—not the brain itself—was deceived. Right and wrong answers—real and false memories—activated different regions of the brain. Genuine memories (*sharp*) turned on areas of the hippocampus and left temporal lobe that are associated, respectively, with memory processing and analysis of auditory information. False memories (*needle*) elicited hippocampal activity, but bypassed the left temporal lobe, activating instead regions in the frontal lobes and cerebellum. These areas, Schacter explains, are involved in the recovery of stored memories and in the monitoring of results for error. One hypothesis is that the subjects, confronted with a false memory, undergo some form of analytical mental struggle, perhaps attempting to resolve misconceptions.

Rewriting the Past

Even ordinary readily accessible memories may not be as accurate as they appear. Our memories appear to be so vivid and so real that it's easy to believe them immutable. It seems that once we stash a remembrance away in the nooks and crannies of the brain, it remains there untouched, as perfectly preserved as a fly in amber. In practice, however, memory, like the state highway system, is in a constant state of reconstruction. Over time we remodel it, reinterpret it, improve upon it, and generally tamper with its original structure and form. The mind does not keep memories in cold storage, but in an incubator. Memories mushroom in the dark.

> *In memory each of us is an artist; each of us creates.*
> Patricia Hampl,
> *A Romantic Education*

Memory can abruptly realign and reverse itself, in the same manner that a change of focus can transform an optical illusion from a pair of female profiles into a Grecian urn. A sudden change of heart or an influx of new information can rewrite the past, revising memories to mesh with the new mind-set. The unlucky hero of *Invasion of the Body Snatchers*, suddenly realizing that all his friends and neighbors have been replaced by pod people from outer space, underwent just such a universal memory turnover. So do the acquaintances of suddenly unmasked murderers, whom one sees standing about on the sidewalk in news clips, rapidly reshuffling memory banks and reversing previous judgments. (*There was always something fishy about Jeffrey* . . .)

> *We never know the whole truth about the past.*
> Niccolò Machiavelli

> *The brain constructs and reconstructs information, creating a highly personal mental artifact and calling it memory.*
> Jeremy Campbell

Just as the past colors the present, so the present colors— and recolors—the past. Grown children who clash with their parents may find memories of childhood plastered over with new impressions. The past becomes gloomier and more dismal; recollections of past injustices loom large. John Kotre, professor at the University of Michigan and specialist in the field of autobiographical memory, cites the story of a young wife and mother who discovered, via private investigator, that her husband was maintaining not one but three separate households: he had both a mistress and another "wife," complete with home and small children. This cataclysmic marital revelation flashed through memory like a blitzkrieg, altering and eradicating segments of the past. Lengthy business trips, casual conversations, inexplicable behavior, and the strapped family finances all took on new meaning. Cherished reminiscences—pledges of affection, romantic evenings, anniversary dinners—became insults and injuries. The past was painfully reborn.

Memories of the bad covered the good, as snow covers grass in the fall.
Ann Jasperson

Even political conversion can rewrite memory. George Goethals and Richard Reckman describe a series of experiments performed at a Massachusetts high school in 1973, in which groups of students were screened for their attitude toward busing as a means of achieving racial equality in the schools. The students, based on preliminary screening, were sorted into same-opinion groups—42 percent of the participants came down on the pro side of the question; 53 percent were con—and each group was then subjected to a series of artfully designed sessions aimed at changing their minds. Pro participants were exposed to convincing anti-busing arguments, backed by the vociferously anti-busing opinions of a "plant" student, a popular school leader. Anti participants got the opposite treatment: seductive pro arguments, also backed by an influential pro student plant. Students who changed their minds following this persuasively mind-bending barrage were then asked to recall their original opinions regarding the issue: "What did you think of busing before attending the discussion sessions?" The reprogrammed teenagers consistently restyled the past, recalling their past opinions as much closer to their present-day attitudes than they actually were. When shown their original test statements, in incontrovertible black and white, the students were universally amazed. Memory, a shameless shape-shifter, had reconstructed itself.

A closely related memory bender is the phenomenon known as hindsight bias—that is, our memory of how confident we were about the truth or falsity of a given statement is altered by the subsequent discovery of whether the statement was actually true or false. If found to be true, we tend to inflate our former degree of confidence in its veracity, remembering ourselves as much more positive than we in fact were at the time. If found to be false, memory hastily backtracks and we remember ourselves as cautiously doubtful. In a study performed under the aegis of Ralph Hertwig at the Max Planck Institute for Psychological Research in Munich, volunteers were read a series of textbook-style factual statements, such as "Prohibition was called 'the noble experiment,'"and asked to rate their confidence in the statements' truth or falsity. The answers were then revealed (in this case, true) and the volunteers were again asked to rate their confidence in their original assessments. People who were proved wrong promptly remembered themselves as more unsure and their recollections of their confidence ratings dropped. People who were proved right, on the other hand, recalled considerably higher levels of confidence than they had actually had.

Hindsight bias also plays a role in the social scene. The skinny nerd in high school who grew up to be a power in the computer industry will be remembered by his/her peers as much more promising and popular than he/she was viewed at the time; the newly successful artist, in retrospect, will be remembered as more talented than originally believed. Memory revels in "I told you so"; it also likes to hedge its bets.

Cryptomnesia

SOME MEMORIES, rather than spin-doctored, may be made up out of whole cloth. Any of us may, in perfect innocence, cherish memories of events that never were. This happens because all of us, no matter how cynical and hardboiled, are at heart shamefully susceptible to suggestion. Plant a hint in the right place and, endlessly gullible, we swallow it whole. This propensity to adopt memories that are not our own is called cryptomnesia, from the Greek for "hidden memory." The *crypto* in such cases is the memory's source. We take, for example, a story told to us by someone else and convert it in our minds into a personal happening, forgetting en route that there ever was a story or a storyteller. Such memories become cuckoos in our mental nests, counterfeits that by all rights belong elsewhere.

Source memory—our memory for where a memory came from in the first place—is notably unreliable. "I'm stunned at how easy it is under laboratory conditions to induce people to remember events that never happened to them," says research psychologist Henry Roediger of Rice University. Simply repeating a fictitious story over and over again will often do the trick. Stephen Ceci and colleagues at Cornell checked this out experimentally, by repeatedly asking a group of children at weekly intervals whether they had ever experienced each of five different events. Four of the events—a trip to Disneyland, for example—had really happened to each child; the fifth, invented by the investigator, consisted of an imaginary accident in which the child got a finger caught in a mousetrap and had to be taken to the hospital. By week 11, the final week of the experiment, a third of the children insisted that they remembered the mousetrap incident, often in detail, with descriptive embellishment: *"The mousetrap is down in the basement, next to the firewood. . . ." "The hospital gave me a little bandage and it was right here. . . ."*

> *The brain invents stories and runs imagined and remembered events back and forth through time.*
> Edward O. Wilson,
> *On Human Nature*

> *If it is necessary to rearrange one's memory or to tamper with written records, then it is necessary to forget that one has done so.*
> George Orwell

Childhood memories often have a cryptomnesic component. Do you really remember, for example, that trip to the circus the summer you were three, or have you invented a memory of the past based on your parents' repeated stories, fleshing it out with pictures from the family photo album and what you now know about circuses? "The tales that get repeated over and over again, around the dinner table, in the car, on the beach, take on a life of their own," writes author Anna Quindlen, "so that after a while they can easily be mistaken for real recollections." The Swiss psychologist Jean Piaget, famed for his studies of childhood development, believed for years that he had been kidnapped as a toddler. He remembered the incident perfectly: the walk along the sunny Champs-Elysées in Paris, a mysterious assailant snatching him from his perambulator, his gallant nurse fighting the attacker off, the providential arrival of a gendarme, armed with a white baton. When Jean turned fifteen, however, the nurse—long since gone from the household and now a saintly soldier in the Salvation Army—wrote a letter to the family, guiltily returning the watch she had received as a reward for her bravery, and confessing that the entire kidnapping tale was a hoax. She had invented it in order to impress Jean's wealthy parents. The incident never happened.

It isn't so astonishing, the number of things I can remember, as the number of things I can remember that aren't so.
Mark Twain

The Curve of Forgetting

WHILE SOME MEMORIES are buried, some invented, and most twisted out of shape, others just plain disappear. The mechanism of this home-and-garden-variety forgetting remains a puzzle. *Why* do memories fade? The oldest and most common explanation for forgetting is decay. If unused, the decay theory holds, memory traces gradually dwindle and disappear. Paths less traveled by in the circuits of the brain do not diverge long: they vanish. The Greek philosopher Plato subscribed to decay theory. Memory, said Plato poetically, is like a wax tablet. As we remember, we etch lines and patterns in the soft surface; then time, a great eraser, slowly smooths the lines away, causing us to forget.

The first experimental studies of memory decay were conducted in the 1880s by German psychologist Hermann Ebbinghaus, who, with true Teutonic thoroughness, invented 2,000 nonsense syllables (RAX, JAF, HUQ, TAJ, ZIN) and doggedly set himself the task of learning them. Ebbinghaus spent years memorizing long lists of these Scrabble rejects and testing his recall ability at various times after the initial learning period. The wealth of results allowed him to develop his famous "curve of forgetting," a graceful, if depressingly steep, roller-coaster slide from competence into near-oblivion. Memory, it seems, decays with awful rapidity: one hour after learning, 56 percent of the assimilated material has gone with the wind; one day

later, 66 percent has evaporated; and after a month, 80 percent
is gone.

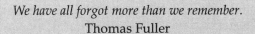

We have all forgot more than we remember.
Thomas Fuller

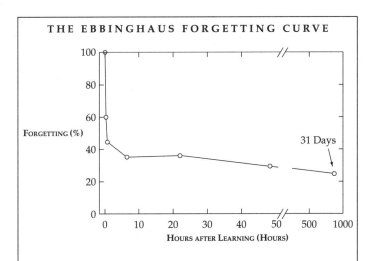

THE EBBINGHAUS FORGETTING CURVE

31 Days

FORGETTING (%)

HOURS AFTER LEARNING (HOURS)

Based on data accumulated in the late nineteenth century by
Hermann Ebbinghaus, the curve of forgetting tells a dismal
tale: one hour after assimilating new information, over half of
it is already forgotten.

My mind lets go a thousand things,
Like dates of wars and deaths of kings.
Thomas Bailey Aldrich

An alternative theory of forgetting—interference—proposes
that memories don't so much disintegrate as lose themselves in
the crowd. Over time, as more and more memories accumulate,

new and old become increasingly indistinguishable. Memories, according to interference theory, are like a vast flock of nearly identical penguins, each so like the other that it becomes impossible to pick one single desired bird out of the homogeneous mass. The more similar memories are in meaning and content, the more likely they are to interfere with each other in this manner. The brain, remembering, generates its own self-defeating camouflage.

An aspect of interference is cue dependency. Forgetting is not only too much muddling multiplication, but a lack of precise retrieval cues—the triggers that activate a specific memory. Tag a recollection with distinctive meaning or eye-catching associations—paint one penguin purple, for example—and it's a likelier candidate for ready recall. Marigold Linton's blurred episodic memories of repeated classroom lectures, racquetball games, and business trips became increasingly inseparable because she lacked distinctive retrieval cues for individual events. Twenty near-identical airplane journeys are difficult, after the fact, to differentiate; while the distinctive trip on which the wings iced over, the oxygen masks dropped into the terrified passengers' laps, and the pilot was forced to make an emergency landing in Hartford—all exciting retrieval cues—is easily remembered.

> *The wisest man I ever knew taught me something I never forgot. And although I never forgot it, I never quite memorized it either. So what I'm left with is the memory of having learned something very wise that I can't quite remember.*
> George Carlin,
> *Braindroppings*

Paying Attention

To REMEMBER SOMETHING in the first place, we have to pay attention to it. Most of us ordinarily ignore much of what takes place around us. We do this through a mechanism called perceptual filtering, which allows us to block out immense amounts of irrelevant input in order to focus on a limited number of important features. Bookworms, lost in the printed page, can thus blot out the world around them, blissfully eliminating from perception the sound of the kids bickering over their Barbie dolls, the smell of dinner burning on the stove, and the pattern of sunbeams in the dust on the coffee table. Birdwatchers, raptly peering through binoculars at a Baltimore oriole, lose sight of the fact that they're up to their ankles in mosquitoes and swamp sludge. Taken too far, perceptual filtering can render us spacily unobservant, a condition that Henry David Thoreau astringently ascribed to most of humankind. In Jerome Lawrence and Robert E. Lee's play *The Night Thoreau Spent in Jail*, the protagonist urges his companions to pay attention to the marvels of the natural world around them:

> In this single pasture, there are *three hundred* distinct and separate varieties of grass. I know; I have catalogued them myself. You look down and you say: "That's grass. Grass is grass." Ridiculous. You have missed the splendid variety of the show. There's

camel grass, candy grass, cloud grass, cow-quake, mouse-barley, fox-tail, Londonlace, devil's knitting needle, feather-top buffalo grass, timothy, and barnyard grass and clovers enough to sweeten the bellies of all the lambs since creation.

> *A man must get a thing before he can forget it.*
> Oliver Wendell Holmes

Deprived of a filter, however, we're in dire straits. Jorge Luis Borges, in "Funes el Memorioso," tells the tale of Irineo Funes, a luckless Argentinian who falls off his horse, knocks himself senseless, and wakes up with a perfect eidetic memory. Nothing—not even the smallest detail—from that moment on could be filtered out or forgotten. Funes remembers every pebble, every blade of grass, every line on every shell on the beach, every word of every conversation. "He remembered the shapes of the clouds in the south at dawn of the 30th of April of 1882," writes Borges, "and he could compare them in his recollection with the marbled grain in the design of a leather-bound book which he had seen only once, and with the lines in the spray which an oar raised in the Rio Negro on the eve of the battle of the Quebracho . . ." Funes eventually was incapacitated by minutiae, unable to see the forest for the pattern of the bark on the trees or the meadow for the three hundred different varieties of grass. The real-life memorist, S, whose phenomenal memory so bowled over Aleksandr Luria, may similarly have lacked a mechanism for perceptual filtering.

The nineteenth-century British historian Thomas Babington Macaulay reputedly had a fabulous memory. One day a visiting friend came upon him in his study, pacing back and forth and reciting, nonstop, hundreds of lines of poetry from an obscure French medieval epic.

"Why, in God's name, Macaulay," the visitor asked, "did you ever bother to memorize all that tedious stuff?"

Macaulay paused in his pacing and threw his friend an agonized look.

"Sir, do you not see," he cried, "that I am doing my best to *forget* it?"

Everyone Knows What a Penny Looks Like

Do you think that you're more observant than the common herd? Any bets that you don't know what a penny looks like? A classic experimental demonstration of perceptual filtering was published in 1979 by researchers Raymond Nickerson and Marilyn Jager Adams, who simply asked their subjects—twenty about-to-be-ashamed-of-themselves American adults—what a penny looks like. Participants were asked to draw a penny, front and back, and were then scored for their ability to remember and locate eight critical penny features.

> Penny Front:
> Head (whose?)
> IN GOD WE TRUST
> LIBERTY
> Date
> Penny Back:
> Building (which?)
> UNITED STATES OF AMERICA
> E PLURIBUS UNUM
> ONE CENT

Hardly anybody, it turned out, had the foggiest idea what a penny really looks like, despite the fact that the U.S. Mint stamps out a cool 39 million of them daily and, accordingly, most of us constantly have our pockets or purses full of them. Of the eight critical penny features, the median number correctly recalled was three, and those three included the two most obvious: the head (Lincoln's, facing right) and the building (the Lincoln Memorial). Almost everybody omitted the word *LIBERTY*, which sits just behind Lincoln's shoulder, and half the subjects pointed Lincoln's head in the wrong direction. Only one subject—an avid penny collector—got all eight features right.

Subjects given a list of forty proposed penny features and asked to identify those that really belonged on a penny did slightly (but not much) better. Practically everybody again omitted the word *LIBERTY*, and various subjects assigned to pennies such non-penny elements as laurel wreaths, sheaves of wheat, the Great Seal of the United States, the Roman numeral I, and the words *WASHINGTON, D.C.* (Nobody, mercifully, voted for *MADE IN TAIWAN*, which the investigators had evilly listed as penny feature number thirteen.) Even when shown pictures of pennies (one right, fourteen wrong), less than half of subjects were able to pick the real penny out of the bogus crowd. The ability to recognize an object, Nickerson and Adams concluded, does not guarantee an accurate memory for detail. What we're most likely to remember seems to be the minimum necessary to allow us to recognize common objects in everyday life. We filter.

The penny collector's banner score demonstrates another side of perceptual filtering: one person's filtered-out irrelevancy is another's life obsession. Memory is quintessentially idiosyncratic—what catches one person's attention, to be tagged for inclusion in long-term memory, passes another by. No two observers ever store quite the same scene. Guests at the garden party, depending on their individual fascinations and foibles, will variously remember, forget, or ignore the hostess's new hat, the cucumber sandwiches, the croquet scores, or the species of beetle infesting the rosebushes.

Steven Rose points out that perceptual filtering adjusts itself to our environment. Children just learning the ins and outs of human survival skills don't filter much of anything; all inputs, to beginners, are equally important. With experience, however, it becomes clear that some aspects of the surroundings are more important than others. The number of tar bubbles in the asphalt, for example, though interesting, is less important perception-wise than that oncoming Mack truck. The street smarts acquired by urban children, points out Rose, comprise a very different set of perceptual and filtering skills than the rural know-how picked up by farm-raised kids. Simply not knowing what to pay attention to may explain why newcomers to the city get their pockets picked and newcomers to the country get kicked by cows.

> *The charm, one might say the genius, of memory is that it is choosy, chancy, and temperamental; it rejects the edifying cathedral and indelibly photographs the small boy chewing a hunk of melon in the dust.*
> Elizabeth Bowen

The Unreliable Eyewitness

F AILURE TO PAY attention, writes Kenneth Higbee, author of *Your Memory: How It Works and How to Improve It*, may be the single most common reason for forgetting. It's the main reason we so often forget the names of people we've just been introduced to—during the crucial exchange, we were inattentive, distracted by the pattern of hula dancers on the stranger's tie or preoccupied with what to say next. Attention and its cattle-prod effect on memory have particular implications for legal testimony, where casually glimpsed events assume life-or-death importance in the courtroom.

The unreliability of inattentive observers was first studied shortly after the turn of the century by William Stern, a German developmental psychologist, who roped his graduate students into acting as sample eyewitnesses in an "event experiment." Stern's fifteen subjects—all innocently attending their first psychology seminar—witnessed a planned event in which T (for "target person"; in reality a conniving fellow student named Lipmann) entered the classroom, handed a manuscript in a manila envelope to the professor, exchanged a few words, selected a book from the bookcase, and rapidly left the room. The next week the students were asked for a detailed account of the T affair. What time did T enter the room? How long did he stay? When did he leave? They were asked to describe T—what color was his hair? what was his approximate age? how was he dressed?—and to list his actions from the time he entered the classroom until (book and hat in hand) he left.

A good third of the student responses were flatly wrong (the women in the class, Stern noted smugly, were particularly prone to error) and almost all were contradictory. G, a male student, wrote:

> A young man unexpectedly entered the room, went up to Dr. Stern, and asked whether he might look something up in one of the volumes in the bookcase. Dr. Stern naturally granted this request. The man (whom I believe I have never seen before, by the way) left the room again after staying for a total of about three minutes. Dr. Stern called after him just as he was leaving, asking him to wait in the anteroom until the end of the seminar. I would estimate that it was around 7:00 or 7:15 in the evening as he left the room.

C, another male, chimed in:

> On Monday, November 9, during Dr. Stern's class, a gentleman entered the Psychology Seminar Room and wished to speak with Dr. Stern. Dr. Stern, although reluctant to interrupt the seminar, did get up and went briefly over to the window with the man who had come in. Then he told him to wait outside. The time was roughly between 7:30 and 7:45.

And L, one of the supposedly unreliable women, reported:

> A gentleman appeared during the lecture, apologizing to Dr. Stern for the interruption that his entrance had created. In addition, he asked whether he might take a book from the library and look something up. Dr. Stern replied, "Please do, and wait

outside for me; I have something else to tell you." The man then took one or two volumes from the bookcase and looked into them as he stood there. Then he took his leave and went out of the room. He was in the room for about seven minutes; it was during the second half of the lecture.

T's hair, which was brown, was described twice as blond and three times as black; his gray jacket was described twice as blue and four times as brown. Four observers forgot or failed to notice his beard (a small pointed number); three said he had a full bushy beard of the sort seen on Santa Claus. Two people said he was wearing spectacles (he wasn't) and one witness mentioned a (nonexistent) cap.

Dr. Stern notwithstanding, some research indicates that, on the attention front, women may have an edge over men. In an attention-assessing study conducted by psychologists Irwin Silverman and Marion Eals at York University, Toronto, subjects—both male and female—were left in an office waiting room for two-minute periods, with no mind-occupying distractions: no magazines, no newspapers, no television. Deprived of such usual waiting-room fare, Silverman and Eals theorized, the subjects would have little to do but kick their heels and observe their surroundings. The women, at least, apparently did so; when the waiting-room occupants were subsequently tested on their knowledge of the room, the women could correctly identify and position 70 percent more objects than the men.

Eyewitness experiments by Elizabeth Loftus and colleagues, however, look uniformly bad for observers. Loftus showed her subjects a series of color slides documenting the successive stages of an automobile accident in which a red Datsun arrives at an intersection, stops, turns right, and creams a pedestrian who is trustfully crossing the street in the crosswalk. Depending on the way in which subjects were subsequently questioned—in some cases, deliberately misleading information was sneaked into the interrogation—up to 80 percent of the witnesses made false assertions about the course of the accident. We don't necessarily internalize all that we see; presence at the scene of the crime does not, by a long shot, guarantee eyewitness accuracy. Prosecutors and defendants in the 80,000 annual U.S. trials that rely primarily on the evidence of eyewitness testimony often stand on psychologically shaky ground.

Memory and the Moody Blues

IF WE CAN'T REMEMBER what takes place before our very eyes, it may be that we were in the wrong mood. Studies by Gordon Bower at Stanford University show that memory retrieval is mood-dependent; that is, incidents are better remembered in the same emotional state in which the original memory was laid down. Persons in cheerful frames of mind have an easier time recalling pleasant memories; persons in the depths of despair are better at retrieving the more miserable segments of their pasts. Bower tested his hypothesis by asking his subjects—all college students—to keep detailed week-long diaries of their emotional ups and downs. The students were then put through a "mood-induction procedure" in the laboratory, designed to nudge them into either an ebullient or a just plain lousy mood. The investigators managed this through a combination of hypnotic and suggestive techniques: participants were shown heartrending movies, played hilarious comedy records, or read a series of up-beat or downbeat self-referential statements, along the lines of "Things have been going very badly for me lately" or "I am feeling lonely, isolated, and depressed." Mood-manipulated students were then tested on their ability to recall events from their diaries. Happy students (comedy record listeners) matched memory to mood, remembering many more pleasant incidents; unhappy students remembered many more miserable and sad incidents.

Bower also had his subjects listen to a story about Happy André, an exuberantly successful and sunny-spirited character, and his alter ego, Sad Jack, a gloomy dweeb with a dismal history of failure. The students then underwent the mood-induction process and, feeling buoyant or dejected, were tested on their memory of the story. Cheerful students had many more memories of the doings of Happy André; downhearted subjects remembered more about Sad Jack. The mood swings of manic-depressive patients similarly affect their memories. Patients on the upswing are better able to retrieve happy memories; patients entering the depressive phase are better at retrieving sad memories.

Jonathan Bargh, a psychologist at New York University, argues that emotions, in the form of unconscious or pre-conscious likes and dislikes, continually affect our thought processes. ("There's nothing that's neutral," says Bargh.) The mind automatically weights all incoming information, instantaneously loading it with a positive or negative tag that, unless we put on the mental brakes by exercising rational evaluation, leads us to make snap judgments. Like greased lightning, we find ourselves loving or loathing Chihuahuas, Volvos, gladioli, or the next-door neighbor. Unconscious predispositions even affect such theoretically valueless items as nonsense words, abstract shapes, and letters of the alphabet. English speakers, for example, much prefer the liquid garble of "juvalamu" to the jagged meaninglessness of "chakaka," and we tend to feel more favorably toward the letters A, B, S, and M than such Scrabble nightmares as Q, X, Z, F, and U. (The two best-loved words in English, according to a poll by the London *Sunday Times*, are *melody* and *velvet*; the two worst, according to the National Association of Teachers of Speech, are *cacophony* and *crunch*.) Unless we're actively paying attention, argues Bargh, such subliminal value weighting can tip us over into unreasoned errors of judgment.

> *Summer afternoon—summer afternoon; to me those have always been the two most beautiful words in the English language.*
> Henry James

The Tramp and the Millionaire

MEMORY ALSO VARIES with physical context. Bower cites the adventures of Charlie Chaplin's Little Tramp in the 1931 silent film *City Lights*, in which the Tramp saves a dejected drunken millionaire (his wife has left him) from drowning himself in the river. The two then spend an intoxicated evening together, drinking, dancing, brawling, driving down sidewalks, and (by mistake) setting a society dowager's gown on fire with a lighted cigar. They part in the wee hours, the best of friends. The next day—"The sober dawn awakes a different man," reads the subtitle—the millionaire, now sober, has forgotten the Tramp, and has his butler throw Charlie out of the house. That afternoon, drunk again, he recognizes the Tramp and greets him ecstatically ("My friend!"). The millionaire's memory is context-dependent: put him back in the condition in which the original memory of the Tramp was laid down (drunk) and the memory immediately becomes accessible.

Psychologists have had a try at *City Lights* in the laboratory (minus the dancing, driving, and inflammatory cigars) and found that tasks learned by subjects while loopily under the influence were best remembered when drunk again. People consistently remember learned material best under the same conditions and in the same surroundings where the original learning took place, which is why students do better on tests taken in their own familiar classrooms. Sometimes one can imagine this posing insurmountable difficulties: in a 1975 British study, sixteen divers were given lists of words to memorize either onshore or in full scuba regalia, submerged in the ocean. Subsequent tests showed that lists learned on land were best remembered on land, while lists learned underwater were best remembered back in Davy Jones's locker.

In Philip MacDonald's mystery novel, *The List of Adrian Messenger*, context-dependent memory saves the day. Adrian Messenger (who doesn't survive past page 22) has plummeted into the sea following an airplane explosion; there, clinging to a makeshift raft, he gasps out crucial clues to a fellow survivor. The fellow survivor, who actually survives, is able to recall, almost verbatim, Messenger's words by imagining himself once more back on the raft in the ocean. "He's got one of those trick memories, thank God," says the detective on the case. "Imagines himself back into the right circumstances and dredges up everything. Almost everything, anyway . . ."

British philosopher John Locke in his "Essay on Human Understanding" describes an inconvenient case of context-dependent memory in a young man who had learned how to dance:

> Having learned to dance, and that to great perfection, there happened to stand an old trunk in the room where he learned. The idea of this remarkable piece of household stuff had so mixed itself with the turns and steps of all his dances, that though in that chamber he could dance excellently well, yet it was only while that trunk was there; nor could he perform well in any other place, unless that or some other such trunk had its due position in the room.

Flashbulbs

O THER MEMORIES GO beyond mere place, mood, and awkward pieces of furniture, forming instantaneously in circumstances so emotionally supercharged that they seem—deceptively—to be branded on the brain. These are referred to by psychologists as "flashbulb memories" from the cameralike flash with which the brain seems to record them. Studies of flashbulb memories usually center on shared experiences of public shock: Pearl Harbor Day, the assassination of President Kennedy, the explosion of the space shuttle *Challenger,* volcanic explosions, earthquakes. In 1899, psychologist F. W. Colgrove set out—thirty-three years after the fact—to chronicle a nineteenth-century public shock, asking 179 persons of appropriate age, "Do you recall where you were when you heard that Lincoln was shot?" Of the interviewees, 127 still retained vivid memories of the awful moment: "I was setting out a rosebush by the door. My husband came in the yard and told me. It was about eleven o'clock A.M." "We were eating dinner. No one ate much after we heard of it." "I was fixing fence, can go within a rod of the place where I stood." "My father and I were on the road to A— in the state of Maine to purchase the 'fixings' needed for my graduation."

Psychologist Roger Livingstone proposes a special neurobiological process for imprinting such crisis moments on the brain, which he calls the "Now Print!" mechanism. The flashbulb memory, Livingstone suggests, is a survival skill, picked up somewhere along the line in early human evolution as a quick means of assimilating all the details of unexpected life-threatening events. Those methodical thinkers who hung around to analyze all the implications of that chance encounter with the cave bear may have been eliminated willy-nilly from the gene pool; far better for the species to imprint all data pertaining to the event in a flash of electrified horror, and then run, to process the new information later in safety.

One would expect such flashbulb memories to be unforgettably accurate and complete—and they seem so; persons recalling where they were when they first heard the news of President Kennedy's assassination preserve the event in photographic detail, right down to the expression on their seatmate's face and the color of their sneakers. Flashbulb memories, however, are just as likely to be fudged, forgotten, or fuzzily distorted as anything else. Immediately after the *Challenger* explosion, a group of Emory University students were asked to write accounts of how they heard the news and where they were at the time. Three years later, asked to remember what they had written, only 7 percent of the students accurately matched their original descriptions, and 25 percent got absolutely everything wrong—despite the fact that the flashbulb experience still seemed clear in their minds. In a similar study at Baylor University, Charles A. Weaver III had a group of college students, two days after the event, complete elaborate questionnaires on where they were when they first heard about the January 16, 1991, bombing that initiated the Persian Gulf war. The surprise and upset generated by this event, Weaver felt, qualified it for flashbulb status. The students were tested on the material in their questionnaires at three months and then one year later. Results showed that even searing flashbulb memories were forgotten, dropping off markedly in accuracy, evolving over time in response to new information much as eyewitness memories can alter in response to after-the-fact input. The mental flashbulb, it seems, takes an impermanent picture.

Forgettable You

"THERE SEEMS," SAYS the *Cambridge Encyclopedia of the English Language*, "to be a universal and deep-rooted drive to give individual names to things." Thus do we set the stage for our own downfall. People, places, and pets are all given names, and so, according to a BBC Radio poll, are houses, cars, yachts, word processors, wheelbarrows, washing machines, house plants, and toothbrushes. Daniel Boone named his rifle; Roy Rogers named his Jeep; King Arthur named his sword; and Eric the Red, lying like a flatfish, named Greenland. An English student living in a hovel abroad even named the resident cockroach (Arnold Schwarzenegger). Most people, asked what they are prone to forget, do not cite presidential assassinations, earthquakes, or alien abductions. Instead they plump for that most common of memory bugbears: proper names. All such names are subject to evaporation at a moment's notice, an occurrence so shamingly frequent that Emily Post covers it in her seminal volume on etiquette under the graceful heading "The Retort Courteous to One You Have Forgotten." Courtesy, however, while preserving the social niceties, won't keep the perennially forgetful from feeling like blithering idiots. "For treachery," writes science editor Roy Herbert, "the brain has no equal, selling its owner down the river of humiliation in a flash, no warning." Roman aristocrats, to avoid this embarrassing fate, were often accompanied on their social rounds by a *nomenclator*, an alert slave whose duty was to surreptitiously supply his master with the names of encountered acquaintances. Aides and assistants today provide such services for forgetful heads of state. In the movie *The American President*, Michael Douglas, in the title role, attempts to greet a White House gardener. Into the dreadful pause that presages the loss of a name leaps his aide, hastily muttering, "Charlie."

While the occasional forgetting of proper names is all in a day's work, chronic name-forgetting is a recognized medical condition with a name all its own—onomastic aphasia, from onomastics, the study of names. Onomastics has a number of petty subdivisions, among them anthropomastics (the study of personal names) and toponomastics (the study of place names), but onomastic aphasics tend not to differentiate among them, forgetting, with equal facility, names of acquaintances old and new, names of streets, towns, and cities, book titles, brand names, and business designations. Author Alun Rees, who claims to suffer from this condition, describes various social ploys used by the name challenged to avoid or delay discovery—the phrase "You two know each other, of course?" followed by silence, usually forces people to introduce themselves, explains Rees. A story told of nineteenth-century statesman Henry Clay is a masterful example of this cagey art. A disappointed lady, the anecdote goes, accused Clay point-blank of not remembering her name. "Madame, I do not," Clay admitted with a gallant bow, "for when we last met, I was certain that your beauty and accomplishments would soon cause you to change it."

If, at a loss for a name, you're willing to risk all on a guess, statistics are slightly on your side. Polls of most popular names show that chances are these days that your addressee is named either Jennifer or Sarah or Michael or Christopher. (This worked better two hundred years ago: 40 percent of colonial American males were named either John or William; 40 percent of females, Mary or Elizabeth.) In the English-speaking world, the best bet for surname is Smith, as in Jennifer or Michael Smith; the runner-up is Johnson or (in New York City) Cohen. This form of guesswork is admittedly risky—even the top ten first names nowadays account for only about 20 percent of the population, and names can be wildly unpredictable. Look at Juice Newton, Ima Hogg, Zaphod Beeblebrox, and Dweezil Zappa. However, in social *extremis*, it may be worth a shot.

> *My memory is so bad that many times I forget*
> *my own name!*
> Miguel de Cervantes,
> *Don Quixote de la Mancha*

> *I cannot tell what the dickens his name is.*
> William Shakespeare,
> *The Merry Wives of Windsor*

> *What a touch of grossness in our race, what a*
> *shortcoming in the more delicate spiritual perceptions, is*
> *shown by the national growth amongst us of such hideous*
> *names as Higginbottom, Stiggins, Bogg.*
> Matthew Arnold

So why do we forget names? Some psychological studies indicate that it has to do with the way the brain processes information. In the 1980s, British psychologist Andrew Young analyzed person-by-person forgetfulness by asking 22 volunteers to keep diaries listing the red-faced details of all the errors they made in recognizing people over a period of seven weeks. Errors, which abounded, were subsequently found to fall into three distinct classes. The volunteers either totally struck out, flatly failing to recognize a familiar person at all; or they recognized a person as familiar, but were unable to place him or her in context ("I know that woman from somewhere"); or they recognized a person fully, but simply could not remember his or her name. Notably absent, Young pointed out, were recognition errors in which the volunteer remembered the person's name— "That's Robert Redford!"—but were unable to come up with any other contextual or biographical details. Names, Young decided, based on such error recognition patterns, were the last stop on the information-processing line.

Young and colleague Vicki Bruce devised a multistep hierarchical model for recognition. Step one—generally rapid—involves recognizing a face as familiar or not. Step two retrieves the stored collection of information that goes with that particular face—"works at that little insurance company on Main Street; plays the violin in the local symphony; breeds canaries." It's in accessing this identity-specific information that we often become confused by contextual cues: the manager of your bank, for example, seen cavorting with a beach ball at the swimming pool, may register as familiar, but might be impossible to place when encountered in a nonbank environment. Processing step three, the clincher, retrieves from memory the familiar person's name.

Dear Sir,—I am in a Madhouse and quite forget your name or who you are.
John Clare

I have become a lost name.
Muriel Rukeyser

The hitch in name retrieval, hypothesizes psychologist Mike Burton of the University of Nottingham, may be due—all those

John Smiths aside—to the very uniqueness of names. Burton and Bruce, who have studied information-processing models using computer simulations, suggest that the brain's system for recognizing individual people consists of clusters of "units," each storing a single item of relevant remembered information. Recognition of Great-Aunt Matilda's face—activation of a "person unit"—turns on a whole battery of associated "information units": "married to Great-Uncle Mortimer," "lives in Charlottesville," "plays the accordion," "horrid little Pekinese dog," "chocolate brownies," and "antimacassars." Many of the Matilda information units are not absolutely unique to the lady herself. "Chocolate brownies" and "antimacassars," for example, may be shared with four other great-aunts and the neighbor down the street; "Charlottesville" and "Pekinese dog" may apply to any number of acquaintances. Such shared units, with their extra dose of interconnections, are, claim Burton and Bruce, more readily activated than unique units, linked only to a single person. Name units, with no additional neural reinforcements—there's only one Matilda Biggle—thus turn on slowly and weakly. "History professor"—a unit with multiple applications—is easier to call up than "Dr. McPherson"; "movie actress" pops up faster than "Emma Thompson" or "Marilyn Monroe."

Other onomastic investigators, including Gillian Cohen of London's Open University, suggest that it's not the uniqueness of names that lays us low, but their essential meaninglessness. Nonsense words like Ebbinghaus's RAX and JAF are much harder to remember than words for which we have meaningful associations (REFRIGERATOR, PTERODACTYL). Proper names, suggests Cohen, fall into the RAX category: Archie Bunker, Isaac Newton, and Isadora Duncan are, at heart, strings of meaningless nonsense syllables. Cohen tested her hypothesis by having subjects memorize lists of names paired with occupations. In some cases, the names doubled as words for meaningful professions: Baker, Butcher, Carpenter, Cook. When subjects learned lists of meaningless names (such as Ryman) paired with meaningful professions (baker), the names proved more difficult to remember than the occupations. When the situation was reversed—meaningful names (Baker) paired with meaningless occupations (ryman)—the names, now provided with a built-in association, were more readily recalled than the occupations.

A Tree Growing Hooks

In GENERAL WE forget the meaningless—which is why those of us without European business interests have long since forgotten the principal products of Portugal—and retain the meaningful. Nonsense syllables are harder to memorize than definable words; scrambled words more difficult than logically ordered sentences. We remember by building on the familiar, adding to an already established network of associations and relationships. The more associations that can be attached to an incoming scrap of information, the more likely that the new tidbit will be remembered. Connect your latest physics lesson to your ability to shoot sugar packets across a restaurant by making a catapult out of your teaspoon, and you'll have a better chance of remembering the equations governing the paths of projectiles. Thus learning builds on learning and memory on memory, like the branching, re-branching, and re-re-branching of an expanding fractal snowflake. "Memory," writes psychologist Peter Russell, "is not like a container that gradually fills up; it is more like a tree growing hooks onto which memories are hung."

> I can never remember things I didn't understand
> in the first place.
> Amy Tan,
> The Joy Luck Club

Associations may be sensory as well as semantic. That physics lesson on trajectories, for example, already associated with such practical equivalents as slingshot projectiles, skeet shooting, and the throwing of bowling balls into the Grand Canyon, may also be linked in memory to the distinctive scorched-rubber smell of the physics laboratory, the measured tick of the classroom clock, and the lurid pattern of purple anemones on the lecturer's Hawaiian shirt. Of all sensory associations, the one with the greatest implication for memory is smell. Odor has the power to send almost all of us around a reminiscent bend. Though the human nose can't hold a candle to that of the average dog, who boasts forty-four times more olfactory cells than we do, with a correspondingly more sensitive sense of smell, we can still be transported into vivid realms of memory by an unexpected sniff. Smell is channeled from the receptor cells of the nasal cavity to the brain's olfactory bulb, a plump podlike structure at the base of the brain, closely connected to the emotion-packed limbic system and the memory-laden hippocampus. The combination is unbeatable: Smell is a sensory umbilical cord linking us to our pasts. Edwin Morris, fragrance expert, writes, "There is almost no short-term memory with smell." Triggered by waves of scent, the switches of memory flash on, illuminating recollections like living dioramas within the mind.

> *Smell is a potent wizard that transports us across thousands of miles and all the years we have lived.*
> Helen Keller

Remembrances are inspired by a whole panoply of odors. While humans are capable of detecting some 10,000 different smells, not all, to the crude human nose, are equally distinctive. Especially recognizable, according to William Cain of Yale and the John B. Pierce Foundation Laboratory, are the aromas of

coffee and peanut butter, of Vicks VapoRub—the gooey
unguent in the electric-blue jar, once so popular for the treatment of chest colds—and of chocolate, baby powder, bub-
blegum, mothballs, Band-Aids—remember all those skinned
knees?—lemons, vanilla, and ("movie smell") buttered popcorn.
Even such a tightfisted curmudgeon as Ebenezer Scrooge fell for
smell. "He was conscious of a thousand odors floating in the
air," wrote Charles Dickens in *A Christmas Carol*, "each one connected with a thousand thoughts, and hopes, and joys, and cares
long, long forgotten." Science writer James Gorman describes
the happy nostalgia brought on by the waxy smell of Crayola
crayons: open a brand-new box filled with yellow-green,
magenta, burnt siena, and gold, he writes, and you'll bring back
that "untouched-coloring-book feeling—you're young, the
world is new, the next thing you know your parents may bring
home a puppy." Charles Dickens, at the smell of paste, experienced the flip side of the coin, unwillingly dragged back in
memory to the bottle factory where he spent a miserable and
poverty-stricken segment of his youth. Others of us dredge up
recollections (of one kind or another) at the smells of chicken
soup, lilies-of-the-valley, bottled ink, motor oil, new-cut hay, or
wet wool.

Truncated as our olfactory senses are, we are still scent
lovers. Cleopatra and Nero were both mad for roses (Nero once
so overloaded a banquet table with rose petals that one of his
dinner guests was asphyxiated); Madame Pompadour loved
hyacinths; the empress Josephine drenched herself in the scent
of violets. Alexander the Great had his tunics spicily soaked in
saffron; Louis XIV had his shirts washed in a broth of nutmeg
and cloves. Sir Walter Raleigh wore strawberry cologne. While
some odors—strawberry cologne—have only personal significance, others seem to have similar effects on us all. The smell of
spiced apple is said to be universally relaxing, lowering blood
pressure in twitchy hypertensives and averting panic attacks in
the ultra-nervous. Lavender, in contrast, perks up the metabolism and makes us more alert; and peppermint—pumped gen-

tly through the ventilation ducts at work—enhances concentration and efficiency. (Periodic puffs of peppermint, researchers find, have about the same effect as an uplifting cup of caffeinated coffee, but without the attendant jitters.)

> *When from a long distant past nothing subsists, after the people are dead, after the things are broken and scattered, still, alone, more fragile, but with more vitality, more unsubstantial, more persistent, more faithful, the smell and taste of things remain poised a long time, like souls, ready to remind us, waiting and hoping for their moment, amid the ruins of all the rest; and bear unfaltering, in the tiny and almost impalpable drop of their essence, the vast structure of recollection.*
>
> Marcel Proust

> *Smells are surer than sights and sounds to make your heart-strings crack.*
>
> Rudyard Kipling

> *Nothing revives the past so completely as a smell that was once associated with it.*
>
> Vladimir Nabokov

Some particularly acute sniffers use their memories of smell professionally. The federal government, for example, still depends on human noses to assess the freshness of fish—a mere 320 molecules' worth of suspect odor is all it takes to damn a hake or catfish, an evanescent whiff as yet undetectable by machine. Perfume chemists depend on a discerning sense of smell, and the incomparable Sherlock Holmes in *The Hound of the Baskervilles* fingered one suspect by the revealing scent of her notepaper (white jessamine). "There are seventy-five perfumes, which it is very necessary that a criminal expert should be able to distinguish from each other," Holmes informs his long-suffering sidekick, Dr. Watson, "and cases have more than once within my own experience depended upon their prompt recognition."

At the opposite end of the scale are those who have lost the ability to smell anything at all, a sensory amnesia known as anosmia. An estimated two million Americans are anosmic—a condition that could be a blessing if you live within spitting distance of a paper mill or garbage dump, but otherwise causes more trouble than it cures. Deprived of smell, we lose taste as well. Apples, onions, and potatoes are all one to the smell-less; red wine, garlic, oranges, and Limburger cheese are reduced to uniform blandness. Taste, smell-wise, is a double whammy: not only do we breathe in odors from loaded forkfuls en route to our mouths, but we get an additional dose during chewing, by the retronasal route—up the pharynx at the back of the mouth and on to the nasal cavity. Food, without smell, is no fun, as anyone knows who has ever eaten gourmet jellybeans in the throes of a heavy cold. Anosmics also lose the ability to smell other human beings—an ability that if not missed in the post-game locker room or on a crowded subway in July may be near essential in the bedroom. The mysterious chemistry of true love, some scientists guess, may consist of volatile molecules romantically whuffed up the nose. Without smell, 25 percent of people lose their sex drive.

Alzheimer's patients, as they inexorably lose memory, also often lose their sense of smell. The two, so closely linked, wither together; as the rooms of memory slowly disappear, so do the scented doors that once opened them to view. At the opposite end of life, smell may be the first memory that we form. Infants, by the time they are two weeks old, have learned to recognize the smell of their mothers: they will turn toward a swab rubbed on their mother's skin, but away from a swab rubbed on a stranger. Mothers, conversely, can recognize the smell of their newborns.

Smell, some studies show, enhances the ability to learn: children given a list of words to memorize, learn and recall more easily if given an accompanying olfactory cue, say a nice scented spurt of white pine. David Smith at Bishop's University in Lennoxville, Canada, tested the ability of subjects to learn lengthy word lists while sniffing either jasmine incense or Lauren perfume. Their performance was reassessed some time later, with either the same scent that had been present during the original learning experience or with the alternative odor. Word-list memory worked best, Smith found, when the scents of the two learning episodes matched. If you routinely do your homework to the smell of chocolate, Lysol, or burned toast, the suggestion is, you'll do better in class or on a test if exposed to the same odor.

Moscow Is Green

For a real memory boost, however, a mixed bag of sensory associations—the more, the better—is ideal, such as the crosslinked array of sight, smell, touch, taste, and sound that appears in the condition known as synesthesia. In synesthesia—from the Greek *syn* (together) and *aisthanesthai* (to perceive)—a stimulus to one sense sets off responses from others. Synesthetics are sensory jumbles: they may hear colors and shapes or feel tastes and smells. To one synesthetic, the taste of chocolate is prickly; to another, the whump of helicopter rotors is a repeating pattern of green loops and the clang of a ringing bell, a forest of red daggers. The most common form of the condition is chromatic-graphemic synesthesia, in which people associate words with colors. The word *Moscow*, explains one such synesthetic, a Welsh painter, is dark gray, with splotches of spinach green and pale blue; *Daniel* is a high-gloss purple, red, and blue; and *Elizabeth*, her own first name, is a "horrid glistening yellow." Author Vladimir Nabokov, in his autobiography, *Speak, Memory*, describes his own "fine case of colored hearing," in which each sound is imbued with a characteristic hue. Long *a*, to Nabokov, had the tint of weathered wood, hard *g* was vulcanized rubber, *n* oatmeal, *k* huckleberry, *m* "a fold of pink flannel," *s* a mix of azure and mother-of-pearl, and *p* unripe apple. Composer Nikolai Rimski-Korsakov heard music in color: C major, for example, was pure white; E major, sapphire-blue; and A-flat major, a muted gray-violet. Michael Watson, subject of neurologist Richard Cytowic's book *The Man Who Tasted Shapes,* has colored orgasms, and describes the taste of quinine as feeling "like polished wood" and of chocolate pie as a series of "cool, smooth columns."

Almost all words have color and nothing is more pleasant than to utter a pink word and see someone's eyes light up and know it is a pink word for him or her too.

Gladys Taber,
Stillmeadow Daybreak

VOYELLES

A noir, E blanc, I rouge, U vert, O bleu: voyelles,
Je dirai quelque jour vos naissances latentes:
A, noir corset velu des mouches éclatantes
Qui bombinent autour des puanteurs cruelles,

Golfes d'ombre; E, candeurs des vapeurs et des tentes,
Lances des glaciers fiers, rois blanc, frissons d'ombelles;
I, pourpres, sang craché rire des lèvres belles
Dans la colère ou les ivresses pénitentes;

U, cycles, vibrements divins des mers virides,
Paix des pâtis semés d'animaux, paix des rides
Que l'alchimie imprime aux grands fronts studieux;

O, suprême Clairon plein de strideurs étranges,
Silences traversés des Mondes et des Anges:
—O l'Oméga, rayon violet de Ses Yeux!

Arthur Rimbaud

VOWELS

Black A, white E, red I, green U, blue O: vowels,
I will tell, one day, of your hidden origins:
A, black hairy corset of glittering flies
Who boom around cruel stenches,

Gulfs of shadow; E, purities of mists and of tents,
Lances of haughty glaciers, white kings, shudders of
        Queen-Anne's-lace;
I, crimsons, spit blood, laughter of beautiful lips
In anger or penitent ecstasies;

U, cycles, divine vibrations of viridian seas,
Peace of pastures scattered with animals, peace of
        wrinkles
That alchemy imprints upon studious foreheads;

O, the last trumpet, filled of strange stridencies,
Silences crossed by Worlds and by Angels:
O, Omega, violet ray of His Eyes!
                    Arthur Rimbaud

S, the Russian journalist whose awesome memory was so impressively described by Aleksandr Luria, was a complex synesthetic who experienced particularly vivid sensory images and associations. Musical tones, to S, had color, texture, and taste. A tone pitched at 250 cycles per second was a velvet cord, tinged a pastel pinkish-orange; a tone at 2000 cycles per second looked like fireworks and tasted like a pickle. The sound of a ringing bell was white, felt rough like a heavy rope, and tasted of salt water. Voices took on similar hues: "What a crumbly, yellow voice you have," S once remarked to a visiting psychologist.

Such powerful multisensory associations serve as built-in memory aids. Synesthetics often have extraordinary memories; they also—life is a trade-off—tend to get lost easily and to have trouble with arithmetic. The majority of synesthetics are female, and most are left-handed. Put all this together and there may be a pattern somewhere, but neurologists have yet to figure it out. They have, however, devised at least two models that explain how the brains of synesthetics operate differently from the brains of the less sensorily endowed. Simon Baron-Cohen and colleagues at London's Institute of Psychiatry suggest that synesthetics are simply crosswired. In the ordinary brain, according to Baron-Cohen, incoming sensory stimuli activate specialized neural "modules" in specific areas of the cerebral cortex. Each module is linked to the others in its group by connective neural pathways. In synesthetics, these pathways have gone interestingly haywire; in lieu of homogeneously linking auditory module to auditory module, for example, synesthetic pathways peel off on curious quests of their own, linking auditory centers to taste, olfactory, or visual modules. Thus an auditory stimulus, such as a blaring flourish of trumpets, activates not only an auditory module, but—via some eccentric crosslink—a visual module as well, eliciting a simultaneous image of red fireworks. Synesthetics, in Baron-Cohen's view, are electrical anomalies; in the household equivalent, the living room light switch would also—always—turn on the stereo.

Richard Cytowic, the neurologist so fascinated by the patchwork senses of synesthetic Michael Watson, holds a different view. In the Cytowic model of the brain, all neural roads lead to a limbic Rome. Cytowic suggests that input from all the senses merges in a coordination center—perhaps the hippocampus—in the brain's limbic system. From there, multiple signals simultaneously activate modules of sensory information stored in scattered spots about the cerebral cortex, producing a single unified perception. In Cytowic's view, we all function alike, but only synesthetics—about 1 in every 500,000 people—become conscious of the limbic mixing process. Synesthetics in effect come on-line a little too early, before the brain has quite finished work. Synesthetics manage to catch the limbic system with its pants down.

John Harrison, a researcher who favors the abnormal crosslinking hypothesis, suggests that the peculiar sensory associations formed by synesthetics may be the result of inadvertent leftovers from infancy. Brain development in growing embryos is ordinarily a matter of enthusiastic overproduction followed by stern cutbacks. Many more neurons are initially born than ultimately survive. The growing brain provides itself with a lush pool of raw material, then discards the excess as it fine-tunes its operational needs. Synesthesia, Harrison suggests, may result from persisting hookups that were intended, in the proper scheme of development, to disconnect, disintegrate, and hit the trash. Some research on infants by Daphne Maurer at the University of Toronto supports this idea, indicating that we may all enter the world trailing, along with our clouds of glory, synesthetic neural pathways. Maurer's work involves shining lights in people's eyes, the sort of thing you yell at your children for doing with an unsupervised flashlight. Flash a light in the eyes of a cooperative (or uncooperative) adult and scanning techniques show an increase in the activity of the visual cortex. Try the same trick on a newborn, however, and brain response, rather than localized in a discrete visual area, is much more diffuse. The baby, write Daphne and Charles Maurer in *The World of the Newborn,* is a synesthetic: "He hears odors, and sees odors, and feels them too. His world is a mêlée of pungent aromas— and pungent sounds, and bitter-smelling sounds, and sweet-smelling sights, and sour-smelling pressures against the skin."

Life Begins in Kindergarten

IF WE DO INDEED start life as juvenile synesthetics—drinking blue milk and gazing at lemon-flavored nightlights—hardly any of us, grown up, can remember the experience. Most people have no memories of the years before their third or fourth birthday, a phenomenon so common that Freud dubbed it "childhood amnesia." Freud attributed the oblivion of toddlerhood to the repression of anxiety-producing sexual and aggressive memories, lustful and murderous feeling that must be gotten safely under wraps before we can safely devote ourselves to the complexities of fingerpaint, Play-Doh, and big-wheel tricycles. Psychologist Ulric Neisser, on the other hand, suggests that childhood forgetfulness may not be so straightforward. We don't just forget the nasty stuff, Neisser points out; we forget *everything*.

> *I can't even remember the name of my kindergarten teacher. The details of my childhood come swimming up at me through some primordial ooze, unanchored by context or plot line: the Good Humor truck bell, a broken nose and the feel of blood in my mouth, my mother in a maternity smock, my father sleeping on the sofa.*
> Anna Quindlen,
> *"How Dark? How Stormy? I Can't Recall"*

Remembered life, according to Neisser, begins in kindergarten. Around the age of five or six, when we begin school, our lives suddenly become predictably structured, and memories—formed on the scaffolding of an organized schedule—become easier to retrieve. There are some problems with this hypothesis—children who attend structured nursery schools starting at very young ages remember no better than kids who spend disorganized preschool years at home—but there is some evidence that memory benefits from established routines. Predictable and repetitive routines allow us to collect our acquired knowledge about the world into scripts—generalized start-to-finish sequences of familiar events that psychologists sometimes refer to as "generic memories" or schemas. Children form scripts for customary activities like eating dinner, going to bed, trips to the playground, and visits to Grandma's house. By adulthood, we have constructed a whole library of such scripts: standard operating procedures for business lunches, blind dates, support group meetings, political confrontations with one's in-laws, and sessions at the neighborhood health club.

Developmental psychologist Katherine Nelson hypothesizes that early memory undergoes an alternating progression, flip-flopping from the unique to the general and back to the unique again. First, says Nelson, the very young assimilate new experience after new experience, a confusing barrage of novelty that, by the age of one, children are beginning to assemble into general patterns that allow them to make sense of the busy world. These general patterns—the scripts—may, as they first form, block the storage of specific memories. Preschoolers around the ages of three or four, finds Nelson, are better at relating the details of their scripts than at describing specific unique episodes from their recent pasts. Three-year-olds, for example, can tell you what *usually* happens at dinner—"We put the plates on the table; I have a red cup; last we have dessert"—but stick at recalling specific dinners past: "Yesterday we had chicken and peas and Daddy told a story about an airplane and I spilled my milk." Nelson suggests that as scripts are in the process of crystallizing, individual memories are simply incorporated into the larger, more general structure, engulfed by the generic mass. Once scripts are fully established and children have an internalized base of working knowledge, however, this indiscriminate absorption ceases. Unique personal memories can now be distinguished from the generalized scripts and stored separately.

MY FIRST THANKSGIVING

I have been asked to recall my first Thanksgiving, which with me is hard to do, as I've seen many. But the very first one I remember was about the year 1864. Father was going to Union village to buy Himself some Boots, and he was to buy me a red dress. I was to be a good girl all day, in hopes of getting a red dress. I tried to do everything I was told to do. But when candlelight came, Father came in from the flax mill, and said he could not get his Boots. Because it was Thanksgiving day, and the Stores were closed. I was heartbroken to think I did not get my red dress. I could not eat my supper.

Mother said it was too bad as I had been a good girl, that day. But they never thought of the Stores being closed. Father patted my head and said don't worry, as he was going to Centre Cambridge in a few days, and would try there, and so he did. But the dress was not red, it was more of a brick red or brown. I was awful disappointed but said nothing, so I never got what I call a red dress. I have found in after years it is best never to complain of disappointments, they are to be.

Grandma Moses
November 21, 1948

A Glowing Orange Box

J UST BECAUSE MOST of us can't remember much pre-three doesn't mean that small children have no memories. Psychologist Marion Perlmutter and colleagues at the University of Michigan found that tots 35 to 38 months old could recall events that had taken place seven and a half months earlier; children 45 to 54 months old could remember events from fourteen and a half months ago. In the very young, recognition memory—"Is this familiar or not familiar?"—clicks on first. Babies six months old can differentiate between the faces of friends and family and those of perfect strangers. As they approach eight to twelve months of age, memory expands and deepens, and recall—an early version of declarative memory—appears. Laraine McDonough and Jean Mandler at the University of California at San Diego showed that eleven-month-olds, between applesauce, strained peas, and naps, are already busy forming long-lasting conscious memories. Twelve babies were treated to demonstrations of what the researchers called "causal sequences"—baby-appealing cause-and-effect activities such as putting a button in a box to make a rattle. Three months later the babies were brought back to the laboratory and allowed to play with the boxes and buttons. All imitated what they had been shown at the original session: they stuffed the button in the box and made a rattle. In a similar study, fourteen-month-olds, happily sitting in their mothers' laps, were shown an assortment of toys by an experimenter, among them an enchanting little box with a translucent orange top. When the experimenter rocked forward and pressed the box with his forehead, a light came on inside, brightly illuminating the orange cover. One week later, when returned to the laboratory and given a chance to play with the box on their own, eight of the twelve babies promptly leaned forward and touched the orange top with their foreheads.

From recall memory, which allows observant infants to remember where Mommy hid the cookies, children gradually develop full-fledged autobiographical memories, personal recollections of their own individual passages through time. Studies attempting to pinpoint just when autobiographical memory first appears find that most people's earliest recollections form around the age of three and a half, with female memories generally extending back a month or two earlier than male. A 1948 poll of earliest memories turned up one woman who claimed a first recollection before the age of one; an occasional individual produces a prebirth or birth memory; and one (male) psychiatrist claims to remember his own conception, including egg-sperm fusion, the long drop down the Fallopian tube, and implantation in the wall of his mother's uterus. For most of us, however, autobiographical memory kicks off around four.

> *In probing my childhood (which is the next best to probing one's eternity) I see the awakening of consciousness as a series of spaced flashes, with the intervals between them gradually diminishing until bright blocks of perception are formed, affording memory a slippery hold.*
> Vladimir Nabokov,
> *Speak, Memory*

Most early memories are visual and most are in living color. Content varies wildly, but a survey of 150 high school and college students showed that most fall into three major categories: trauma, such as being injured, frightened, or lost; transition, as in the birth of a new brother or sister, or a move to a new house; and trivia. Vladimir Nabokov's first memory—vividly trivial—is of a walk with his parents down a sun-dappled avenue of trees: it took place, he recalled, the summer he was four. His mother wore a soft pink dress; his father was in dazzling military uniform, white tricked out with glittering gold. The small Nabokov walked between them, holding a hand of each, flickering in and out of sunlight with each step. "I see my diminutive self as celebrating, on that August day 1903, the birth of sentient life," wrote a much older Nabokov, looking back some forty-four years later.

First Memories

FIRST MEMORIES, no matter how insignificant—a second-long vision, say, of splashing in the bathtub with plastic boat and rubber duck—are thought by some psychologists to reveal essential truths about ourselves. "The first memory will show the individual's fundamental view of life," wrote psychologist Alfred Adler. Adler's own first memory was of being propped, ill and neglected, on a bench, watching his stronger and healthier brother at play; he grew up to invent a school of psychology based on the inferiority complex. Golda Meir's telling first memory was of Russian Jews being overrun by Cossacks on horseback; Dwight Eisenhower's, an appropriately soldierly recollection, was of bravely beating off an attacking gander with a broomstick. Albert Einstein recalled being given a compass at the age of four, and his fascination with the mysterious and permanent pointing of the needle to the north. Thomas Jefferson's earliest recollection—a transitional memory—was of a move that took place when he was two: he was handed up to a slave on horseback, he remembered, and carried on a pillow to the new family plantation, fifty miles away. Henry David Thoreau's was of a trip to Walden Pond: "When I was four years old, as I well remember, I was brought from Boston to this my native town, through these very woods and this field, to the pond. It is one of the oldest scenes stamped on my memory." Theodore Roosevelt's earliest memory, which proved him as obstreperous a four-year-old as Rough Rider, politician, and president, was of (mild) trauma:

> I bit my elder sister's arm. I do not remember biting her arm, but I do remember running down to the yard, perfectly conscious that I had committed a crime. From the yard I went into the kitchen, got some dough from the cook, and crawled under the kitchen table. In a minute or two, my father entered from the yard and asked where I was. The warm-hearted Irish cook had a characteristic contempt for "informers," but although she said nothing she compromised between informing and her conscience by casting a look under the table. My father immediately dropped on all fours and darted at me. I feebly heaved the dough at him, and, having the advantage of him because I could stand up under the table, got a fair start for the stairs, but was caught halfway up them. The punishment that ensued fitted the crime, and I hope—and believe—that it did me good.

Since each of us retains such cinematically vivid snippets from our early years, why is so much of childhood forgotten? Some psychologists argue that there's nothing mysterious about it: over time, people simply forget things, and childhood, for most of us, was a good long time ago. Others suggest that childhood forgetting is less attrition than judicious, if unconscious, selection. According to psychologist John Kihlstrom of the University of Wisconsin, adult personality leads to a selectivity of memory: people remember past episodes that reinforce their adult perceptions of themselves. The content of early memories thus shifts and changes with the changing present. Happy, well-adjusted adults, researchers find, tend to have pleasant earliest memories; anxious and depressed adults tend to recall anxious and depressed early happenings. A study in which the earliest memories of elderly persons were screened both before and after their admission to institutions or nursing homes showed a marked reshaping of recollections. Post-institutionalization, earliest memories took a turn for the worse; new themes of loss, loneliness, pain, and death predominated. The remembered past was a function of the experienced present.

> *Old paint on canvas, as it ages, sometimes becomes*
> *transparent. When that happens it is possible, in some*
> *pictures, to see the original lines: a tree will show through*
> *a woman's dress, a child makes way for a dog, a large boat*
> *is no longer on an open sea. That is called pentimento*
> *because the painter "repented," changed his mind.*
> *Perhaps it would be as well to say that the old conception,*
> *replaced by a later choice, is a way of seeing and then*
> *seeing again.*
> Lillian Hellman,
> Pentimento

Some neurobiologists hypothesize that childhood amnesia may have a straightforwardly organic explanation. Though humans are born with all the neurons they'll ever have, the newborn brain is not yet fully functional. In the first months of life, synapses by the thousand are formed and pruned away; critical development periods come and go. Most notable among these is the developmental window for learning language, which seems to swing open somewhere around eighteen months of age and to slam shut by the time children are ready to enter school. Children, once the language window opens, have to get while the getting is good: if the syntax of at least one language is not learned during this crucial period, language skills will be impaired for life. Autobiographical memory—the ability to string episodes of our lives together into a coherent narrative—

seems to develop in tandem with language, implying that certain new capacities are common to both.

The solidification of episodic memories into recollections that can last a lifetime may also depend on the maturation of the hippocampus, that vaguely seahorselike organ on the underside of the temporal lobes that functions in the transfer of certain kinds of information from short-term to long-term memory. Some evidence shows that the hippocampus isn't fully up and running until the age of four or five. Perhaps childhood forgetting results not from memories lost, but from memories never properly installed. Most early memories may be temporarily jerry-rigged by the developing brain; only when mature mental machinery becomes available can truly permanent memories form and survive.

There's some suggestion that the smarter we are, the earlier our first permanent memories form. Researchers Patrick Rabbitt and Lynn McInnis, in a study of 377 volunteers ranging in age from 54 to 83, found that the earliest memories of high-IQ subjects occurred at much younger ages than those of people with low IQs. Mean age at first memory for smart volunteers was 3.14 years, as opposed to 4.79 years for the not-quite-so-smart volunteers. Exceptionally gifted children—those mental superstars with IQs upward of 180—usually have both prodigious and extremely early memories. One gifted youngster, Adam, could remember his prenatal days; and most of the children studied had memories going back to the ages of 12 to 18 months. One teenaged girl could recall in great detail an incident that happened when she was 15 months old: she had swallowed a splinter and been rushed to the hospital. She remembered the conversation she had with her mother, how she felt and her impressions of what her mother felt, what she was wearing, the trip to the hospital, meeting the doctor, and what the doctor said. Gifted children display not only early episodic memories, but early semantic memories too. One child could recite passages from storybooks at the age of 12 months; another could recite nursery rhymes at the age of 18 months. A third, aged two and a half, memorized and recited a very long Australian epic poem. Perhaps, suggest the investigators, these results indicate that brighter brains mature more rapidly. More intelligent brains, whose systems come on-line earlier in development, may "wake up earlier" than their less on-the-ball peers.

Mythmaker and Archivist

ONCE MEMORIES BEGIN to accumulate in permanent storage, we embark on the lifelong process of creating and recreating mental autobiographies, using—in lieu of pencil, paper, and word processor—the cell assemblies of the brain. Autobiographical memory, writes psychologist John Kotre, is "memory for the people, places, objects, events, and feelings that go into the story of your life." Autobiographical memory encompasses your first day of school, your grandmother's raisin pies, your first fishing trip, your college sweetheart, and your last summer's oceanside vacation—weaving them all into a continuous and more or less true tale. Autobiographical memory, however, despite its convincing aura of accuracy, is more historical novel than history. For one thing, in the realm of memory, we are all stars, planted squarely and triumphantly at the center of the action. Psychologist Anthony Greenwald explains that in the making of memory, we're all "totalitarian egos": we remember ourselves as important and assign ourselves central roles in successful decisions or performances. Conversely, we weasel out of failure. Autobiographical memory is big on scapegoats: "we" win, but "they" lose. The totalitarian ego, ever eager to put its best foot forward, determinedly clears our memories of blame. Author Fay Weldon discusses this self-serving process in the context of Jane Austen's novel *Emma*. The spoiled protagonist of the story has just attended a picnic, where she has disgraced

herself by being cruel to the annoying but kindhearted Miss
Bates. She's sorry later, but her attempts to make amends are
rejected, and Emma is left with her guilt. It's just such moments
of shame and discomfort that we strive to smooth over in memory, recalling them, says Weldon, "after a fashion, but never
quite, as it were, head-on. The mind slips away, hastily gets
round, somehow, like a car going into rapid reverse, grating its
gears, when it encounters these small, scraping memories. . . ."
In autobiographical memory, we become better than we really
are. In accident reports and insurance claims, we tend never to

> *as I was crawling*
> *through the holes in*
> *a swiss cheese*
> *the other*
> *day it occurred to*
> *me to wonder*
> *what a swiss cheese*
> *would think if*
> *a swiss cheese*
> *could think and after*
> *cogitating for some*
> *time I said to myself*
> *if a swiss cheese*
> *could think*
> *it would think that*
> *a swiss cheese*
> *was the most important*
> *thing in the world*
> *just as everything that*
> *can think at all*
> *does think about itself.*
> Don Marquis,
> *archys life of mehitabel*

be at fault: trees and telephone poles maliciously leap out at us, fence posts and stop signs suddenly appear before us, and pedestrians fling themselves in our paths. "An invisible car came out of nowhere, struck my car, and vanished," Richard Lederer quotes one such totalitarian insurance claimant in his book *Anguished English.* "A pedestrian hit me and went under my car."

Autobiographical memory, according to Kotre, is in a constant state of struggle between opposing forces: a "mythmaker" that, in striving to turn our lives into a good story, favors poetic license, exaggeration, and embellishment; and an "archivist," a Jiminy Cricket–like stickler for historical truth. (The mythmaker may produce face-saving excuses, but the archivist knows damn well who drove head-on into that tree.) The mythmaker, however, given the malleability of memory and the merciful nature of time, has ample scope for plying its inventive trade. What we remember and how we remember it are both the result of a mental editing process, during which a good deal of memory is left in the discard pile on the cutting room floor. It's this mental rewrite process, unique for each one of us, that causes different people to remember the same events in very different ways. A classic example, according to psychologist Daniel Schacter, is the Senate confirmation hearing of Supreme Court Justice Clarence Thomas, at which Thomas was accused of repeated sexual harassment by law professor Anita Hill. Viewers assumed that one of the pair was lying, says Schacter, but, given the malleability of memory, the very opposite may have been the case. Both may have been telling the truth according to their own lights, presenting two different takes on what was once a common reality.

"And then you remember," said my mother, "the first Sunday after they were married, Vic brought her into town to dinner and when he came into Grandmother Dinsmore's house we said, 'Where's Carrie?' and he said, 'She's out in the car. She's afraid to come in.'"

This was time-polished family lore. I leaned against a sagging split-rail fence, drinking in the evening, while my mother and Ruby stood in the lane, going through the story, point and counterpoint. With confident boredom I expected the ending I had always heard, which was my mother saying, "And so I went out and brought her in."

And then, instead, I heard Ruby's urgent, rather throaty voice saying, "And so I went out and brought her in."

The voice went through my mind with the flash of an old-fashioned explosion of nitrate powder, taking a photograph inside on a dark night, only the exposure in this case, literally the exposure of what must have been a lie, was a double exposure on a film I had thought developed and yellowed and filed long ago. There was one image, vivid as everything my mother always told, of herself, slim and pretty in her 1930s dress, hurrying down the walk to the Ford . . . where Carrie sat. Then there was another image superimposed on it of Ruby's large white face, dark eyes, and dark hair.

Which image recorded the event?

Jeffrey Simpson,
American Elegy

Recording the present, re-creating the past, imagining the future—all are acts of imagination, of conjuring.

Roberta Israeloff,
Lost and Found

The Hill of Reminiscence

In PART, WHAT we remember depends on how old we are.
A method known as the "Crovitz procedure," named after
psychologist Herbert Crovitz, who popularized it in the 1970s,
is sometimes used to study the relationship between memory
and age. It involves asking participants to produce memories
related to certain cue words: window, flower, coin, snow-
storm, tree, fire, mountain, picture, yard. After running
through several dozen of these, subjects are asked to assign
approximate dates to each remembered incident. Once dated,
psychologist David Rubin found that the memories fall into
reproducible patterns. Twenty- and thirty-something-year-old
subjects come up with a high proportion of recent memories,
the number dropping off sharply with time and eventually
tailing off into the nothingness of childhood amnesia.
Graphed, the results look a lot like Ebbinghaus's famous
forgetting curve, a steep slope arching from near-complete
retention into forgetfulness. Subjects in their fifties and seven-
ties, however (no data is available for the forties and sixties),
show a downshift in the curve. Older participants produce a
large proportion of memories from the second and third (and
occasionally first) decades of life. This mass of early-life
memories generates a dromedarylike hump toward the bottom of the forgetting curve, which Rubin dubbed the "hill of
reminiscence."

THINGS THAT AROUSE A FOND MEMORY OF THE PAST

Dried hollyhock.
The objects used during the Display of Dolls.
To find a piece of deep violet or grape-colored material that has been pressed between the pages of a notebook.
It is a rainy day and one is feeling bored. To pass the time, one starts looking through some old papers. And then one comes across the letters of a man one used to love.
Last year's paper fan.
A night with a clear moon.
The Pillow Book of Sei Shōnagon

The first ten or twelve years are just one triumph after another, and the giddy glow of accomplishment lights up our ambitions for the rest of our lives, even if our later achievements are always a little ambiguous, a little clouded, compared with the ringing clarity of learning to climb stairs, flip a light-switch, or ride a two-wheeler.
Barbara Holland,
Endangered Pleasures

One possible contributor to the emergence of this hill, which pops up along with menopause, midlife crises, and bifocals, is the "serial position effect," a memory phenomenon that affects not only the makeup of autobiographical memory, but our ability to recall the items on a grocery list, the names of the presidents of the United States, and (in chronological order) the titles of Shakespeare's plays. In learning a series of items, how well we remember each depends on its position in the series. We tend to remember the first and last items on a list best (the "primacy" and "recency" effects), but to forget the items in the bland middle. Chances are, in an attempt to list the presidents in order, you'll do well at the beginning (Washington, Adams, Jefferson) and the end (Reagan, Bush, Clinton), but will fall down in the middle over such poorly positioned executives as James K. Polk, Rutherford B. Hayes, and Warren G. Harding. In presidential lists, there's usually at least one ray of light in the dim interior: most people manage to remember middleman Abraham Lincoln. Lincoln, a sudden spike in the midst of a monotonous trough of forgetfulness, is an example of the "von Restoroff effect" (eponymously named for the psychologist who first quantified it): that is, when an outstandingly eye-catching item (such as Lincoln) is embedded in an otherwise homogeneous mush, it will be disproportionately remembered. Spend a couple of minutes studying the following list and then, in no particular order, try to recall as many of the listed items as possible:

> house dog wind chair cat gate day
> door rabbit moon Komodo dragon car
> girl flower walk egg tree candle street
> shirt light cup sheep book apple hat

You're most likely to remember the first words in the series (house, dog, wind) and the last (book, apple, hat), and—due to the von Restoroff effect—that peculiarly attention-getting Komodo dragon.

A more compelling explanation for the bulging early hill in middle- to old-age memory is the very nature of the memories themselves. During our teens and twenties—the "hill" period—we are experiencing the bulk of our life's "first-times": first leap off the high diving board, first day of college, first apartment, first meeting with your future parents-in-law. All these firsts—usually novel and emotion-packed experiences—are great grist for memory's mill. Their uniqueness and intensity make them stand out; first times are indelible. Second, third, and fourth times seldom fare as well; nobody remembers the runners-up.

Repeated episodes, as demonstrated so exhaustively by indefatigable diary-keeper Marigold Linton, do not flourish. As experiences multiply and the number of first-time encounters drops off, the hill of reminiscence similarly slopes downward into neglectful absentmindedness.

Remembering Days and Years

For most of us, putting a definitive date to some long-cherished memory is more difficult than it sounds. By and large, none of us remembers by calendar time. Marigold Linton's extensive records of her personal memories over a twelve-year time period showed that the memories were arranged chronologically for about five years, then they underwent an organizational change, reshuffling themselves by content and subject matter. Long-term memory does not arrange itself along a timeline; in our mental storage bins "when" is forgotten much more easily than "what." We remember the details of a vacation at the Grand Canyon or a business trip to Japan, but struggle to recall when each took place—1990? 1991? Memory for dates seems to follow the normal plunge of the forgetting curve: the longer ago an event took place, the less likely we'll be able to remember its day, month, or year. Furthermore, those dates we do manage to dredge up are likely to be erroneously edged forward in time, a common phenomenon known as "forward telescoping," in which past events are believed to have occurred more recently than they really did. It's forward telescoping that gets us into trouble on medical forms with questions such as "At any time in the past five years, have you had any major surgery?"

Try recalling, for example, the dates of John Kennedy's assassination, the first moon landing, the eruption of Mount Saint Helens, the murder of John Lennon, the wedding of Prince

Charles and about-to-be princess Di, the explosion of the space shuttle *Challenger,* and the Oklahoma City bombing. Rather than attacking such chronological problems head-on—a flat feat of memory retrieval—most date-seekers use a process of reconstruction, using recall cues from their personal lives. "Let's see now, it must have been in the fall because the woodstove was burning and we'd just put the storm windows up . . ." "That was the year we were living in the blue house in California . . ." "It was right after Michael's seventh birthday party . . ." We're best at recalling month of the year, followed by day of the week and hour of the day, probably because of their higher quota of associative cues. ("I was making the children's Halloween costumes . . ." "We had just planted the garden . . ." "It was the day of the town Historical Society meeting . . ." "It happened right after the six o'clock news . . .") We're worse at remembering years and worst of all at recalling days of the month. September seventeenth, for example, doesn't mean much to most of us unless it happens to be our birthday, wedding anniversary, or the historic repeat of the day lightning struck the barn.

> *In the South the war is what* A.D. *is elsewhere; they date from it.*
> Mark Twain

> *I was brought up in a country vicarage, after all. They date things by events, they don't date them by years. They don't say "That happened in 1930" or "That happened in 1925" or things like that. They say, "That happened the year after the old mill burned down" or "That happened after the lightning struck the big oak and killed Farmer James" or "That was the year we had the polio epidemic." So naturally, of course, the things they remember don't go in any particular sequence.*
> Agatha Christie,
> *By the Pricking of My Thumbs*

I observe my neighbors and it seems to me that they are content to live on, registering and employing each day but not in the least distinguishing one day beyond another, and, although that is obviously the best way of passing time, it makes, I feel, for little or no excitement. Even a major event (like our hurricane, or the time we had the flood, or that terribly heavy snow when all the electricity was out for three days) tends to become, by the next day, only a remembered landmark—"That was two days, I recollect, before the hurricane, because we had all those raspberries to set out . . ."—and even the last trump will, I am afraid, make no more of an impression on our community (". . . well, now, let's see; that there bugle blowed around about three in the afternoon, and I remember the day because it was the day I's supposed to hammer on the boards on that there gate, and here it's been six weeks since that ol' bugle and there hangs the gate right now . . ."). When I think about it, I can only remember the year Laurie was born because I was waiting to get a new winter coat.

Shirley Jackson,
Life Among the Savages

Memory and Age

THOSE OF US WITH the longest pasts, conventional dogma holds, have the hardest time of all remembering. Somerset Maugham, inadvertently illustrating the forgetfulness of age, gave a speech at the Garrick Club in London on the occasion of his eightieth birthday that began with the resoundingly upbeat statement "There are many virtues in growing old." This delivered, Maugham paused, looked down at the table, fiddled with his notes, coughed, and shifted nervously back and forth from foot to foot. The pause grew to embarrassing length while Maugham, stymied, struggled silently to remember what came next. Finally he cleared his throat and spoke. "I'm just trying to think what they are," he said.

> *There is a wicked inclination in most people to suppose an old man decayed in his intellects. If a young or middle-aged man, when leaving a company, does not recollect where he laid his hat, it is nothing; but if the same inattention is discovered in an old man, people will shrug up their shoulders, and say, "His memory is going."*
> Samuel Johnson

Most studies of memory in old age do indicate gradual age-related changes in the capacities and composition of the brain.

None, however, suggest that aging is an inevitable dive into what Shakespeare in *As You Like It* characterized so crushingly as "second childishness and mere oblivion." Barring stroke or such brain-devastating ailments as Alzheimer's disease, Parkinson's disease, and multiple sclerosis, the brain pretty much manages to hold its own. Giuseppe Verdi was still composing operas in his eighties, and Robert Frost was writing poems; George Bernard Shaw was writing plays in his nineties; Georgia O'Keeffe was painting pictures; and Pablo Casals was playing the cello. Oliver Wendell Holmes, Jr., without batting an eye, dominated the Supreme Court until his retirement at the age of 91. Bertrand Russell, aged 89, spent a vocal week in prison for civil disobedience. Somerset Maugham wrote his last book at 84; Frank Lloyd Wright designed his last building at 89. Leopold Stokowski founded the American Symphony Orchestra at 80, recorded twenty albums in his nineties, and—an incurable optimist—signed a six-year recording contract at the age of 96.

Winston Churchill, well into his eighties, dropped in on a session of the House of Commons. He attracted so much attention that the debate then in progress was disrupted, causing one irritable MP to mutter resentfully to his neighbor, "After all, they say he's potty."

Churchill fixed him with a cold eye.

"They say he can't hear either," he retorted.

Some researchers claim that age-related memory loss is a cruel hoax, behavior brought on by social expectations rather than by demonstrable physical deterioration. (Other behaviors of the same socially encouraged ilk include "all little girls like pink" and "all little boys like football.") Older Americans, according to Becca Levy and Ellen Langer of Harvard University, grow forgetful in response to our culture's negative stereotypes of old age. Levy and Langer tested their hypothesis by comparing the memories of average elderly Americans to older deaf Americans—under the assumption that the deaf are relatively protected from the slurs of the anti-age mainstream culture—and to elderly Chinese citizens, from a culture where the old are highly respected. Both deaf Americans and Chinese outremembered elderly Americans with normal hearing; and the elderly Chinese, unfazed by time, performed as well on memory tests as did young Chinese. If Grandma can't find her pince-nez, Levy and Langer's results imply, it's because nobody expects her to. A Dutch study from the University of Limberg found similar, if not quite identical results. All memory loss in the normal elderly, the Dutch researchers found, was due to either mild head injuries, the after-effects of general anesthesia, or "social drinking." Those who avoided whacks on the skull, too many whiffs of ether, and college beer bashes were unimpaired, stubbornly holding their own with younger subjects even into extreme old age.

The opposition—notably a Washington-based medical group, the Memory Assessments Clinic, Inc.—claims that up to 50 percent of over-fifty Americans may suffer from memory loss, a condition ominously referred to in capitals as Age-Associated Memory Impairment, or AAMI. The old, mentally as well as physically, aren't quite as speedy as the young. With age, the rate of cognitive processing declines, which means that it generally takes longer to retrieve information from memory. The elderly eventually get where they're going, but in doing so they're tortoises in comparison to the youthful hares. Learning—the ability to transfer new information into memory—also becomes increasingly difficult with age, down 50 percent, one researcher finds, between the ages of 25 and 75. (But by no means impossible: Leo Tolstoy, at 67, took up the bicycle; Queen Victoria, at 68, began learning Hindustani.) Still, Paul Baltes and colleagues at the Max Planck Institute in Berlin found that seventy-year-olds are three to four times slower than twenty-year-olds at memorizing word lists; and researchers at the National Institute on Aging found that subjects in their late sixties to mid-seventies were impaired in their ability to memorize and recognize new faces.

> *My memory is like camphor. It evaporates with time.*
> Dominique Lapierre

> *Memory is often not so much lost as hard to find.*
> Steven Rose

> *I cannot sing the old songs now!*
> *It is not that I deem them low:*
> *'Tis that I can't remember how*
> *They go.*
> C. S. Calverley

Neurons and Canaries

ATTEMPTS TO CORRELATE memory loss in the elderly with structural changes in the brain remain on shaky ground. With age, our (possibly) irreplaceable neurons begin to dribble away, to the tune of—according to one scare-mongering gerontologist—100,000 cells per day from the age of thirty on. If this is true, by the time we become octogenarians, we will have lost close to two billion brain cells, only a little less than 2 percent of our total neuronal complement. Neuronal loss is not uniform throughout the brain, however; some regions seem more susceptible to atrophy than others. Neurons tend to blink out in the substantia nigra and locus coerulus—areas in the brain stem that are hard-hit in patients with Parkinson's disease—and in the limbic system. The hippocampus is thought to lose about 5 percent of its neurons each decade in the second half of life; this loss, since the hippocampus plays such an important role in memory and learning, may be a factor in age-related memory impairment. Or maybe not: some researchers have noticed that as hippocampal neurons bite the dust, their still-healthy neighbors sprout a new lush crop of connective dendrites. The guess is that this new growth is a compensatory mechanism, the means by which the brain creatively battles the ravages of time. The brain does not go gentle into that good night. It sprouts.

While neurobiological dogma has held for years that neurons in the adult human brain do not reproduce themselves, more recent evidence suggests that such may not be quite the case. Some potential for fertility may remain. Indications of such a possibility originally came from the brain of the canary, the little butter-yellow finch famed for his versatile repertoire of song. *His* is the operative word here: ordinarily only male canaries— after some initial coaching from their fathers and a few months of practice—learn to sing. Nonvocal females, however, when injected with the male hormone testosterone, also acquire the ability to burst operatically into song. Unscrupulous pet store owners in the 1930s, with a little hormonal funny business, managed to foist a lot of commercially worthless females off on would-be songbird owners. (All went well for the first few weeks; then the testosterone wore off and female song petered out.) This low trick eventually attracted the attention of Fernando Nottebohm at Rockefeller University, whose wholly aboveboard research interests centered on the biological basis of birdsong. Nottebohm and an interested graduate student, Steven Goldman, produced some melodiously masculinized female canaries of their own, and injected them with a radioactively labeled compound—tritiated thymidine—which, they hoped, would allow them to identify any changes in the new singers' brains. The radiolabel told a neurobiologically unexpected tale: the singing females had enlarged male-style song centers in their brains, populated with brand-new actively reproducing neurons.

Since the bird brain harbored neurons still capable of multiplying, hopeful researchers proceeded to probe the brains of other animals in search of fertile precursor cells. Mice and rats, it turns out, have some, as do tree shrews and macaque monkeys. Adult shrews and monkeys, in fact, were shown to produce new neurons in the brain's hippocampus— the first evidence to date of cellular reproduction in a part of the brain involved in learning and memory. Since macaques, as primates, are evolutionary cousins of human beings, the results suggest, says Elizabeth Gould of Princeton University, that we too may have the capacity for hippocampal cell division. Human neurons, perhaps, have not reached an irreversible dead end.

Serenity, Sugar, and Sage

Pending the perfection of a technique to stimulate division of dwindling brain cells, however, age-related memory loss must be tackled in other—simpler—fashions. A stress-free life may help memory in the long run: cortisol, a hormone released by the adrenal glands in response to danger, threat, and upset, is a killer when it comes to memory-forming neurons. Sonia Lupien of Rockefeller University and colleagues recently studied a group over sixty years old, one subset of whom—presumably all under stress—produced 50 percent more cortisol than the rest. In maze tests, which required good memory skills, the high-cortisol subjects performed poorly relative to their more laid-back peers. Stress, it seems, along with all its other ill effects, makes us forgetful.

Dieting also appears to be a downer for memory. According to Mike Green of the British Institute of Food Research, dieters do much worse than nondieters on tests of memory, reaction time, and mental-processing capacity. Test scores of the dieters, said Green, were equivalent to those of test takers who had just polished off two stiff drinks of alcohol—both were poor—but he attributed lousy performance in the dieters' case to anxiety. Unsuccessful dieters, those desperate types living on celery and Melba toast, but still not whittling off the pounds, were both the most anxious and the most forgetful of all.

The biochemical basis of stress-induced forgetfulness may be a disruption in LTP—long-term potentiation, the synaptic strengthening believed to be important in learning and the formation of associative memories. Neurobiologist Richard Thompson created a population of chronically stressed rats by subjecting the animals to a series of inescapable electrical shocks over a period of seven days. At the end of this period, cells in the hippocampi of the strung-out rats had lost the ability to generate LTP. Robert Sapolsky of Stanford points out that stress also starves the brain: the glucocorticoid stress hormones, such as cortisol, reduce the cellular uptake of sugar. Stressed neurons, Sapolsky finds, experience a 20 to 30 percent drop in energy, enough to have an adverse effect on learning and memory.

While stress shrinks memory, a dose of sugar—as found in such weight-watcher's no-nos as jelly doughnuts, banana cream pie, and chocolate éclairs—markedly enhances it. In one series of sugary experiments, psychologist Paul Gold of the University of Virginia had volunteers listen to an audiotaped prose passage, then drink a glass of lemonade laced with either glucose—real sugar—or with saccharine, an artificial sugar substitute. Twenty-four hours later, when participants were asked to recall details of the passage they had heard on the previous day, the sugar drinkers came up with 53 percent more information than their sugar-free compatriots. It's not clear how glucose exerts its memory-boosting effect. It may simply act as an extra shot of brain fuel; active neurons demand high quantities of blood sugar. Or, as some studies suggest, it may enhance the neuronal release of acetylcholine, a neurotransmitter important in memory formation.

Neurons communicate with each other via chemicals: neurotransmitter molecules, released by the axon of one nerve cell, send a signal to the next neuron in line. About 15 percent of the brain's neurons produce the neurotransmitter acetylcholine, notably those of the memory-involved hippocampus and amygdala. In lab rats, drugs that block the action of acetylcholine also eliminate rodent memory; and acetylcholine-producing cells seem to be particularly sensitive to the ravages of memory-eradicating Alzheimer's disease. Such observations led researchers to propose treating memory disorders with drugs that enhance acetylcholine's effects. If drugs that block acetylcholine inhibit memory, the rationale ran, perhaps acetylcholine boosters will have the opposite effect. One such potential enhancer, to the vast delight of dedicated herbalists, is sage oil, squeezed from the plant that seventeenth-century plantsman John Gerard farsightedly claimed "helpeth a weake braine or memory and restoreth them being decayed in a short time."

Sage oil moves in subtle ways: rather than interacting head-on with acetylcholine itself, transforming it into an enhanced supermolecule, sage instead targets acetylcholinesterase, the enzyme that ordinarily breaks down and disposes of excess acetylcholine in the brain. In other words, sage beats off acetyl-choline's biological attackers, allowing the neurotransmitter to survive for longer periods of time in the dangerous world of the synaptic cleft. Acetylcholinesterase, however, is not the nervous system's version of the bad guy in the black hat. Effective synaptic transmission is a hit-and-run affair: secreted neurotransmitter erupts across the synaptic cleft, sends its signal, and gets out of there, to make way for the next message en route. Acetylcholinesterase ordinarily performs an essential mopping-up function, preventing the signal molecules from loitering beyond their allotted time.

Too much of this enzyme, on the other hand, is far from wonderful: excess acetylcholinesterase, like the unstoppable water-toting broom in *The Sorcerer's Apprentice,* floods the synapse, eliminating neurotransmitter molecules before they've had a chance to do their job. Large quantities of acetylcholinesterase build up in the brains of Alzheimer's patients, suggesting that the disease-associated memory loss may be due at least in part to such overdestruction of neurotransmitter. The drug Tacrine, which alleviates some of the early memory-dissolving symptoms of Alzheimer's disease, is an acetyl-cholinesterase blocker.

There's rosemary, that's for remembrance; pray, love, remember: and there is pansies, that's for thoughts.
William Shakespeare,
Hamlet

Smart Drugs

Drugs that purport to boost memory and cognitive skills are called "smart drugs" by the socially snappy and "nootropics" (from the Greek for "acting on the mind") by the clinically conscientious. Many of these chemicals have been shown to increase learning ability in laboratory animals— treated rats, for example, get better at running mazes—but it's unclear how well the smarter-rat effect translates to human beings. Clinical studies of smart drugs—though pharmacological hope springs eternal—remain largely equivocal.

Nootropics presently fall into three general classes. The first includes those drugs that increase blood flow to the brain. Such blood-flow boosters dilate blood vessels, which theoretically ups the supply of oxygen and glucose to feeble, underfed neurons. The better-nourished cells become more active, contributing to increased memory skills and mental alertness. The second class—neurotransmitter enhancers—are more specific. These act to increase active levels of various neurotransmitters, the neuron-to-neuron message-carrying molecules that are spat into the synapse in response to electrical impulse. Enhancers are a mixed pharmaceutical bag: some, like Tacrine, boost active levels of acetylcholine; others target alternative neurotransmitters, such as glutamate, serotonin, and dopamine. The third class of nootropics are calcium channel blockers, which act to keep calcium ions firmly out of cells. Interest in calcium blockers as memory drugs rose from studies of the ubiquitous maze-trotting rat: in geriatric rodents, researchers found, accumulated defects in the neuronal membrane ion channels (they stayed open all the time) led to a lethal buildup of calcium inside brain cells. Since the timed opening and closing of calcium channels is an essential step in the intracellular memory-forming process, channel breakdown was suspected as a factor in old-age memory loss. Calcium channel blockers improved memory in old rats, but evidence is still sparse and sketchy for comparable effects in human beings. If such channel blockers prove effective, however, one possible bet for the forgetful is ginseng—the vaunted cure-all over which Chinese provinces once went to war. Ginseng, said to prevent aging, contains a compound that blocks calcium channels.

Perhaps the best bet among memory uppers these days is a class of compounds collectively known as ampakines, from the lab of Gary Lynch and colleagues at the University of California at Irvine. Ampakines are named for their bolstering effect on AMPA receptors—a class of receptors that bind the neurotransmitter glutamate, found on the post-synaptic nerve cell membrane. Over 90 percent of the synapses in the memory-monitoring hippocampus are fueled by glutamate—and it's just these synapses that seem most sensitive to the depredations of old age. Glutamate synapse number in the hippocampi of the elderly may plunge by as much as 40 percent—a nervous-making loss that may explain Grandma's inability to find her spectacles and Grandpa's failure to recall the neighbors' names. Ampakines, studies show, may be just the medicine to shore up such faltering brainpower. Rats, fed doses of Lynch's memory pill, remember their lessons twice as well as their drug-free peers, as evidenced by their masterful abilities to track down Froot Loops hidden in the tunnels of a maze. Human volunteers on ampakines similarly exhibit memory boosts. Younger subjects upped their scores on tests of short-term learning and recall—memorizing lists of nonsense syllables, for example—by about 20 percent; elderly subjects quadrupled their test scores, attaining levels comparable to those of volunteers in their early thirties.

Another candidate for potential brain-boosting is the sex hormone estrogen, the steroid that governs the female repro- ductive cycle. Estrogen, produced by the ovaries, plunges post- menopause from 300 micrograms a day to zilch; with its departure, women become prone to osteoporosis, heart disease, hot flashes, depression, and—the latest in this dismal parade— memory loss. Barbara Sherwin and Diane Kampen at Montreal's McGill University recently investigated the effect of estrogen on memory by reading short prose selections to post-menopausal women (aged fifty-five and older), then—after a thirty-minute wait—asking the participants to repeat back details of the selec- tions they had heard. Women on estrogen replacement therapy did markedly better on this test of verbal memory than did their estrogen-less peers. Jerome Yesavage and colleagues at Stanford found a slight memory edge of estrogen takers in the ability to recall names and memorize word lists; and Uriel Halbreich, of the State University of New York at Buffalo, found that estrogen treatment—and the more of it, the better—enhanced women's scores on a range of cognitive tests evaluating memory, reaction time, verbal skills, mental alertness, and reasoning ability. In one of these, a simulated driving test in which the participants had to react quickly to an unexpected array of road hazards and obstacles, estrogen-less women initially performed poorly; after two months of estrogen therapy, however, their scores rivaled those of younger drivers in their twenties. The explanation for the mind-expanding effects of estrogen—provided, that is, that women function like rats—is twofold: estrogen both promotes the growth of synaptic connections in the hippocampus and prevents deterioration and death of acetylcholine-producing neurons throughout the brain. According to Meharvan Singh and James Simpkins at the University of Florida, ovarectomized rats, who produce no estrogen, gradually cease to produce a protein called nerve growth factor (NGF). After three estrogen- less months, NGF levels in the now-menopausal rats had dwindled rapidly, to 45 percent of normal. NGF is a poor protein to lose. As its name implies, it is essential for the health and growth of acetylcholine-producing neurons. Deprived of it, these cells begin to wither and die, and, as they kick the bucket, rodent females become increasingly absentminded. Rats on estrogen are twice as good at solving mazes and learning to avoid electrical shocks as their estrogen-less peers. Estrogen therapy, unfortunately, has its drawbacks—it increases, for example, the risk of endometrial cancer—which means that it's not the memory booster for everyone. Men, incidentally, get a steady dose of estrogen throughout life: it's manufactured as needed from the male sex hormone, testosterone.

Mental Aerobics

Open to nearly everybody is the brain-boosting option for healthful exercise. According to some studies, elderly persons who regularly perform some kind of aerobic exercise score better on cognitive tests than couch potatoes. Some researchers, on the other hand, hold that physical exercise, while undeniably beneficial, cannot substitute for exercise of the mind.

> *A sound mind in a sound body, is a short but full*
> *description of a happy state in this world.*
> John Locke,
> *"Some Thoughts Concerning Education"*

Almost any form of enriching mental activity—reading the Great Books, for example, or becoming a leading light of the local debating society—may contribute to overall memory enhancement. Psychologist Arthur Shimamura at the University of California, Berkeley, has experimental evidence that a challenging mental life does indeed bolster some aspects of memory. Shimamura recruited 72 of his professorial peers on the Berkeley campus and gave them a series of memory and cognitive tests. The oldest of the group, the "senior professors," aged 60 to 71, Shimamura found, were unable to keep up with the younger faculty in such tasks as memorizing names and faces, or in tests of reaction time in which test takers were required—as fast as possible—to punch the proper computer button in response to a flashed instruction on the monitor screen. They equaled their younger colleagues, however—and markedly outperformed nonprofessionals of their own age group—in memory tests that demanded mental planning, problem solving, and the recall of the details of recorded text passages. Mental exercise, as provided by a challenging job environment, seems to keep at least some subsets of memory vigorously green. Cognitive skills, the suggestion is, deteriorate if neglected: when it comes to the brain, it's a matter of use it or lose it.

Konrad Adenauer, chancellor of West Germany at the age of eighty-nine, visited his doctor for treatment of a miserable cold. The doctor, who couldn't help much, became increasingly annoyed at Adenauer's demands for a cure. "I'm not a magician," the frustrated doctor finally cried. "I can't make you young again!"

"I haven't asked you to," snapped Adenauer. "All I want is to go on getting older."

Encouragingly, lots of people don't seem to lose much of it at all. The elderly, according to neuroscientist Richard Thompson, display a very wide range of memory capabilities, with those at the upper end of the scale equaling or surpassing the performances of youngsters in their twenties. In general, however, encoding strategies—the methods by which new information is squirreled away—and retrieval speed—the rate at which stored material is accessed—both inevitably drop off with increasing age, which means that the old have more trouble than the young at assimilating new skills. (The over-sixties are more likely to have that blinking clock on their VCRs; it's the ten-year-olds who learn how to program the things.) Math skills tend to dribble away as we inexorably approach our eighties, but vocabulary resolutely holds its own, as does the vast stockpile of general knowledge that, once we've accumulated enough of it, comes to be known as "wisdom."

Psychologist Warner Schaie has been conducting for the past forty years—the project began with his doctoral dissertation—a longitudinal study of mental abilities, tracking hundreds of subjects from a Seattle-based HMO in their mental and physical progression through time. Every seven years, the volunteers take a battery of tests assessing their verbal and numeric reasoning, spatial skills, perceptual speed, and memory. To date, this is the largest study of its kind; most age-related studies are cross-sectional, comparing groups of different persons in different age groups, rather than studying the same people as they age. Schaie, over the years, has accumulated data on over 5,000 people. Results indicate the importance of three factors in age-related mental deterioration. The first is mental lifestyle. "A person who stops solving problems arrives at a point where he can't solve problems," Schaie explains, pointing out that the mentally active, such as bridge players and crossword addicts— who participate regularly in problem-solving activities— perform better with age on cognitive tests than their less challenged peers. The second is chronic disease: the healthy, unsurprisingly, do better at maintaining their mental abilities than the perennially sick. Lengthy stays in the hospital, according to Schaie, are particularly pernicious for mental function, perhaps due to the long periods of enforced inactivity and understimulation. The third factor is cognitive style, a mode of mental operation that ranges, in Schaie's studies, from the rigidly restricted to the creatively flexible. Flexible thinkers, whom Schaie defines as having "the ability to adapt and roll with life's punches," are much more likely to hold their own with advancing age.

The crucial decade, according to the Schaie studies, seems to be the fifties: persons who remain mentally active and alert between fifty and sixty tend to stay that way. The ideal gifts for a fiftieth birthday party might be mind-expanders: puzzles, books, chess sets, French lessons, telescopes, and carpentry tools.

ANTIDOTES FOR AGING MEMORY

1. Keep working. The mental challenges and social interactions of a job are mental boosters.
2. Stay physically fit. Exercise, jog, play badminton, ride a bicycle, swim, take an aerobics class.
3. Take a class in something. Tackle Mandarin Chinese, flower arranging, or astronomy.
4. Learn to play the piano—or the clarinet, the guitar, or the Celtic harp.
5. Be flexible; go with the flow; learn to take life as it comes. Be able to answer no to the question "Do you insist on having a place for everything and everything in its place?"
6. Turn off the TV.
7. Socialize. Volunteer at the local hospital, public school, library, or animal shelter. Invite people over for dinner.
8. Play bridge, Go, or chess. Do crossword puzzles.
9. Read.
10. Enjoy as many new and rich experiences as possible.

An ounce of prevention is worth a pound of cure.
Traditional saying

FOOD FOR THOUGHT

The act of vividly recalling a patch of the past is something that I seem to have been performing with the utmost zest all my life, and I have reason to believe that this almost pathological keenness of the retrospective faculty is a hereditary trait.

VLADIMIR NABOKOV,
Speak, Memory

Bumps on the Head

SOME OF US ARE undeniably better at remembering than others. Witness how a brisk game of Trivial Pursuit separates the sheep from the goats; always, as the rest of us grope slowly through the gluey tangles of our memory banks, there's one recall superstar blithely spouting out the name of the inventor of penicillin, the identity of the only mammal to have four knees, and the geographical location of Tobago. Some specialists claim that such maddening expertise is more a matter of technique and training than of any innate ability. Others—science being the contentious discipline that it is—say otherwise.

ENVIABLE PEOPLE

One has been learning a sacred text by heart; but, though one has gone over the same passage again and again, one still recites it haltingly and keeps on forgetting words. Meanwhile one hears other people, not only clerics (for whom it is natural) but ordinary men and women, reciting such passages without the slightest effort, and one wonders when one will ever be able to come up to their standard.

The Pillow Book of Sei Shōnagon

Among the earliest proponents of the view that memory is born, not made, was Franz Josef Gall, the eighteenth-century German pseudoscientist whose obsessive interest in mapping the brain led to the bumpy art of phrenology. Gall's neurological raison d'être was localization. All human personality traits and qualities of mind, he believed, were housed in specific locations on the surface of the brain. An over- or underdose of any particular trait would reveal itself, Gall hypothesized, as a corresponding lump or hollow on the skull, detectable by the judicious trained hand. Accordingly, armed with calipers, he examined the heads of countless personalities, using the accumulated data to produce elaborate, though sadly illusory, diagrams of the human brain. In each, the brain was divided into a patchwork of forty-six sections, each devoted to a mental trait or personality attribute: wit, courage, benevolence, mirthfulness, politeness, combativeness, loyalty, patriotism, ambition. Destructiveness curled around the top of the ear; bibativeness—the bump of drunkards—lurked over the temple; veneration perched smack on top of the skull; and memory dwelt just behind the forehead. Destiny, it seemed, lay in the shape of one's head. Show an outsized bump of amativeness, for example, and chances are you're a Don Juan; a bulge over the region devoted to acquisitiveness and you may have a tendency to stick your fingers illegally in the till. A bulging forehead and large protruding eyes, Gall proclaimed, were certain indications of superior memory.

Phrenology was received with enthusiasm in Europe—except in France, where Napoleon curtly pronounced it a fraud, and among medical anatomists, who protested poor-sportishly that the brain at no point comes in contact with the inner surface of the skull, thus rendering all those vaunted bumps and hollows psychologically and physiologically meaningless. Undeterred, phrenology made an even bigger splash in America where, throughout the first half of the nineteenth century, traveling phrenological shows toured the country, feeling the bumps of the populace and pronouncing upon their probable dispositions. (At least one practitioner enlivened the proceedings by providing, for demonstration purposes, a dwarf and a seven-foot-four-inch-tall giant.) Phrenological converts included Horace Mann, founder of the American public school system, Henry Ward Beecher, noted preacher and brother of Harriet Beecher Stowe, and Allan Pinkerton, head of federal intelligence during the Civil War and founder of the eponymous Pinkerton detective agency. General George McClellan admired the system enough to have all potential Union spies phrenologically screened (presumably for bumps of loyalty, patriotism, courage, and caution) before sending them out to infiltrate Confederate encampments.

Results, though interesting, were often howlingly inaccurate. Mark Twain, for example, whose bumps were professionally prodded shortly after the author leaped to literary fame with the publication of "The Celebrated Jumping Frog of Calaveras County" in 1865, was found to be strikingly deficient in a sense of humor. Phrenology, under the accumulated weight of such public embarrassments, gradually disappeared from view, and Gall's unreliable prognostications on memory—pop-eyed people remember no better than the rest of us—fell by the scientific wayside.

School: Con and Pro

For all Gall's faults, the phrenologists at least did consider memory a mental asset—a desirable bump, on a par with the beneficial lumps of conjugality, friendship, and sublimity. Non-phrenologists, however, sometimes gave the subject a different spin. A good memory, argued a Dr. Delannay in 1879, presenting his theory to the Société de Biologie in Paris, is inevitably correlated with a low degree of intelligence. Thus, pointed out the doctor, Africans, Chinese, Italians, and Russians all possess notably better memories than the intellectually superior (but absentminded) French; women possess better memories than men; and lumbering peasants from the provinces have better memories than cultured urbanites from Paris. Lawyers, tellingly, have better memories than doctors; callow adolescents have better memories than older and wiser adults; and clerics, in crushing finale, have better memories than practically everybody.

While this thesis clearly presents an appealing out for the perennially vague, no evidence to date supports the view that forgetfulness goes hand in hand with brains. Gifted children, modern studies show, tend to have excellent memories; conversely, so do the victims of savant syndrome, a rare medical condition in which astonishing "islands of genius," characterized by phenomenal feats of memory, stand out from a background of otherwise severely limited mental ability. Originally called "idiot savants," such patients were first formally described by J. Langdon Down, the nineteenth-century London psychiatrist who also first characterized Down's syndrome. Savant syndrome sufferers include lightning calendar calculators, lightning calculators, musical prodigies, and memorists— Down mentions a young boy who "could read an entire book and ever more remember it"—all of whom are mentally handicapped in all but their single field of spectacular expertise. Nineteenth-century examples include a slave boy named "Blind Tom" who, though limited to a vocabulary of less than 100 words, was an expert pianist, with a musical repertoire of over 5,000 pieces. He was said to have been able to reproduce a twenty-page musical composition after hearing it only once. (At the age of eleven, he played at the White House for President James Buchanan.) Harold Ellis Jones of Columbia University described, in the 1920s, a savant syndrome patient known as K, a thirty-eight-year-old with an estimated mental age of eleven, who had a phenomenal mathematical memory. His accomplishments, wrote Jones, included memorizing the populations, according to the 1920 census, of every town and city in the United States with a population over 5,000, the county seats of every county in the United States, the distances of every major city in the country from New York and Chicago, the populations of 1,800 foreign cities, and the statistics on 3,000 mountains and rivers. Psychiatrist Oliver Sacks describes John and Michael, twins, who share the ability to perform lightning calendar calculations. Given a date any time in the last or next 40,000 years, the twins can determine, almost instantly, what day of the week it fell (or will fall) on. Neither twin, however, has an IQ above 60.

While memory, studies of such patients indicate, can operate independently from intelligence, Dr. Delannay's conviction that dolts never get lost and stupid schoolchildren win all the poetry recitation contests is patently wrong. Some results, however, do suggest that school does our memories no good. Socrates, who seems to have avoided it and thus never wrote anything whatsoever down, once said (according to Plato, who did): "The discovery of the alphabet will create forgetfulness in the learners' souls, because they will not use their memories; they will trust to the external written characters and not remember of themselves." Socrates, it seems, may have been correct. In the late 1970s, Ernest Frederick Dube, at work on his doctoral dissertation at Cornell University, compared the memories of illiterate children from rural villages in Botswana to those of literate African and American schoolchildren. The children were all told long and detailed stories—among them the story of Maakga the Hunter and Inkanyamba the Snake, an 18-episode, 99-theme folktale that ends (happily) with the (hostile) Snake being burnt to ashes—and then were asked to repeat the story back to the investigator, first immediately after telling, then one week and finally one month later. The African youngsters—all from a nontechnological society with a strong cultural background in traditional storytelling—beat the Americans hands down. Even the lowest-scoring of the African groups topped the American children. Within each group, the most intelligent children displayed the best memories (so much for Dr. Delannay) and the illiterate village children, who depended more on the exercise of memory in their daily lives, had the best memories of all. Culture and intelligence, Dube concluded, are determining factors for good memory; formal schooling isn't—and may even be a detriment.

> *It is only when we forget all our learning that we begin to know.*
> Henry David Thoreau

The greater picture, however, is complex, and few researchers would suggest that in quest of better memories we dash out en masse, lemminglike, and quit school. Studies of middle-aged women have shown that number of years of past schooling and present school attendance both correlate positively to performance on memory tests—that is, Ph.D.'s, as a general rule, have better memories than high school dropouts; and persons currently struggling through Economics 101, Introduction to Art History, or French Cooking Made Easy remember better than those spending their spare time watching sitcom reruns on television. Such results, however, may have less to do with education *per se* than with the fact that people who do best in school may be those who have devised the most effective personal memory strategies.

> *The older generation may have little formal education, but they have a great store of learning handed down by word of mouth. Through them are preserved many old English and Scotch ballads and dances. Even their language, quaint to lowlanders, is an Anglo-Saxon survival.*
> Federal Writers' Project, North Carolina

Pictures Worth a Thousand Words

MEMORY STRATEGIES, if you haven't stumbled upon them on your own, can be learned; and memory can be markedly improved through training. Some evidence suggests that memory enhancement courses increase performance by 40 to 50 percent. Most strategies involve either methods for improving attention and concentration—tricks for getting new information into memory in the first place—or methods for enhancing memory organization, which eases the sometimes agonizing process of recall or retrieval. Classically, all techniques that help us remember things better—from the piece of string tied around the finger on up—are referred to as mnemonics, from the Greek *mneme*, to remember.

Memory expert Danielle Lapp of Stanford University suggests that memory is best thought of as a chain of essential links, beginning with the need to know, and proceeding through interest, motivation, attention, concentration, and finally internal organization. A need to know something (the directions for disarming the burglar alarm on your rental car, for example, presently blatting away insanely in the Holiday Inn parking lot) or an interest (how *does* a cuckoo clock work anyway?) motivates you to pay attention to incoming information, concentrating on the details such as to store them, in organized and readily retrievable fashion, in long-term memory.

Attention takes effort, but it's worth it. "An object once

attended to will remain in memory," wrote William James confidently, "whereas one inattentively allowed to pass will leave no traces." The spacily inattentive allow experience to slide by without conscious awareness; memories thus formed are doomed for destruction, insubstantial as sandcastles built on the beach in the teeth of the incoming tide. Combating such memory dissolution calls for active observation: active observers think about the meaning of the subject at hand, associate it with personal emotions, elaborate upon individual details. Which paintings do you remember best after a culturally uplifting stroll through the art museum: those you winged past with a cursory glance or those that had an emotional impact, before which you stood awhile and thought?

> *Remembering does not happen as a matter of course whenever a person is exposed to information.*
> Richard Saul Wurman,
> *Information Anxiety*

> *Just as eating against one's will is injurious to health, so study without a liking for it spoils the memory, and it retains nothing it takes in.*
> Leonardo da Vinci

Most memory trainers agree that attention—and the chance of channeling an item into long-term memory—is enhanced by forming mental images. The forming of pictures in the mind's eye—and the gaudier and more dramatic the mental picture, the better—is an almost surefire path into permanent storage. One of the earliest studies of visual imagery and memory was conducted, in offhand fashion, by Sir Francis Galton, the English anthropologist whose long career—he lived to be eighty-nine—was annoyingly overshadowed by his brilliant first cousin,

Charles Darwin. Galton, despite continual invidious comparisons with cousin Charles, carved out considerable scientific territory of his own: he devised the modern technique of weather mapping, with its lines of advancing and retreating high and low pressure zones; he invented the dog whistle; and he demonstrated the uniqueness of fingerprints, eventually designing a system of print identification that proved invaluable to the detectives of Scotland Yard. He spent the latter half of his life studying human heredity, concentrating particularly on the inheritance of intelligence, which he felt could be maximized if people would only breed properly: he thus invented and named the science of eugenics, a concept that has plagued mankind ever since. Less damagingly, he came up with a method for measuring boredom, by surreptitiously observing a subject and counting number of fidgets per minute. This only worked, Galton cautioned, for the middle-aged, since "children are rarely still, while elderly philosophers will sometimes remain rigid for minutes altogether." Galton used to conduct his boredom research during long lectures at the Royal Geographical Society.

In 1883, Galton became interested in mental imagery, which he sought to assess by sending a questionnaire to one hundred men, asking each to recall his breakfast that morning in as much detail as possible, employing visual and auditory imagery and sensations of smell, touch, and taste. Those respondents who were best able to remember their morning meal, Galton found, produced a wealth of descriptive and sensory images, from the slippery feel of the linen tablecloth to the tangy fragrance of the lemon marmalade, the clash of the silver serving utensils (this was, after all, aristocratic England), the smell of the kippers, the color of the china teacups, and the rustle of the pages of the morning London *Times*. Others, whose memory of breakfast was definitely fuzzy, could produce only vague images, and a few respondents, for whom breakfast was a blank, could produce no images at all.

Memory prefers the concrete, and favors the picture over the thousand words. The brain's childish predilection for illustration means that mental images stick with us. Create a picture of an object, name, word, task, or (trickier) abstract concept, concentrate on it for a few seconds, and it embeds itself in the mind. To memorize a recipe for pumpkin bread, for example, Danielle Lapp suggests first visualizing each of the required ingredients: flour (in that yellow tin canister with the poppies on the front), vegetable oil (big plastic bottle, always sticky), sugar (blue and white bag), a can of pumpkin (orange label), raisins (red box), and spice bottles of cinnamon, nutmeg, and cloves. Then picture yourself preparing the recipe in sequence: run through the process of getting out mixing bowls and spoons, combining oil and sugar, adding flour, and so on. Such image formation and mental rehearsal enhance memory.

SHAKESPEARE'S MOST FAMOUS RECIPE

Double, double toil and trouble;
Fire, burn; and cauldron bubble.

Fillet of a fenny snake,
In the cauldron boil and bake;
Eye of newt, and toe of frog,
Wool of bat, and tongue of dog,
Adder's fork, and blind-worm's sting,
Lizard's leg, and howlet's wing;
For a charm of pow'rful trouble
Like a hell-broth boil and bubble.

Double, double toil and trouble;
Fire, burn; and cauldron bubble.

Scale of dragon, tooth of wolf,
Witch's mummy, maw and gulf
Of the ravined salt-sea shark,

Root of hemlock, digged i' the dark,
Liver of blaspheming Jew,
Gall of goat, and slips of yew
Slivered in the moon's eclipse,
Nose of Turk, and Tartar's lips,
Finger of birth-strangled babe
Ditch-delivered by a drab:
Make the gruel thick and slab.
Add thereto a tiger's chaudron
For the ingredients of our cauldron.

Double, double toil and trouble;
Fire, burn; and cauldron bubble.

Cool it with a baboon's blood,
Then the charm is firm and good.

While a tour of the everyday kitchen won't give you much help in visualizing the ingredients of Shakespeare's famous recipe, Shakespeare, however, has provided plenty of powerful potential mind pictures for aid in memorization: "lizard's leg," "scale of dragon," and "witch's mummy" are all startling, strange, and conducive to the formation of distinctive—if somewhat gruesome—mental images. Shakespeare also thoughtfully provides memorists with the additional cues of poetic rhyme and rhythm.

Howdy Doody and Homer

FOOLISH, EXAGGERATED, emotional, or sexually explicit images—which show what kind of minds we human beings have—are remembered even better. The more senses you can bring into play in the formation of to-be-remembered images, the more effective those images become. ("Develop your sensory awareness," writes Danielle Lapp bolsteringly, "and you will easily compensate for the decline in perception which may occur with age.") Poetry is more memorable than prose, and song more memorable than poetry, because of their added auditory dimensions: rhythm, rhyme, and melody are all powerful cues to lollygagging memory. It's no idle fluke that adroit marketing departments favor the memory-clinging advertising jingle. If you can carol "Have you driven a Fo-ord lately?" or "The best part of waking up is Folger's in your cup," or warble the theme songs to *The Howdy Doody Show*, *Sesame Street*, or *The Brady Bunch*, you've been the recipient/victim of powerful multiple auditory stimuli. Music may be a deliberate, as well as an inadvertent, learning tool. Educators nowadays teach the multiplication tables, the parts of speech, and United States and world geography in unforgettable song. In the 1993 remake of the movie *Born Yesterday*, an increasingly politically enlightened Melanie Griffith sets the Bill of Rights to music; and master satirist Tom Lehrer, in bouncy Gilbert and Sullivan style, has written a memorably musical version of the Periodic Table of

Elements, a rare melodic mnemonic for the budding chemist.
Poetry, writes Robert Pinsky, is a technology for remembering. Before writing came to the fore, poetry ruled the world—
information packaged in readily memorizable form that could
be passed from generation to generation. Homer's chanted *Iliad*,
writes Marshall McLuhan, was the "cultural encyclopedia" of
preliterate Greece; and the books of the Old Testament, says
archaeologist Benjamin Mazar, were ancient long before they
were written down, mnemonic "song stories" over three thousand years old passed unaltered through time from fathers to
sons. The art of the medieval troubadors was poetry and song:
these peripatetic performers traveled from town to town, enter-
taining the populace with juggling acts, magic tricks, and near-
interminable stories in rhyme, each dramatic, repetitive, and
easily memorizable. Poetry was the most prominent memory
aid of the day. Up through the fourteenth century, practically
everything except legal documents—a historically stodgy
genre—was written in rhyme. French merchants learned all the
rules of commercial arithmetic through a collection of 137
rhyming couplets; English farmers went about their business
according to the instructions of Thomas Tusser, whose *Hundred
Points of Husbandry* (later, due to popular demand, expanded to
Five Hundred Points) were all written in unforgettable verse:

> In May get a weed-hook, a crotch and a glove,
> and weed out such weeds, as the corn do not love,
> For weeding of winter corn, now it is best;
> but June is the better for weeding the rest.

Tusser's rhythmic jingles stuck in the agrarian memory like
burrs to wool socks.

Most of us, in the recesses of our brains, have squirreled
away surprising amounts of poetry. "Even a crowded elevator"—Pinsky again—"could probably collaborate to produce a
fairly good-sized anthology of interesting verse." Some of this
verse was forced upon us in the threatening milieu of junior

high school English class; some of it we acquired on purpose on our own; and a good deal simply slid slyly into our neural networks by osmosis. In the latter category are hundreds of nursery rhymes, Sunday School hymns (in multiple verses), dirty limericks ("There was a young lady from Harrow . . ."), and the words to those popular songs that have any. More challenging compositions include such soulful ditties as Joyce Kilmer's "Trees" ("I think that I shall never see/A poem lovely as a tree"), great chunks of Henry Wadsworth Longfellow's "The Song of Hiawatha" ("By the shore of Gitche Gumee/By the shining Big-Sea-Water"), Robert Frost's "Stopping By Woods on a Snowy Evening" ("Whose woods these are I think I know/His house is in the village though"), Lewis Carroll's "Jabberwocky" (" 'Twas brillig and the slithy toves/Did gyre and gimble in the wabe"), Edgar Allan Poe's "The Raven" ("Once upon a midnight dreary/As I pondered weak and weary"), and Samuel Taylor Coleridge's "Xanadu" ("In Xanadu did Kubla Khan/A stately pleasure dome decree").

The all-time favorite poem in the English language, according to William Harmon, who bases the score on number of appearances in anthologies, is William Blake's "The Tyger," which first appeared in the poet's *Songs of Experience* in 1794. Last in line (no. 100 in popularity) is Walter de la Mare's eerie "The Listeners"; in between are "The Passionate Shepherd to His Love" (no. 12, Christopher Marlowe), "I Wandered Lonely as a Cloud" (no. 42, William Wordsworth), "Ode on a Grecian Urn" (no. 49, John Keats), and the entire "Rime of the Ancient Mariner" (no. 84, Samuel Taylor Coleridge). This last has some particularly catchy verses, often highlighted by explanatory margin notes. "The ancient Mariner inhospitably killeth the pious bird of good omen," for example, accompanies

> "God save thee, ancient Mariner!
> From the fiends that plague thee thus!—
> Why look'st thou so?"—With my crossbow
> I shot the ALBATROSS.

Repeat and Rehearse

THE MEDIEVAL *jongleurs*, who gathered periodically to participate in Olympic recitation contests, were masters of memory, able to repeat a poem of several hundred lines after hearing it only three times. Memorization comes less easily to those of us raised in a print-based, rather than an oral, culture. Danielle Lapp suggests that would-be rememberers begin by reading their chosen poem or prose passage aloud—with gestures and feeling—thus adding auditory and kinesthetic ("muscle") cues to the memory. Form mental images of the concepts discussed or described: picture Wordsworth's host of golden daffodils, Poe's raven (a glaring black creature), or the shattered wreck of the statue ("Two vast and trunkless legs of stone") in Shelley's "Ozymandias." That done, most verbatim memorization is next a matter of repetition and rehearsal. This generally works best taken slowly, like dieting or exercise: learn one new verse a day, for example, each time reviewing and rehearsing the previous days' verses. Recite the verses or phrases aloud; call up your original mental images; use emotional and sensory cues. And, once you've finally mastered "Paul Revere's Ride," "Miniver Cheevy," or "Do Not Go Gentle Into That Good Night," don't stop there. Continued practice—overlearning—improves and enhances memory and retrieval speed. It's overlearning that explains the unshakable permanence of so many childhood memorizations: the Pledge of Allegiance, the Boy Scout Laws, the words to "Jesus Wants Me for a Sunbeam," and "Eenie Meenie Minie Moe."

THE TYGER

Tyger! Tyger! burning bright
In the forests of the night,
What immortal hand or eye
Could frame thy fearful symmetry?

In what distant deeps or skies
Burnt the fire of thine eyes!
On what wings dare he aspire?
What the hand dare seize the fire?

And what shoulder, & what art,
Could twist the sinews of thy heart?
And when thy heart began to beat,
What dread hand? & what dread feet?

What the hammer? what the chain?
In what furnace was thy brain?
What the anvil? what dread grasp
Dare its deadly terrors clasp?

When the stars threw down their spears
And water'd heaven with their tears:
Did he smile his work to see?
Did he who made the Lamb make thee?

Tyger! Tyger! burning bright
In the forests of the night,
What immortal hand or eye,
Dare frame thy fearful symmetry?

William Blake

First read the poem aloud. For an added memory boost, be dramatic about it: use facial expressions, motions, gestures.

Then reread, forming distinctive mental images of the concepts or objects mentioned or described in the verses.

Take it slowly. Material is best memorized in manageable chunks. Poems, for example, should be absorbed one to two verses at a time. Some studies show that learning is maximized when ten-minute breaks are taken between chunks. Relax and don't rush it.

During each memory session, repeat and rehearse previously learned material. Continue rehearsal even after you've become word perfect: overlearning strengthens memory.

THE GETTYSBURG ADDRESS

Fourscore and seven years ago our fathers brought forth on this continent, a new nation, conceived in Liberty, and dedicated to the proposition that all men are created equal.

Now we are engaged in a great civil war, testing whether that nation or any nation so conceived and so dedicated can long endure. We are met on a great battlefield of that war. We have come to dedicate a portion of that field, as a final resting place for those who here gave their lives that that nation might live. It is altogether fitting and proper that we should do this.

But, in a larger sense, we cannot dedicate—we cannot consecrate—we cannot hallow—this ground. The brave men, living and dead, who struggled here, have consecrated it far above our poor power to add or detract. The world will little note nor long remember what we say here, but it can never forget what they did here. It is for us, the living, rather to be dedicated here to the unfinished work which they who fought here have thus far so nobly advanced. It is rather for us to be here dedicated to the great task remaining before us—that from these honored dead we take increased devotion to that cause for which they gave the last full measure of devotion; that we here highly resolve that these dead shall not have died in vain; that this nation, under God, shall have a new birth of freedom; and that government of the people, by the people, for the people, shall not perish from the earth.

Abraham Lincoln
November 19, 1863

Techniques for memorizing prose are similar to those for memorizing poetry (see "The Tyger," page 275). Prose, however, without poetry's rhythm and rhyme, is generally more difficult to learn verbatim.

THE MOZART EFFECT

For an added memory boost, try accompanying memory sessions with a bout of classical music. A series of experiments performed by researchers Frances Rauscher and Gordon Shaw at the University of California, Irvine, have shown that children and adults, exposed to as little as ten minutes of complex classical music—Rauscher and Shaw favored Mozart piano sonatas—display significant boosts in spatial-temporal reasoning abilities. This discovery, promptly dubbed "the Mozart effect," was subsequently shown to have a host of related mind-building effects. Music students, for example, were variously found to have elevated IQ and SAT scores, enhanced self-concepts, and better math and reading skills. Manuscript editors listening to classical music increased their mistake-fingering abilities by 21.3%; AT&T, by creative use of classical music, managed to cut employee training time in half; and Don Campbell, author of *The Mozart Effect*, reports that Baroque music has a positive effect on everything from anxiety to dyslexia to post-surgical recovery rates. Listening to Mozart has also been said to increase the ability to memorize prose, poetry, the correct spellings of words, and foreign language vocabulary.

> *I have discovered that it is of some use when you lie in bed at night and gaze into the darkness to repeat in your mind the things you have been studying. Not only does it help the understanding, but also the memory.*
> Leonardo da Vinci

> *A teacher who can arouse a feeling for one single good action, for one single good poem, accomplishes more than he who fills our memory with row on rows of natural objects classified with name and form.*
> Johann Wolfgang von Goethe

While faithful practice solidifies the memory for individual works of art—say, "The Face on the Barroom Floor"—practice *per se* doesn't do much for memory in general. Memory, annoyingly, does not behave like a muscle and does not respond to mental calisthenics. In the late 1800s, psychologist William James set out to see if mental exercise would improve his memory. He spent some weeks flexing his brain by memorizing passages from Victor Hugo's works, then spent thirty-eight days memorizing selections from Milton, and then returned to Hugo again—at which point, to his dismay, he found that his memory rate was somewhat slower than it had been in the first place. More recently, a group of volunteer twelve-year-olds spent half an hour a day for six weeks memorizing poetry, scientific formulae, and geographic distances, with—frustratingly—no noticeable improvement in memory rate or retention. What *does* improve with practice, however, is the ability to relearn material once absorbed: that Sanskrit course, now ostensibly forgotten, that you took in a fit of elective curiosity back in college should make it easier for you to relearn the same material again today. One ambitious psychologist tested this hypothesis on his young son by reading Greek to the child from the time he was fifteen months old until the age of three. The boy was tested for his ability to memorize the original passages and comparable new ones at the ages of 8, 14, and 18. At 8, the son took 27 percent as many trials to memorize the old passages as the new; at 14, 8 percent; and at 18, a mere 1 percent. Familiarity may breed contempt, but in memory it also breeds expertise.

> *Memory's like an athlete; keep it in training; take it for cross-country runs.*
> James Hilton

The Crushed Banquet Hall

Memory techniques, if not memory itself, can also be improved with practice; dedicated users become increasingly adroit at the tricks of recall. The vast majority of memory techniques aim at enhancing memory organization. New concepts are tied to structured mental frameworks, setting them up for easy recall, rather than being flung higgledy-piggledy into the dusty attics of the cerebrum. This organizational process, in its many creative forms, is known as elaborative encoding. The more elaborate the associations formed as information is filed—encoded—in the brain, the more likely that it will be readily remembered in the future.

> *A man should keep his little brain attic stocked with all the furniture he is likely to use, and the rest he can put away in the lumber room of his library, where he can get it if he wants it.*
> Arthur Conan Doyle,
> *Five Orange Pips*

Among the oldest of these memory organizers is the "method of loci," in which items to be remembered are deliberately associated with a series of visualized places or locations (in

Latin, *loci*). The invention of memory techniques—the ancient "art of memory"—is classically attributed to a poet named Simonides of Ceos who lived in the fifth century B.C. Simonides, an ancient Greek Elvis, was much in demand in his heyday and was reportedly the first Greek poet with enough popular clout to demand payment for his performances. Payment, then as now, was occasionally a bone of contention, and at one particularly acrimonious banquet, thrown by a Thessalonian nobleman named Scopas, was even refused. Simonides had written a poem in praise of the host and of the gods Castor and Pollux; Scopas mean-spiritedly offered the poet half the previously agreed-upon price, saying that the gods—who, after all, had starred in half the poem—could pay the remainder. At that incendiary moment, a message arrived for Simonides, saying that two young men with urgent business were waiting to see him outside. Simonides went to meet his visitors; while he was gone, the roof of the banquet hall fell down, crushing all within. (The two mysterious young men, the implication was, were Castor and Pollux, revenging themselves on Scopas for his pettiness.) Scopas and all his luckless guests were flattened beyond recognition, but Simonides was able to identify the bodies for the grieving next of kin by recalling at which place each guest had sat at the banquet table—the first recorded exercise of the method of loci. The story fails to mention whether or not Simonides had any further payment problems. One suspects not.

The method of loci is most apropos for learning lists of items, especially lists in specific order. Most commonly it involves imagining a familiar street or building—your own home, for example—and "placing" items to be remembered in sequential order through its rooms. The Roman orators, who gave their prolonged speeches in the challenging days before notes on index cards, remembered the order of points in their talks by associating each with the well-known shops and structures of the Forum. A stirring introduction recalling your family's valiant sacrifices for the empire, for example, might be represented by a sword and shield propped dramatically at the door of the wine seller's shop; a nasty comparison with the decadent youth of today might be recalled by imagining a foppish gambler lolling in front of the next-door bakery; a plea for stricter educational standards remembered by a stack of scrolls and inkpots on the front step of the fruit merchant. And so on, simultaneously, in matched pairs, down the street and through the speech. Mark Twain on lecture tour through small- and large-town America routinely spent a pre-speech hour in the local town park, organizing thoughts for his upcoming performance by associating each with a park feature: one image sitting on a park bench, for example; another leaning against the Civil War monument; a third perched memorably on top of the bandstand. John Dean, whose prolific memory attracted so much attention during the Watergate hearings of 1973, used a variant of the method of loci to recall the sequence of wheelings and dealings in and around the Nixon White House. Dean kept a newspaper clipping file from the time of the kickoff Watergate break-in in June 1972 through the beginning of the Senate Committee investigation some nine months later. By relating his personal doings to the collected newspaper articles (the loci), he was able to piece together a reasonably reliable account of his activities over time. The interrogating chief investigator, Senator Inouye of Hawaii—not a Simonides man—didn't quite catch on:

> SENATOR INOUYE: Are you suggesting that your testimony was primarily based upon press accounts?
> DEAN: No sir, I am saying that I used the press accounts as one of the means to trigger my recollection of what had occurred during given periods of time.

Historically, such memory triggers were not everyone's cup of tea. The eighth-century English cleric Alcuin of York, imported by Charlemagne to shore up the sagging intellectual performance of the dissolute French clergy, seems to have ignored mnemonics, centering his memory instruction on a pithy admonition in favor of temperance: "Avoid drunkenness." (He also emphasized the importance of good handwriting.) Erasmus, the foremost scholar of the northern Renaissance, was cool toward artificial memory strategies, obviously feeling that they lured budding theologians from the scholastic straight and narrow. "Though I do not deny that memory can be helped by places and images," wrote Erasmus, "yet the best memory is based on three most important things, namely study, order, and care." Still, even if Erasmus considered them cheating, use of memory-boosting places and images was generally permissible, if not taken too far. Loci went over the line, however, in the case of Giordano Bruno, the sixteenth-century ex–Dominican friar whose politically and theologically incongenial works included

> The art of memory, with its rhetorical antecedents and its magical burgeonings, is very much an affair of imaginary places, or of real places transmuted into visual images. Since childhood, I have enjoyed an uncanny memory for literature, but that memory is purely verbal, without anything in the way of a visual component. Only recently, past the age of sixty, have I come to understand that my literary memory has relied upon the Canon as a memory system. If I am a special case, it is only in the sense that my experience is a more extreme version of what I believe to be the principal pragmatic function of the Canon: the remembering and ordering of a lifetime's reading. The greatest authors take over the role of "places" in the Canon's theater of memory, and their masterworks occupy the position filled by "images" in the art of memory.
>
> Harold Bloom,
> *The Western Canon*

three volumes on memory techniques. Bruno's memory strategies were all methods of loci, but the loci he chose as memory anchors—magical images of stars, hallways lined with statues of Roman gods and goddesses—looked, to the church authorities, suspiciously like witchcraft. For this, along with multiple other heresies (Bruno, in six different countries, had managed to enrage Protestants, Catholics, Aristotelians, Oxonian scholars, English aristocrats, and astronomers), he was imprisoned for several years in Venice. Finally, after an interminable O. J. Simpson–like trial, he was burned at the stake in 1600.

Memory Houses

As GIORDANO BRUNO languished in jail (or worse), Renaissance craftsmen were perpetuating the method of loci in socially approved fashion by building the peculiar structures known as "memory theaters." In mnemonics as taught in the Roman academies or medieval universities, memory buildings were all in the mind. Users accustomed themselves to pass through them in imagination in some habitual sequence, studying in the course of this mental journey the images of the various memory cues neatly arranged inside. The Renaissance memory theaters, however, were solid wood: gigantic and elaborate dollhouses, each divided into many memory-jogging rooms and compartments. The most famous of these was an immense model created in the early 1500s by Giulio Camillo of Bologna, who spent most of his life either working on his theater or soliciting funds for its support. Completed, the theater was big enough to hold two people and was a mass of little boxes and carved images, variously designed to represent eternal truth from the birth of the universe through all the stages of creation. Unfortunately, Camillo never managed to write the promised accompanying instruction manual explaining the many features of his mnemonic creation, and after his death in 1544, the theater vanished from history. Records also exist of a notable English memory theater, built during the reign of James I and modeled after

Shakespeare's famous Globe. The miniature Globe, like its larger namesake, did not survive.

Intriguing as the thought of your own little wooden memory house may be, most loci advocates suggest that beginning memorizers simply establish within their minds a detailed mental image of a familiar house, room, or street. Draw a mental map, and proceed—always in the same order—from chosen place to chosen place. This works, memory experts explain, for any familiar dwelling area. If you've chosen a single room— your study, for example—as a memory theater, loci may include, clockwise around the walls, the door, the bookcase, the desk chair, the desk, your framed college diploma, the floor lamp, the window, the fax machine, the computer monitor, and the filing cabinet. Whole-house loci can be spread out a bit, and, depending on your socioeconomic group, may include entrance hall chandelier, Italian drawing room, butler's pantry, ballroom, servants' elevator, and wine cellar or woodshed, chicken coop, root cellar, junked Chevrolet, dog kennel, and outhouse. To be effective, loci of whatever degree must be permanent. If you are a constant rearranger of furniture, and that distinctive green velvet chair in the parlor is likely to end up in the guest bedroom next week, avoid it in favor of immovable objects. Choose the grand piano, the refrigerator, the fireplace, and the ceiling fan. Once you've selected a list of loci, learn them. Review them in order: make repeated mental tours, always traveling in the same direction, stopping in sequence at each one.

When you are ready to memorize, begin by making a numbered list of your loci in order, then a list of the items you need or want to remember. Then pair your first locus with the first item on your list, forming as clear and vivid a mental image as possible. The technique works for lists as mundane as "Things to Get from the Grocery Store"—visualize an enormous heap of potatoes blocking the front door, a leafy head of lettuce nodding on the living room sofa, a bottle of liquid dish soap frothing bubbles over the dining room table, and toothpaste squeezing itself out in coils down the cellar stairs—to such wholly serious and uplifting lists as the (26) Amendments to the Constitution, Benjamin Franklin's List of (13) Virtues, the Ten Commandments, and the (38) plays of Shakespeare.

THE BILL OF RIGHTS

For learning a list in order, an effective mnemonic technique is the method of loci, in which each item to be remembered is associated, in ordered fashion, with familiar locations, such as the arrangement of furniture in your living room, the layout of rooms in your home, or the sequence of buildings along a well-known street.

As you read your list, use your imagination as vividly as possible. Associate distinctive mental images with each listed item and its "location."

Review and rehearse.

To memorize the first ten amendments to the Constitution, for example, your list of selected loci might include, in familiar order, the furnishings of your living room:

1. Couch
2. Rocking chair
3. Coffee table
4. Fireplace
5. Green armchair
6. Magazine rack
7. End table
8. Floor lamp
9. Leather armchair
10. Bookcase

Once the order of loci has been comfortably established (you always start at the couch, for example, and circle the room counterclockwise), begin forming mental images, associating the first item on your to-be-memorized list (Amendment 1) with locus no. 1 (Couch).

Amendment 1: Freedom of Religion, Speech, and the Press; Right of Assembly

Congress shall make no law respecting an establishment of religion, or prohibiting the free exercise thereof; or abridging the freedom of speech, or of the press; or the right of the people peaceably to assemble, and to petition the government for a redress of grievances.

Locus 1: Couch

Imagine a bishop in full clerical regalia, including a towering mitre, sitting on the couch reading the newspaper. He is annoyed by the woman sitting next to him, who is making a loud political speech through a megaphone. Next to her, a small group of protesters has assembled, cheering and waving big, brightly colored signs.

Amendment 2: Right to Keep and Bear Arms

A well-regulated militia, being necessary to the security of a free State, the right of the people to keep and bear arms, shall not be infringed.

Locus 2: Rocking chair

Imagine a toppling stack of rifles in the rocking chair, each equipped with a glittering bayonet.

Amendment 3: Quartering of Troops

No soldier shall, in time of peace be quartered in any house, without the consent of the owner, nor in time of war, but in a manner to be prescribed by law.

Locus 3: Coffee table

Visualize a uniformed soldier perched on the coffee table, equipped with mess kit, sleeping bag, duffel bag, and large fluffy pillow. Then mentally cross them all out with a red X.

Amendment 4: Limiting the Right of Search

The right of the people to be secure in their persons, houses, papers, and effects, against unreasonable searches and seizures, shall not be violated, and no warrants shall issue but upon probable cause, supported by oath or affirmation, and particularly describing the place to be searched, and the persons or things to be seized.

Locus 4: Fireplace

Picture a large wooden door blocking the fireplace, heavily barred and padlocked, with a sign tacked on it reading "Trespassers Keep Out." Pounding on the door, imagine a police officer waving a search warrant.

Amendment 5: Trial by Jury; Respect for Private Property

No person shall be held to answer for a capital, or otherwise infamous crime, unless on a presentment or indictment of a grand jury, except in cases arising in the land or naval forces, or in the militia, when in actual service in time of war or public danger; nor shall any person be subject for the same offense to be twice put in jeopardy of life or limb; nor shall be compelled in any criminal case to be a witness against himself, nor be deprived of life, liberty, or property, without due process of law; nor shall private property be taken for public use, without just compensation.

Locus 5: Green armchair

Sitting in the green armchair, imagine a judge in black robes and pounding a gavel, while before him a self-incriminating criminal, wearing a T-shirt labeled with the number 2, babbles "I did it!"

Amendment 6: Rights of Accused Persons

In all criminal prosecutions, the accused shall enjoy the right to a speedy and public trial, by an impartial jury of the State and district wherein the crime shall have been committed, which districts shall have been previously ascertained by law, and to be informed of the nature and cause of the accusation; to be confronted with the witnesses against him; to have compulsory process for obtaining witnesses in his favor, and to have the assistance of counsel for his defense.

Locus 6: Magazine rack

Balancing on top of the magazines, imagine a complete miniature courtroom, with judge, jury, and opposing lawyers. Have each jury member wear a sandwich board reading "Speedy Trial."

Amendment 7: Rules of Common Law

In suits at common law, where the value in controversy shall exceed twenty dollars, the right of trial by jury shall be preserved, and no fact tried by jury, shall be otherwise reexamined in any court of the United States than according to the rules of common law.

Locus 7: End table

Imagine a sign reading "Common Law" propped on the end table, surrounded by a flapping border of twenty-dollar bills.

Amendment 8: *Prohibition of Excessive Bail, Fines, Unusual Punishments*

Excessive bail shall not be required, nor excessive fines imposed, nor cruel and unusual punishments inflicted.

Locus 8: Floor lamp

Transform the lamp into an Iron Maiden or a stake, with the lampshade still in place. Surround the lamp with bushel baskets overflowing with coins. Label each basket "Bail" or "Fines."

Amendment 9: *Rights Retained by the People*

The enumeration in the Constitution of certain rights shall not be construed to deny or disparage others retained by the people.

Locus 9: Leather armchair

Cram several imaginary people into the leather armchair. Imagine that each holds a large box, labeled "More Rights!" Suspend a cartoon bubble over each person's head, containing the word "Mine!"

Amendment 10: *Powers Reserved to the States*

The powers not delegated to the United States by the Constitution, nor prohibited by it to the States, are reserved to the States respectively, or to the people.

Locus 10: Bookcase

Picture, stretched across the front of the bookcase, a large multicolored map of the United States. Add a couple of citizens vigorously rubber-stamping the phrases "States' Rights" and "Reserved" all over it.

Imagination grows by exercise and contrary to common belief is more powerful in the mature than in the young.
W. Somerset Maugham

Mnemonics

NoT ALL MEMORY strategies demand the architectural inventiveness of the method of loci. Most common mnemonics are short, snappy little numbers, relying on simple letter or rhyming cues. Rhymed mnemonics, the Burma Shave signs of memory, include all the helpful little jingles most of us picked up in elementary school: "I before E / Except after C / Or in rhyming with A / As in neighbor and weigh" falls into this category, along with "Thirty days hath September / April, June, and November / When short February's done / All the rest have thirty-one." (There's another version that explains the occurrence of leap year, but it's bumpier and less memorable.) The seminal date in American history—regardless of the value you place on it—is easily locked in memory with "Columbus sailed the ocean blue / In fourteen hundred ninety-two," and young Brits, who have over nine hundred years' worth of regal first names to absorb, do so with:

> Willy, Willy, Harry, Ste,
> Harry, Dick, John, Harry Three,
> One, Two, Three Neds, Richard Two,
> Henry Four, Five, Six—then who?
> Edward Four, Five, Dick the Bad,
> Harries Twain and Ned the Lad,

Mary, Bessie, James the Vain,
Charlie, Charlie, James again.
William and Mary, Anna Gloria,
Four Georges, William, and Victoria,
Ned Seventh ruled till 1910,
When George the Fifth came in, and then
Ned went when Mrs. Simpson beckoned,
Leaving George and Liz the Second.

Translated into historical respectability, this mnemonic ditty lists all the rulers of England in chronological order from William the Conqueror through Elizabeth II (minus Oliver Cromwell, who was a Protector, and doesn't count).

A second simple class of mnemonics is based on acronyms, in which each letter of a word—invariably shown in attention-getting capital letters—stands for a name or other desirable item of information. HOMES, for example, is an old stand-by for recalling the name of the Great Lakes (Huron, Ontario, Michigan, Erie, Superior); ROY G BIV for the colors of the visible spectrum (Red, Orange, Yellow, Green, Blue, Indigo, Violet); and FACE for the notes on the spaces of the treble clef.

The notes on the lines of the treble clef—EGBDF—inconsiderately spell nothing, and thus are an excellent illustration for the third simple mnemonic technique: acrostic-style mnemonics. In these, the first letter of each word making up a (usually silly, senseless, or sexist) sentence stands for a name or other item to be remembered. Thus, for the lines of the treble clef, Every Good Boy Does Fine or Every Good Boy Deserves Fudge or Elephants Go Belly Dancing Fridays or Empty Garbage Before Dad Flips. American presidents, whose ungainly collection of last names do not convert readily to rhyme, can be remembered through an assortment of memory-jogging sentences: "Washington And Jefferson Made Many A Joke," for example, translates into Washington, Adams, Jefferson, Madison, Monroe, Adams again (John Quincy), and Jackson; "Very Heavy Tennis Players Throw Fast Purple Balls" into Van Buren,

Harrison, Tyler, Polk, Taylor, Fillmore, Pierce, Buchanan. The geologic time periods (Cambrian, Ordovician, Silurian, Devonian, Carboniferous, Permian, Triassic, Jurassic, Cretaceous, Paleocene, Eocene, Oligocene, Miocene, Pliocene, Pleistocene, and Recent) can be recalled with the mnemonic triple-header "Camels Often Sit Down Carefully. Perhaps Their Joints Creak. Persistent Early Oiling Might Prevent Permanent Rheumatism." The infuriatingly incorrect is often most eminently memorizable: astronomers remember star classification, from hottest to coolest (Types O, B, A, F, G, K, and M) with "Oh Be A Fine Girl, Kiss Me"; medical students learn the names of the nerves that pass through the superior orbital fissure of the skull (lachrymal, frontal, trochlear, superior, nasal, inferior, and abducent) with "Lazy French Tarts Sit Naked In Anticipation" and the eight bones of the surprisingly complicated human wrist (navicular, lunate, triangular, pisiform, multiangular greater, multiangular lesser, capitate, hamate) with "Never Lower Tillie's Pants, Mother Might Come Home."

The seasonal verse:

> How I wish I could recapture pi.
> Eureka! cried the great inventor.
> Christmas pudding, Christmas pie
> Is at the problem's very center.

allows those who might not otherwise remember it to recite the value of pi to 21 places (3.141592653589793223846). The number of letters in each word of the jingle corresponds to a number in the mathematical sequence (How = 3; I = 1; wish = 4; and so on). It doesn't work as fluidly as some mnemonics—first-time users find themselves counting surreptitiously on their fingers to figure out how many letters there are in "Christmas"—but it is still head-and-shoulders above what R. P. and J. R. Cody have dubbed the world's worst mnemonic. The disaster in question—

$$S = .027465 + .157692K + .000159446K^2$$

is said (tongue firmly in cheek) to be an "easy guide" for those classical musicians who simply cannot remember the Köchel numbers of Mozart's symphonies. S, in the above mnemonic equation, is the symphony number; K the Köchel number. Take calculator in hand, say Cody and Cody, and the answer will be no more than 2 off, 85 percent of the time.

SEVEN DWARFS AND EIGHT TINY REINDEER

Lists can be memorized by inventing simple sequential mnemonics, such as composing sentences in which the first letter of each word in the sentence represents the first letter of a name in the list. A sentence to jog your memory for the names of Disney's Seven Dwarfs must include words starting with the letters B, D, D, G, H, S, and S: say, Big Dogs Dine Greedily on Ham Sandwiches and Soup. For added boost in this case, the Dwarfs' names come with their own built-in images—it's easy to visualize a Bashful or a Sneezy. Included, for practice purposes, is a list of Rejected Dwarfs—characters proposed for the original Disney animation who never made it into the script.

The Seven Dwarfs: Bashful
                    Doc
                    Dopey
                    Grumpy
                    Happy
                    Sleepy
                    Sneezy

Suggested But Rejected by Disney Dwarfs:
                    Baldy

Biggo-Ego
Burpy
Gabby
Jumpy
Nifty
Puffy
Stubby
Stuffy
Wheezy

Eight Tiny Reindeer: Blitzen
Comet
Cupid
Dancer
Dasher
Donder
Prancer
Vixen

The names of Clement Moore's eight tiny reindeer, first mentioned in the nineteenth-century poem "A Visit From Saint Nicholas," can be memorized list-fashion, though most memorists may prefer the memory-jogging cues of the original rhyme:

On, Dasher! On Dancer!
On, Prancer and Vixen!
On, Comet and Cupid!
On, Donder and Blitzen!

Number Codes

MOST NUMBER-REMEMBERING techniques involve devising number codes in which each number is paired with a specific concrete object. Numbers/objects can then be used to form visual associations with the items to be remembered. (It's easier than it sounds.) Some systems recommend that code objects be chosen that rhyme with the numbers they represent. In buckle-my-shoe-style rhyming code, 1 = gun, 2 = shoe, 3 = tree, 4 = door, 5 = hive, 6 = sticks, and so on up through 10 = hen. Code numbers are then paired with items to be remembered in a more or less imaginative visual image: when trying to retain "5 bottles of brandy," for example, one foolish-sounding but effective tactic is to picture a snifter of Courvoisier precariously balancing on top of a beehive (hive = 5). To remember multidigit numbers—say, 326, the number of your TWA flight to Heathrow—the code objects may be used sequentially, to form a picture story. A number code user would visualize, for example, a towering tree (3) with shoes (2) dangling leaflike from its branches, while on the ground below a crowd of barefoot people try to bat them down with sticks (6).

Storytelling, no matter how rudimentary, is a powerful memory tool: it helps us organize thoughts in coherent order and allows us to add sensory and emotional special effects to what might otherwise be a stream of featureless khaki-colored data. S, the near-legendary Russian memorist, was able to memorize enormous (and senseless) mathematical equations by inventing narrative stories associated with the numbers and functional signs. Faced with:

$$N \cdot \sqrt{d^2 \times \frac{85}{vx}} \cdot \sqrt[3]{\frac{27b^2 \cdot 86x}{n^2v \cdot \pi264}} \, n^2b = sv \, \frac{1624}{32^2} \cdot r^2s$$

S, in seven inventive minutes, came up with an image-laden tale beginning with the irritable exploits of a gentleman named Neiman. "Neiman (N) came out and jabbed at the ground with his cane (.). He looked up at a tall tree which resembled the square-root sign, and thought to himself: "No wonder the tree has withered and begun to expose its roots. After all it was here when I built those two houses" (d^2)." The action continues through Neiman's financial and real estate ruminations, the appearance of a stranger (x) in a black cape trying to break down the fence surrounding a girls' school, and a visit to S's childhood classroom where he writes on the blackboard and is annoyed by two students (r^2) chattering behind him.

[Francie] liked numbers and sums. She devised a game in which each number was a family member and the "answer" made a family grouping with a story to it. Naught was a babe in arms. He gave no trouble. Whenever he appeared you just "carried" him. The figure 1 was a pretty baby girl just learning to walk, and easy to handle; 2 was a baby boy who could walk and talk a little. He went into family life (into sums, etc.) with very little trouble. And 3 was an older boy in kindergarten, who had to be watched a little. Then there was 4, a girl of Francie's age. She was almost as easy to "mind" as 2. The mother was 5, gentle and kind. In large sums, she came along and made

everything easy the way a mother should. The father, 6,
was harder than the others but very just. But 7 was mean.
He was a crotchety old grandfather and not at all account-
able for how he came out. The grandmother, 8, was hard
too, but easier to understand than 7. Hardest of all was 9.
He was company and what a hard time fitting him into
family life!

   When Francie added a sum, she would fix a little story
to go with the result. . . . Each single combination of num-
bers was a new setup for the family and no two stories were
ever the same.

                         Betty Smith,
                    A Tree Grows in Brooklyn

An alternative number code—a favorite for visual thinkers—bases the code objects on the shapes, rather than the sounds, of individual numbers. Straight-up-and-down 1 is represented by a fence post, spear, or telephone pole; 2, a swan or goose; 3, a pitchfork or trident; 4, a sailboat; 5, a spread hand; 6, a coiled snake, and so on. For the number 2,144, you picture a goose waddling toward a fence post, to which are tied a pair of bobbing sailboats.

   1 = spear
   2 = goose
   3 = pitchfork
   4 = sailboat
   5 = hand
   6 = snake
   7 = flag
   8 = hourglass
   9 = snail
   0 = plate

A phonetic code associates the numbers 0 through 9 with letters of the alphabet:

1 = t (single vertical line) or d

2 = n (two downstrokes)

3 = m (three downstrokes)

4 = r (last letter of word *four*)

5 = l (Roman numeral L = 50)

6 = soft g or j (6 looks vaguely like capital G), or the sound-alike sh or ch

7 = k (k looks like two 7's back to back) or hard g

8 = f (a cursive f has two 8-like loops) or the f-sound-like ph or v

9 = p or b (either of which looks like a 9, turned backward or upside-down)

0 = z (which stands for zero) or s (which looks sort of like z)

Multidigit numbers, using this phonetic code, can be converted—with a little imagination—into more memorable words. 515 (ltl), for example, transforms into "little"; 436 (rmg) into "rummage"; 8093 (fzbm) into "fuzz bomb." (You're looking for memorable here, not elegant.)

Long strings of numbers can be converted into phrases and sentences, complete with concrete imagery. Try 572438519086326. First dissect the string into manageable 3- or 4-digit chunks: 572-438-519-086-326. Match each number with its letter code: lkn-rmf-ltp-sfg-mng. Then convert each letter group to a word. There are usually several possibilities for each letter combination. "Lkn," for example, could morph into liken, looking, leaking, locking, or Lincoln; "rmf" into remove, Romanoff, or earmuff. Thus, with practice and imagination, 572438519086326 can move smoothly from lkn-rmf-ltp-sfg-mng to the memory-sticking "Lincoln's earmuffs light up a surfing mango"—with accompanying lush image of Honest Abe in phosphorescent ear gear illuminating a surfboard-riding tropical fruit. None of these images, luckily, need be shared—memory formation is a private act—and all that emerges for public display should be the impressively accurate end result, traced backward from bizarre presidential image to descriptive sentence to individual letter groups to, in triumphant grand finale, the remembered string of numbers.

Number codes are the best bet for memorizing such slippery but essential strings of digits as Social Security numbers, license plate numbers, bank account and credit card numbers, purchase order numbers, and zip codes. They're also good for equally slippery, but less essential, values. Try memorizing these:

Distance from Earth to the Moon	233,812 miles
Height of Mount Everest:	29,028 feet
Length of the Nile River	4,145 miles
Area of the Pacific Ocean:	64,186,300 square miles
Speed of sound:	741.5 miles per hour
Speed of light:	186,282.4 miles per second
Distance light travels in a year:	5,878,499,834,000 miles

Teddy Rosebelt

Names—the bête noire of the forgetful on social occasions—are best remembered through "substitute words" and their corresponding images. Some names lend themselves readily to association, without much effort from us. A Mr. Carpenter, Ms. Bell, or Dr. Wolfe, for example, come with built-in mental images. For an onamastic memory boost, visualize a busy builder hung about with saws and hammers, a clanging Liberty Bell, and the toothy bane of Little Red Riding Hood at the crucial moment of introduction. Harry Lorayne's *Memory Book* lists 600 common American surnames (excluding the egregious Smith) with proposed memory-jogging substitutes. These include "collie" for Collins, "duck" for Donald, "Old Mother" for Hubbard, "Mack truck" + "decoy" for McCoy, "rose in iceberg" for Rosenberg, "trace E" for Tracy, and "blood test" for Wasserman. The system reputedly works for any name, though some, such as Mayakovsky, Czerwinski, Yananopoulos, and Cheremisinoff, require more effort than others.

The substitute word system also works for names other than those of new acquaintances. Patricia Gordon and Reed Snow propose a system of word substitution and imagery for learning state capitals. "Make a movie in your mind," write Gordon and Reed, followed by cinematic explanations for how to remember Tallahassee, Florida (picture *Lassie* mopping the kitchen *floor* with a *towel*), Montgomery, Alabama (a *mountain* of *gum* with an *owl* perched on top), and Indianapolis, Indiana (*Indians* juggling *apples*). Will Cleveland and Mark Alvarez in *Yo, Millard Fillmore!* describe a similar method for memorizing the names of the presidents of the United States, beginning with the Father of Our Country, who is represented by a giant *washing* machine capable of washing a *ton* of grubby clothes. Cleveland and Alvarez also employ the technique of linkage, tying each presidential association to the next in line such that all 42 are memorized in precise order. Washington's oversized washing machine, for example, is filled with sloshing Bohr *atoms* (Adams), which are then fished out and fried on an outdoor grill by a *chef's son* (Jefferson) in puffy white hat. The heat for the grill comes from a trapped *mad sun* (Madison).

Word substitutions and associative links—no matter how humiliatingly simple-minded—are time-tested and effective memory aids. Memory has no pride and feels no shame at allowing us—all respectable adults—to remember "Theodore Roosevelt" by picturing a stuffed teddy bear wearing a belt made out of red roses. (Teddy Rosebelt, get it?) "We lose much of the power of the brain if we consider ourselves too elegant to accept help through associations, for example, mnemonics," writes medical professor Wolf Seufert. "The brain functions like that on its own all the time."

LADIES AND GENTLEMEN, THE PRESIDENTS OF THE UNITED STATES . . .

1. George Washington
2. John Adams
3. Thomas Jefferson
4. James Madison
5. James Monroe
6. John Quincy Adams
7. Andrew Jackson
8. Martin Van Buren

9. William Henry Harrison
10. John Tyler
11. James K. Polk
12. Zachary Taylor
13. Millard Fillmore
14. Franklin Pierce
15. James Buchanan
16. Abraham Lincoln
17. Andrew Johnson
18. Ulysses S. Grant
19. Rutherford B. Hayes
20. James Garfield
21. Chester A. Arthur
22. Grover Cleveland
23. Benjamin Harrison
24. Grover Cleveland
25. William McKinley
26. Theodore Roosevelt
27. William Howard Taft
28. Woodrow Wilson
29. Warren G. Harding
30. Calvin Coolidge
31. Herbert Hoover
32. Franklin D. Roosevelt
33. Harry S. Truman
34. Dwight D. Eisenhower
35. John F. Kennedy
36. Lyndon Johnson
37. Richard Nixon
38. Gerald Ford
39. Jimmy Carter
40. Ronald Reagan
41. George Bush
42. William Clinton

A useful mnemonic trick for memorizing lists of names is word associations: sound-alikes or puns. In a list of presidential names, for example, George Washington might be associated with WASHING a TON of grubby underwear or gold nuggets; John Adams with ADAM, biting the fatal apple, or ATOMS; and so on.

For learning lists in order, use linkage: tell a simple story that connects each item on the list to the next in line. Stories, no matter how foolish, are powerful memory cues.

Use vivid visual imagery.

Review and rehearse.

Memory Aids

Forgetters of the future may be able to weasel around the low tastes of the biological memory by using electronic memory aids. External memory aids have been around for millennia, in a range of creative forms from the scratches on the cave wall (= 1 mammoth) to the Filofax, the datebook, the diary, and (for those who can't recall when they started baking the muffins) the buzzer on the kitchen stove. The wave of the twenty-first century, however, may be a combination of camcorder and computer technology, endlessly recording and storing the details of our daily lives. Xerox's EuroParc laboratory in Cambridge, England, has already completed a number of experimental "memory prostheses," among them an electronic diary (called "Pepys") that produces a minute-to-minute record of a person's movements by tracking his or her "smart card" identification badge with infrared sensors. Admittedly, this generates an impoverished memory record compared to Samuel Pepys's famous diary, with its banquets, barge trips, card parties, dalliance with serving wenches, overexpenditures on gold lace and velvet cloaks, and worries about the plague. Pepys, Xerox-style, is basically an activity log. Its understated entries include such snippets as "8.15: Attended event in main conference room with Winterbottom, Smith, and Wang [36 minutes]." As such, Pepys is a memory-trigger rather than a memory substitute. It provides a referential time framework for the day's occupations, but it's still up to human memory to recollect just how you, Winterbottom, Smith, and Wang spent those 36 minutes. An improved VIP version of Pepys, named Vepys, adds a videocamera to the system, which photographs badge-wearers at ten-minute intervals throughout the day, providing an additional flurry of visual memory cues. An even more elaborately enhanced system, Forget-Me-Not, includes a telephone-pager-sized personal computer equipped with a diary cross-referencing system for retrieval of specific past activities.

For all their talents, however, the geeks of the Information Age have yet to produce a viable rival to the versatile human brain—and few of us, for all our fuzzy imperfections, would willingly turn our memories over to machines. Human memory is not a computer. It is an artist and an inventor, a dream spinner and a poet, always in motion, never still. Most of all, memory is a storyteller, fabricating for each of us the ever-absorbing tale of our own lives. "Time," wrote Marcus Aurelius, perhaps the wisest of all Roman emperors, "is a sort of river of passing events, and strong is its current; no sooner is a thing brought to sight than it is swept by and another takes its place, and this too will be swept away." Through memory, however, we can still return upstream, and nothing that we choose to keep is ever wholly lost. We are what we remember.

> *There is no life of a man, faithfully recorded, but is a heroic poem of its sort, rhymed or unrhymed.*
> Thomas Carlyle

> *This story's about you.*
> Horace

BIBLIOGRAPHY

Ackerman, Diane. *A Natural History of the Senses.* New York: Random House, 1991.

Agranoff, Bernard W., Roger E. Davis, and John J. Brink. "Chemical Studies on Memory Fixation in Goldfish." *Brain Research* 1 (1966): 303–9.

Alkon, Daniel L. "Memory Storage and Neural Systems." *Scientific American,* July 1989, 42–50.

———. *Memory's Voice.* New York: HarperPerennial, 1992.

Altman, Lawrence K. "Research Dispels Myth That Brain in Adults Is Unable to Renew Itself." *New York Times,* 18 April 1995.

Baddeley, Alan. "Working Memory." *Science,* 23 January 1992, 556–59.

Baltes, Paul. "Wise and Otherwise." *Natural History,* February 1992, 50–51.

Barinaga, Marcia. "To Sleep, Perchance to . . . Learn?" *Science,* 29 July 1994, 603–4.

Bartsch, D., M. Ghirardi, P. A. Skehel, K. A. Karl, S. Herder, M. Chen, C. H. Bailey, and E. R. Kandel. "CREB-2ATF-4 as a repressor of long-term facilitation in *Aplysia:* Relief of repression converts a transient facilitation into a long-term functional and structural change." *Cell* 83 (1995): 979–92.

Blackmore, Susan. "Alien Abduction: The Inside Story." *New Scientist,* 19 November 1994, 29–31.

Blakeslee, Sandra. "The Mystery of Music: How It Works in the Brain." *New York Times,* 16 May 1995.

Blakeslee, Sandra. "Traffic Jams in Brain Networks Result in Verbal Stumbles." *New York Times,* 26 September 1995.

Bliss, T. V. P., and G. L. Collingridge. "A synaptic model of memory: Long-term potentiation in the hippocampus." *Nature* 232 (1993): 31–39.

Bourtchuladze, Roussoudan, Bruno Frenguelli, Julie Blendy, Diana Cioffi, Gunther Schutz, and Alcino J. Silva. "Deficient Long-Term Memory in Mice with a Targeted Mutation of the cAMP-Responsive Element-Binding Protein." *Cell* 79 (1994): 59–68.

Bower, B. "Conscious Memories May Emerge in Infants." *Science News,* 5 August 1995, 86.

Bower, Gordon. "Mood and Memory." *American Psychology,* February 1981, 129–48.

Burke, James. *The Day the Universe Changed.* Boston: Little, Brown and Co., 1985.

Burton, Mike. "Good Morning, Mr. . . . er." *New Scientist,* 1 February 1992, 39–41.

Byers, Duncan, Ronald L. Davis, and John A. Kiger, Jr. "Defect in cyclic AMP phosphodiesterase due to the *dunce* mutation of learning in *Drosophila melanogaster.*" *Nature* 289 (1/8 January 1981): 79–81.

Calder, Nigel. *The Mind of Man.* New York: Viking, 1970.

Calvin, William H., and George A. Ojemann. *Conversations with Neil's Brain.* New York: Addison-Wesley, 1994.

Campbell, Don G. *The Mozart Effect.* New York: Avon, 1997.

Campbell, Jeremy. *Grammatical Man.* New York: Simon and Schuster, 1982.

Cohen, Jonathan D., W. M. Perlstein, T. S. Braver, L. E. Nystrom, D. C. Noll, J. Jonides, and E. E. Smith. "Temporal dynamics of brain activation during a working memory task." *Nature* 386 (10 April 1997): 604–8.

Concar, David, and Andy Coghlan. "Is There Money in Lost Memories?" *New Scientist,* April 1993, 20–22.

Connolly, John B., and Tim Tully. "You Must Remember This." *The Sciences*, May/June 1996, 37–42.

Courtney, S. M., L. G. Ungerleider, K. Keil, and J. V. Haxby. "Transient and sustained activity in a distributed neural system for human working memory." *Nature* 386 (10 April 1997): 608–11.

Crick, Francis. *The Astonishing Hypothesis*. New York: Simon and Schuster, 1995.

Crick, Francis, and Christof Koch. "The Problem of Consciousness." *Scientific American*, September 1992, 153–59.

Cytowic, Richard E. *The Man Who Tasted Shapes*. New York: Warner Books, 1993.

Damasio, Antonio R. *Descartes' Error: Emotion, Reason, and the Human Brain*. New York: G. P. Putnam's Sons, 1994.

Damasio, Antonio R., and Hanna Damasio. "Brain and Language." *Scientific American*, September 1992, 89–95.

De Haan, Edward, and Freda Newcombe. "What Makes Faces Familiar?" *New Scientist*, February 1991, 49–52.

Desimone, Robert. "The Physiology of Memory: Recordings of Things Past." *Science*, 9 October 1992, 245–46.

Dudai, Yadin, Yuh-Nung Jan, Duncan Byers, William G. Quinn, and Seymour Benzer. "*Dunce*, a mutant of *Drosophila* deficient in learning." *Proceedings of the National Academy of Sciences* 73 (May 1976): 1684–88.

Ebbinghaus, Hermann. *Memory: A Contribution to Experimental Psychology*. New York: Dover Publications, 1964.

Egeth, Howard E. "What Do We Not Know About Eyewitness Identification?" *American Psychologist*, May 1993, 577–80.

Elias, Marilyn. "When to Worry About Forgetting." *Harvard Health Letter*, 1 July 1992.

Ericsson, K. Anders, William G. Chase, and Steve Faloon. "Acquisition of a Memory Skill." *Science*, 6 June 1980, 1181–82.

Ezzell, Carol. "Memories Might Be Made of This." *Science News*, 25 May 1991, 328–30.

Fackelmann, Kathleen. "Forever Smart: Does Estrogen Enhance Memory?" *Science News*, 4 February 1995, 74–75.

Ferraro, Susan. "You Must Remember This." *New York Times Education Supplement*, 9 April 1989.

Ferry, Georgina. "Networks on the Brain." *New Scientist*, 16 July 1987, 54–58.

Fischbach, Gerald D. "Mind and Brain." *Scientific American*, September 1992, 48–57.

Fogler, Janet, and Lynn Stern. *Improving Your Memory*. Baltimore: Johns Hopkins University Press, 1988.

Folkers, Elizabeth, Peter Drain, and William G. Quinn. "Radish, a *Drosophila* mutant deficient in consolidated memory." *Proceedings of the National Academy of Sciences* 90 (September 1993): 8123–27.

Freedman, David H. "In the Realm of the Chemical." *Discover*, June 1993, 69–76.

———. "Quantum Consciousness." *Discover*, June 1994, 89–98.

Freeman, Walter J. "The Physiology of Perception." *Scientific American*, February 1991, 78–85.

Friedman, William J., and Arnold J. Wilkins. "Scale Effects in Memory for the Time of Events." *Memory & Cognition* 13 (1985): 168–75.

Gardner, Howard. *The Mind's New Science*. New York: Basic Books, 1987.

Gold, Paul E. "Sweet Memories." *American Scientist* 75 (1987): 151–55.

Golding, David. "The Secret Life of the Neuron." *New Scientist*, 18 August 1988, 52–55.

Goldman-Rakic, Patricia S. "Working Memory and the Mind." *Scientific American*, September 1992, 111–17.

Goleman, Daniel. "Brain May Tag All Perceptions With a Value." *New York Times*, 8 August 1995.

———. "Peak Performance: Why Records Fail." *New York Times*, 11 October 1992.

Gorman, James. *The Man With No Endorphins*. New York: Penguin Books, 1985.

Gould, Stephen Jay. *The Mismeasure of Man*. New York: W. W. Norton & Co., 1981.

Greenfield, Susan A. *Journey to the Centers of the Mind*. New York: W. H. Freeman, 1995.

Hacking, Ian. *Rewriting the Soul: Multiple Personality and the Sciences of Memory*. Princeton: University Press, 1995.

Hartson, William. *Drunken Goldfish & Other Irrelevant Scientific Research*. New York: Sterling Publishing, 1987.

Herbert, Roy. "What a Piece of Work Is Whatsitsname!" *New Scientist*, 21/28 December 1991, 30–31.

Herold, Mort. *Memorizing Made Easy*. Chicago: Contemporary Books, 1982.

Higbee, Kenneth L. *Your Memory: How It Works and How to Improve It*. Englewood Cliffs, N.J.: Prentice-Hall, 1988.

Hilts, Philip J. *Memory's Ghost: The Strange Tale of Mr. M and the Nature of Memory*. New York: Simon and Schuster, 1995.

Hinton, Geoffrey E. "How Neural Networks Learn From Experience." *Scientific American*, September 1992, 145–51.

Holmes, Bob. "When Memory Plays Us False." *New Scientist*, 23 July 1994, 32–35.

Hooper, Judith, and Dick Teresi. *The 3-Pound Universe*. New York: Jeremy P. Tarcher, 1992.

Horne, James. *Why We Sleep: The Functions of Sleep in Humans and Other Mammals*. London: Oxford University Press, 1989.

Howe, Michael. "Perspiration Beats Inspiration." *New Scientist*, 24/31 December 1988, 58–60.

Huyghe, Patrick. *Glowing Birds*. Boston: Faber and Faber, 1985.

———. "Voices, Glances, Flashbacks: Our First Memories." *Psychology Today*, September 1988, 48–52.

Ingram, Jay. *The Science of Everyday Life*. New York: Viking, 1989.

Jaffe, Klaus. "Effect of Cycloheximide on Protein Synthesis and Memory in Praying Mantis." *Physiology & Behavior* 25 (1980): 367–71.

Jaroff, Leon. "Lie of the Mind." *Time*, 29 November 1993, 52–59.

Johnson, Mark. "Memories of Mother." *New Scientist*, 18 February 1988, 60–62.

Kandel, Eric R., and Robert D. Hawkins. "The Biological Basis of

Learning and Individuality." *Scientific American*, September 1992, 79–86.

Kandel, Minouche, and Eric Kandel. "Flights of Memory." *Discover*, May 1994, 32–38.

Karni, A., D. Tanne, B. S. Rubenstein, J. J. M. Askenasy, and D. Sagi. "Dependence on REM Sleep of Overnight Improvement of a Perceptual Skill." *Science*, July 1994, 679–82.

Kempermann, G., H. G. Kuhn, and F. H. Gage. "More hippocampal neurons in adult mice living in an enriched environment." *Nature* 386 (3 April 1997): 493–95.

Ketchum, Richard M. "Memory as History." *American Heritage*, November 1991, 142–48.

Kotre, John. *White Gloves: How We Create Ourselves Through Memory.* New York: The Free Press, 1994.

Krampe, R. T., and K. A. Ericsson. "Maintaining excellence: deliberate practice and elite performance in young and older pianists." *Journal of Experimental Psychology*, 125 (December 1996): 331–59.

Lapp, Danielle C. *Don't Forget!* New York: Addison-Wesley, 1995.

LeDoux, Joseph E. "Emotion, Memory, and the Brain." *Scientific American*, June 1994, 50–57.

Levelt, W. J., and L. Wheeldon. "Do speakers have access to a mental syllabary?" *Cognition* 50 (April–June 1994): 239–69.

Levin, Lonny R. Pyung-Lim Han, Paul M. Hwang, Paul G. Feinstein, Ronald L. Davis, and Randall R. Reed. "The Drosophila Learning and Memory Gene Rutabaga Encodes a Ca2+/-Calmodulin-Responsive Adenylyl Cyclase." *Cell*, 7 February 1992, 479–89.

Livermore, Beth. "Build a Better Brain." *Psychology Today*, 1 September 1992, 40–46.

Llinás, R. R., and D. Paré. "On Dreaming and Wakefulness." *Neuroscience* 44 (1980): 521–35.

Loftus, Elizabeth F., and Geoffrey R. Loftus. "On the Permanence of Stored Information in the Human Brain." *American Psychologist* 35 (May 1980): 409–20.

Loftus, Elizabeth F., and Wesley Marburger. "Since the eruption of Mt. St. Helens, has anyone beaten you up? Improving the accuracy of retrospective reports with landmark events." *Memory & Cognition* 11 (1983): 114–20.

Lorayne, Harry, and Jerry Lucas. *The Memory Book.* New York: Dorset Press, 1974.

Lynch, G., R. Granger, J. Ambros-Ingerson, C. M. Davis, M. Kessler, and R. Schehr. "Evidence that a positive modulator of AMPA-type glutamate receptors improves delayed recall in aged humans." *Experimental Neurology* 145 (May 1997): 89–92.

Luria, A. R. *The Mind of a Mnemonist.* Cambridge: Harvard University Press, 1968.

Malinow, Roberta. "LTP: Desperately Seeking Resolution." *Science,* 18 November 1994, 1195–96.

Mansfield, Howard. *In the Memory House.* Golden, Colo: Fulcrum Publishing, 1995.

Mark, Vernon H., and Jeffrey P. Mark. *Reversing Memory Loss.* New York: Houghton Mifflin, 1992.

McCrone, John. "Don't Forget Your Memory Aide." *New Scientist,* 5 February 1994, 32–36.

———. "Maps of the Mind." *New Scientist,* 7 January 1995, 30–34.

———. "Quantum States of Mind." *New Scientist,* 20 August 1994, 35–38.

McLuhan, Marshall, and Quentin Fiore. *The Medium Is the Massage.* New York: Bantam Books, 1967.

Menzel, Randolf, and Jochen Erber. "Learning and Memory in Bees." *Scientific American,* July 1978, 102–10.

Miller, G. A. "The magical number seven, plus or minus two: Some limits on our capacity for processing information." *Psychological Review* 63 (1956): 81–96.

Milner, Peter M. "The Mind and Donald O. Hebb." *Scientific American,* January 1993, 124–29.

Mishkin, Mortimer, and Tim Appenzeller. "The Anatomy of Memory." *Scientific American,* June 1987, 80–89.

Montgomery, Geoffrey. "Molecules of Memory." *Discover,* December 1989, 46–55.

Motluk, Alison. "The Sweet Smell of Purple." *New Scientist,* 13 August 1994, 33–37.

Neimark, Jill. "It's magical. It's malleable. It's memory." *Psychology Today,* 1 January 1995, 44–52.

Neisser, Ulric. *Memory Observed.* New York: W. H. Freeman, 1982.

Norman, Donald A. *Learning and Memory.* New York: W. H. Freeman, 1982.

Nyberg, L., A. R. McIntosh, R. Cabeza, R. Habib, S. Houle, and E. Tulving. "General and specific brain regions involved in encoding and retrieval of events: what, where, and when." *Proceedings of the National Academy of Sciences* 93 (October 1996): 11280–85.

Ornstein, Robert, and Richard F. Thompson. *The Amazing Brain.* Boston: Houghton Mifflin, 1984.

Parkin, Alan J. *Memory and Amnesia.* New York: Basil Blackwell, 1987.

Rabbitt, Patrick, and Lynn McInnis. "Do Clever Old People Have Earlier and Richer First Memories?" *Psychology and Aging* 3 (1988): 338–41.

Rauscher, F. H., G. L. Shaw, and K. N. Ky. "Music and spatial task performance." *Nature,* 14 October 1993, p. 611.

Rauscher, F. H., G. L. Shaw, L. J. Levine, E. L. Wright, W. R. Dennis, and R. L. Newcomb. "Music training causes long-term enhancement of preschool children's spatial-temporal reasoning." *Neurological Research,* February 1997, pp. 2–8.

Rees, Alun. "If Only I Could Remember Her Name." *New Scientist,* 24/31 December 1994, 72–73.

Rensch, B. "The Intelligence of Elephants." *Scientific American,* February 1957, 44–49.

Restak, Richard M. *The Modular Brain.* New York: Simon and Schuster, 1994.

Richardson, Sarah. "The Brain-Boosting Sex Hormone." *Discover,* April 1994, 30–31.

Rose, Steven. *The Making of Memory.* Garden City, N.Y.: Doubleday, 1992.

———. "Memories and Molecules." *New Scientist,* 27 November 1988, 40–44.

———. "No Way to Treat the Mind." *New Scientist,* 17 April 1993, 23–26.

Rosenfield, Israel. *The Invention of Memory.* New York: Basic Books, 1988.

Russell, Peter. *The Brain Book.* New York: Penguin Books, 1979.

Sacks, Oliver. *The Man Who Mistook His Wife for a Hat.* New York: Summit Books, 1985.

———. *The Anthropologist on Mars.* New York: Knopf, 1995.

Sagan, Carl. *The Dragons of Eden.* New York: Ballantine Books, 1977.

Schacter, Daniel L. "Memory Wars." *Scientific American,* April 1995, 135–39.

———. *Searching for Memory.* Basic Books, 1996.

Schooler, C., E. Neumann, L. J. Caplan, and B. R. Roberts. "A time course analysis of Stroop interference and facilitation: comparing normal individuals and individuals with schizophrenia." *Journal of Experimental Psychology* 126 (March 1997): 19–36.

Selkoe, Dennis J. "Aging Brain, Aging Mind." *Scientific American,* September 1992, 135–42.

Shanks, David. "Remembrance of Things Unconscious." *New Scientist,* 24 August 1991, 39–42.

Squire, Larry R. *Memory and Brain.* New York: Oxford University Press, 1987.

Stromeyer, Charles F. "Eidetikers." *Psychology Today,* November 1970, 76–80.

Terr, Lenore. *Unchained Memories.* New York: Basic Books, 1994.

Tootell, R. B., J. B. Reppas, A. M. Dale, R. B. Look, M. I. Sereno, R. Malach, T. J. Brady, and B. R. Rosen. "Visual motion aftereffect in human cortical area MT revealed by functional magnetic resonance imaging." *Nature* 375 (May 1995): 139–41.

Treffert, Darold A. *Extraordinary People.* New York: Harper & Row, 1989.

Tully, T., T. Preat, S. C. Boynton, and M. Del Vecchio. "Genetic Dissection of Consolidated Memory in Drosophila." *Cell,* 7 October 1994, 36–47.

Tulving, Endel. "Remembering and Knowing the Past." *American Scientist* 77 (1989): 361–67.

Tulving, Endel, and Daniel L. Schacter. "Priming and Human Memory Systems." *Science* 247 (1990): 301–6.

Vines, Gail. "Exercise Your Mind." *New Scientist*, 18 March 1989, 60–63.

Wells, G. L. "What do we know about eyewitness identification?" *American Psychologist* 48 (1993): 553–71.

Wilson, M. A., and B. L. McNaughton. "Reactivation of hippocampal ensemble memories during sleep." *Science* 265 (29 July 1994): 676–79.

Winson, Jonathan. "The Meaning of Dreams." *Scientific American*, November 1990, 86–96.

Wright, Lawrence. *Remembering Satan.* New York: Knopf, 1994.

Wurman, Richard Saul. *Information Anxiety.* Garden City, N.Y.: Doubleday, 1989.

Yates, Frances A. *The Art of Memory.* Chicago: University of Chicago Press, 1966.

Yin, J. C. P., M. Del Vecchio, H. Zhou, and T. Tully. "CREB as a memory modulator: induced expression of a dCREB2 activator isoform enhances long-term memory in *Drosophila.*" Cell 81 (1995): 107–15.

Yin, J. C. P., J. S. Wallach, M. Del Vecchio, E. L. Wilder, H. Zhou, W. G. Quinn, and T. Tully. "Induction of a dominant negative CREB transgene specifically blocks long-term memory in *Drosophila.*" Cell 79 (1994): 49–58.

Young, Stephen. "Brain Cells Hit the Big Time." *New Scientist*, 5 February 1994, 23–27.

———. "The Body's Vital Poison." *New Scientist*, 13 March 1993, 36–40.

Zeki, Semir. "The Visual Image in Mind and Brain." *Scientific American*, September 1992, 69–76.

PERMISSIONS

Grateful acknowledgment is made for permission to reproduce the following previously published material:

"The Brain" by Emily Dickinson, in *The Complete Poems of Emily Dickinson*, ed. Thomas H. Johnson, Little Brown & Company. Used with permission.

"Absentminded" by Walter Hard, in *Vermont People* (1981), Vermont Books, Inc., Publishers, Middlebury, Vermont.

"Nonsense Equation" in *The Mind of a Mnemonist* by A. R. Luria, Basic Books, 1968. Copyright © Professor Michael Cole.

"Archygrams," from *the lives and times of archy and mehitabel* by Don Marquis. Copyright 1927, 1930, 1933, 1935, 1950 by Doubleday, a division of Bantam Doubleday Dell Publishing Group, Inc. Used by permission of Doubleday, a division of Bantam Doubleday Dell Publishing Group, Inc.

"My First Thanksgiving," by Grandma Moses. Copyright © 1948 (renewed 1976) Grandma Moses Properties Co., New York.

"L'Envoi" and "You Were Perfectly Fine" by Dorothy Parker, from *The Portable Dorothy Parker* by Dorothy Parker, introduction by Brendan Gill. Copyright 1928, renewed © 1956 by Dorothy Parker. Used by permission of Viking Penguin, a division of Penguin Books USA, Inc.

Excerpts from study by William Stern in *Memory Observed: Remembering in Natural Contexts* by Ulrich Neisser. Copyright © 1982 by W. H. Freeman and Company. Used with permission.

INDEX

REBECCA RUPP lives in Vermont with her husband and three sons, with whom she shares a tractor, a telescope, and a toboggan. She has a Ph.D. in cell biology, has written for many national magazines, and has published several books, including *Red Oaks and Black Birches* and *Everything You Never Learned About Birds*. She forgets things unless she writes them down.